entre nous

EUROPEAN PERSPECTIVES

On Thinking-of-the-Other **entre nous**

Emmanuel Levinas

*Translated from
the French by
Michael B. Smith
and Barbara Harshav*

Columbia University Press

NEW YORK

Publishers Since 1893

New York   Chichester, West Sussex

Copyright © 1998 Columbia University Press

Entre Nous: Essais sur le penser-à-l'autre (c) Editions Grasset & Fasquelle 1991

Columbia University Press wishes to express its appreciation of assistance
given by the government of France through Le Ministère de la Culture
in the preparation of this translation.

Library of Congress Cataloging-in-Publication Data
Levinas, Emmanuel.
    [Entre nous. English]
    Entre nous : on thinking-of-the-other / Emmanuel Levinas ;
    translated from the French by Michael B. Smith and Barbara Harshav.
        p.   cm. -- (European perspectives)
    Includes bibliographical references and index.
    ISBN 0-231-07910-9 (cloth : alk. paper).
    1. Philosophy. I. Title. II. Series.
    B2430.L483E5813 1998
    194--dc21

∞

Casebound editions of Columbia University Press books are printed
on permanent and durable acid-free paper.
Printed in the United States of America

Designed by Chang Jae Lee

c 10 9 8 7 6 5 4 3 2 1

EUROPEAN PERSPECTIVES

A Series in Social Thought and Cultural Criticism

Lawrence D. Kritzman, Editor

EUROPEAN PERSPECTIVES presents English translations of books by leading European thinkers. With both classic and outstanding contemporary works, the series aims to shape the major intellectual controversies of our day and to facilitate the tasks of historical understanding.

Translators' Acknowledgments

entre nous

Michael B. Smith wishes to thank Berry College for its encouragement and support and Martha Reynolds of the Memorial Library for her professional assistance. And he is very grateful for the forbearance of his wife, Helen, whose spouse was, for the larger part of a summer, "lost in translation."

Barbara Harshav wishes to thank Professor Robert Gibbs, of Princeton University, who good-naturedly devoted much time and effort to this project.

Author's Preface

entre nous

The essays in this volume are arranged in chronological order of their appearance in various philosophical publications. "Is Ontology Fundamental?," dating from 1951, gives a general sense of what will be discussed in the subsequent essays. The rationality of the human psyche is explored in the intersubjective relation, the relationship of one person to another, in the transcendence of the "*for-the-other*" initiating the "ethical subject," which initiates the *entre-nous*.

What motivates these pages is not some urgent need to return to ethics for the purpose of developing *ab ovo* a code in which the structures and rules for good private conduct, public policy, and peace between nations would be set forth, however fundamental the ethical values implied in these chapters may appear to be. The main intent here is to try to see ethics in relation to the rationality of the knowledge that is immanent in being, and that is primordial in the philosophical tradition of the West; even if ethics—ultimately going beyond the forms and determinations of ontology, but without rejecting the peace of reason—could achieve a different form of intelligibility and a different way of loving wisdom;[1] and perhaps even—but I will not go that far—the way of Psalm 111:10.

I will set out from being in the verbal sense of that word: neither from "beings"[2]—physical objects, living bodies, human individuals—nor physical objects, living bodies, human individuals—nor from nature, which encompasses them all in one way or another in its totality.

I will set out from being in the verbal sense of the word, in which being is suggested and understood, in a sense, as a process of being, an event of being, an adventure of being. A remarkable adventure! The event of being is in a concern with being; it would appear to be its only way of being, in its *élan* which is "essentially" finite and completely absorbed in this concern with being. In a sense, the only thing at issue for the event of being is the being of that very being. To be as such is, from the first, to be preoccupied with being, as if some relaxation were already necessary, some "tranquilizer," in order to remain—while being—unconcerned about being. To be: already an insistence on being as if a "survival instinct" that coincided with its development, preserving it, and maintaining it in its adventure of being, were its meaning. The tensing of being back onto itself, a plot in which the reflexive pronoun, -self, is bound up.[3] An insistence before all light and decision, the secret of a savagery excluding deliberation and calculation, violence in the guise of beings who affirm themselves "without regard" for one another in their concern to be.

Origin of all violence, varying with the various modes of being: the life of the living, the existence of human beings, the reality of things. The life of the living in the struggle for life; the natural history of human beings in the blood and tears of wars between individuals, nations, and classes; the matter of things, hard matter; solidity; the closed-in-upon-self, all the way down to the level of the subatomic particles of which physicists speak.

But behold! The emergence, in the life lived by the human being (and it is here that the human, as such, begins—pure eventuality, but from the start an eventuality that is pure and holy), of the devoting-of-oneself-to-the-other. In the general economy of being in its inflection back upon itself, a preoccupation with the other, even to the point of sacrifice, even to the possibility of dying for him or her; a responsibility for the other. Otherwise than being! It is this shattering of indifference—even if indifference is statistically dominant—this possibility of one-for-the-other, that constitutes the ethical event. When human existence interrupts and goes beyond its effort to be—its Spinozan *conatus essendi*[4]—there is a vocation of an existing-for-the-other stronger than the threat of death: the fellow human being's existential adventure matters to the *I* more than its own, posing from the start the *I* as responsible for the being of the other; responsible, that is, unique and elect, as an *I* who is no longer just any individual member of the human race. It is as if the emergence of the human in the economy of being upset the meaning and plot and philosophical rank of ontology: the in-itself of being-persisting-in-being goes beyond itself in the gratuitousness of the outside-of-itself-for-the-other, in sacrifice, or the possibility of sacrifice, in the perspective of holiness.

entre nous

Is Ontology Fundamental?

one

The Primacy of Ontology

The primacy of ontology among the branches of knowledge would appear to rest on the clearest evidence, for all knowledge of relations connecting or opposing beings to one another implies an understanding of the fact that these beings and relations exist. To articulate the meaning of this fact—i.e., to take up once again the problem of ontology, which is implicitly resolved by each one of us, even if by forgetting about it—would seem tantamount to constructing a fundamental knowledge without which all philosophical, scientific or common fields of knowledge are naive.

The dignity of contemporary ontological research is derived from the urgent and original nature of that evidence; relying on it, thinkers have immediately risen above the "illuminations" of literary coteries to breathe once again the air of the great dialogues of Plato and Aristotelian metaphysics.

To question this fundamental evidence is a daring enterprise. But approaching philosophy through this critique has at least the virtue of returning to its source, beyond the problems and pathos of literature.

Contemporary Ontology

What is unique about the revival of ontology by contemporary philosophy is that the knowledge of being in general—or fundamental ontology—assumes a situation of fact for the mind that knows. A reason liberated from temporal contingencies, a soul coeternal with Ideas—such is the self-image of a form of reason unaware or forgetful of itself: a naive reason. Ontology, "authentic" ontology, coincides with the facticity of temporal existence. To understand being as being is to exist in this world. Not that this world, through the hardships it inflicts on us, elevates and purifies the soul, enabling it to acquire a receptivity to being. Nor that this world inaugurates a history, the unfolding of which would be the only thing that could make the idea of being thinkable. This world acquires its ontological privilege neither from the ascesis it entails nor the civilization to which it gives rise: already in its temporal concerns an understanding of being is discernible. Ontology is accomplished not in the triumph of man over his condition, but in the very tension in which that condition is assumed.

This possibility of conceiving contingency and facticity not as facts presented to intellection but as the act of intellection—this possibility of demonstrating the transitivity of understanding and a "signifying intention" within brute facts and data (a possibility discovered by Husserl, but attached by Heidegger to the intellection of being in general) constitutes the great novelty of contemporary ontology. Henceforth, the understanding of being implies not just a theoretical attitude, but the whole of human behavior. The whole man is ontology. His scientific work, his affective life, the satisfaction of his needs and his work, his social life and his death articulate, with a rigor that assigns a determined function for each of these aspects, the understanding of being, or truth. Our entire civilization emanates from this understanding—be it in the form of the forgetting of being. It is not because there is man that there is truth. It is because being in general is inseparable from its *disclosedness*; it is because there is truth, or, if you like, it is because being is intelligible, that there is humanity.

The return to the original themes of philosophy (and here, too, Heidegger's work remains impressive) proceeds, not from a pious decision to return at last to I know not what *philosophia perennis*, but from a radical attention to the pressing preoccupations of today. The abstract question of the meaning of being *qua* being and contemporary issues coalesce spontaneously.

The Ambiguity of Contemporary Ontology

The identification of the understanding of being with the fullness of concrete existence initially risks drowning ontology in existence. This philosophy of existence, which Heidegger rejects as a designation of his own work, is merely the counterpart—but an inevitable one—of his conception of ontology. Historical existence, which interests the philosopher in that it is ontology, is of interest to human beings and literature because it is dramatic. When philosophy and life are confused, we no longer know whether we are interested in philosophy because it is life, or whether we care about life because it is philosophy. The essential contribution of the new ontology may appear in its contrast to classical intellectualism. To understand a tool is not to see it, but to know how to use it; to understand our situation in reality is not to define it, but to be in an affective state. To understand being is to exist. All this seems to indicate a break with the theoretical structure of Western thought. To think is no longer to contemplate, but to be engaged, merged with what we think, launched[1]—the dramatic event of being-in-the-world.

The comedy begins with our simplest gestures. They all entail an inevitable awkwardness. Reaching out my hand to pull a chair toward me, I have folded the arm of my jacket, scratched the floor, and dropped my cigarette ash. In doing what I willed to do, I did a thousand and one things I hadn't willed to do. The act was not pure; I left traces. Wiping away these traces, I left others. Sherlock Holmes will apply his science to this irreducible coarseness of each of my initiatives, and thus the comedy may take a tragic turn. When the awkwardness of the act is turned against the goal pursued, we are in the midst of tragedy. Laius, in attempting to thwart the fatal predictions, undertakes precisely what is necessary to fulfill them. Oedipus, in succeeding, works toward his own misfortune. It is like an animal fleeing in a straight line across the snow before the sound of the hunters, thus leaving the very traces that will lead to its death.

Thus we are responsible beyond our intentions. It is impossible for the attention directing the act to avoid inadvertent action. We get caught up in things; things turn against us. That is to say that our consciousness, and our mastery of reality through consciousness, do not exhaust our relationship with reality, in which we are present with all the density of our being. It is the fact that, in Heidegger's philosophy, our consciousness of reality does not coincide with our dwelling in the world that has created a strong impression in the literary world.

But the philosophy of existence immediately fades away before ontology. This fact of being launched, this event to which I am committed, bound as I am to what was to be my object with bonds that cannot be reduced to thoughts, this existence—is interpreted as understanding. Hence the transitive character of the verb to know is attached to the verb to exist.[2] The first sentence of Aristotle's *Metaphysics*, "All men by nature desire to know," remains true for a philosophy that, without due consideration, was thought to be contemptuous of intellect. Ontology not only crowns our practical relations with being, as the contemplation of essences in Book X of *Nicomachean Ethics* crowns virtues: it is the essence of all relation with beings, and even of all relation in being. Does not the fact that beings are "open" belong to the very fact of their being? Our concrete existence is interpreted in function of its entrance into the "openness" of being in general. We exist in a circuit of intelligence with the real; intelligence is the very event articulated by existence. All misunderstanding is simply a deficient mode of understanding. Thus, the analysis of existence and of what is called its *haecceity* (*Da*) is nothing but the description of the essence of truth, of the condition of the very intelligibility of being.

The Other as Interlocutor

No meaningful language can argue in favor of a divorce between language and reason. But we may legitimately wonder whether reason, posited as the possibility of meaningful language, necessarily precedes it—whether language is not based on a relationship that is prior to understanding, and that constitutes reason. The following pages attempt in a very general way to characterize this relation, which cannot be reduced to understanding—even one resembling the understanding Heidegger delineated beyond classical intellectualism.

For Heidegger, understanding ultimately rests on the *openness* of being. Whereas Berkeley's idealism perceived in being a reference to thought because of the qualitative contents of being, Heidegger perceives being's intelligibility in the (formal, as it were) aspect of the fact that beings *are*—in their work of *being*, in their very independence. This does not imply a prerequisite dependence with regard to a subjective thought, but a kind of vacancy awaiting its occupant, which is opened by the very fact that beings are. Heidegger thus describes, in its most formal structure, the articulations of vision, in which the relation of the subject to the object is subordinate to the relation of the object to light—which is not an object. Thus the understanding of a being consists in going beyond that being—precisely into openness—and perceiving it upon the *horizon of being*. Which is to say that, in Heidegger, understanding rejoins the great tradition of Western philosophy: to understand the particular being is already to place oneself beyond the particular. To understand is to relate to the particular, which alone exists, through knowledge, which is always knowledge of the universal.

We cannot set personal preferences against the venerable tradition Heidegger continues. We cannot *prefer* a relation with beings as a condition for ontology to the fundamental thesis that every relation with a particular being assumes an intimacy with, or a forgetting of, being. As soon as we are engaged in reflection (and precisely for the very reasons that, since Plato, have subordinated the sensation of the particular to the knowledge of the universal) it seems that we are reduced to subordinating the relations between beings to the structures of being, metaphysics to ontology, the existentiell to the existential. Moreover, how can the *relation* to a *being* be anything, initially, but the understanding of it as a being—the fact of freely letting it be as a being?

Except for the other. Our relation with him certainly consists in wanting to understand him, but this relation exceeds the confines of understanding. Not only because, besides curiosity, knowledge of the other also demands sympathy or love, ways of being that are different from impassive contemplation, but also because, in our relation to the other, the latter does not affect us by means of a concept. The other is a being and counts as such.

Here the advocate of ontology will object that to use the term "a being" is already to insinuate that beings concern us on the basis of a revelation of being, and that, consequently, placed in the opening onto being, the being in question is already set within a milieu of understanding. What, in fact, does the independence of a being mean, if not its reference to ontology? For Heidegger, to relate to beings *qua* beings means to let beings be, to understand them as independent of the perception that discovers and grasps them. It is precisely through that understanding that they are given as beings and not just as objects. To Heidegger, being-with-the-other-person—*Miteinandersein*—thus rests on the ontological relation.

We reply: Is our relation with the other a *letting be?* Is not the independence of the other achieved through his or her role as one who is addressed? Is the person to whom we speak understood beforehand in his being? Not at all. The other is not first an object of understanding and then an interlocutor. The two relations are merged. In other words, addressing the other is inseparable from understanding the other.

To understand a person is already to speak to him. To posit the existence of the other by letting him be is already to have accepted that existence, to have taken it into account. "To have accepted," and "to have taken into account" do not come down to an understanding, a letting be. Speech delineates an original relation. The point is to see the function of language not as subordinate to the *consciousness* we have of the presence of the other, or of his proximity, or of our community with him, but as a condition of that conscious realization.

It is true that we still have to explain why the event of language can no longer be situated at the level of understanding. Why not expand the notion of understanding, following a procedure with which we have become familiar through phenomenology? Why not present our addressing of the other as a feature belonging to our the understanding of him?

That seems impossible to me. The handling of everyday objects, for example, is interpreted as understanding them. But the expansion of the notion of knowledge is justified, in that example, by our going beyond known objects. This going beyond is achieved in spite of all the pretheoretical involvement in the handling of "equipment." In handling, beings are transcended in the very movement that grasps them, and, in that "beyond" necessary for presence "to hand" we recognize the very itinerary that is characteristic of understanding. This going beyond is not due solely to the prior appearance of the "world" whenever we touch what can be handled, as Heidegger would have it.[3] It is also delineated in the *possession* and *consumption* of the object. There is nothing of the sort in my relationship with the other. There, too, if you will, I understand being in the other, beyond his or her particularity as a being; the person with whom I am in relation, I call being, but in calling him *being*, I call upon him. I do not just think that he is, I speak to him. He is my *partner* within a relation that was only to have made him present to me. I have spoken to him, that is, I have overlooked the universal being he incarnates in order to confine myself to the particular being he is. Here the principle "before being in relation with a being, I have to have understood him as being," loses its strict application: in understanding this being, I simultaneously tell him my understanding.

Man is the only being I cannot meet without my expressing this meeting itself to him. That is precisely what distinguishes the meeting from knowledge. In every attitude toward the human being there is a greeting—even if it is the refusal of a greeting. Here perception is not projected toward the horizon (the field of my freedom, my power, my property) in order to grasp the individual against this familiar background: it refers to the pure individual, to a being as such. And that signifies precisely, to put it in terms of "understanding," that my understanding of a being as such is already the expression I offer him or her of that understanding.

This impossibility of approaching the other without speaking means that here thought is inseparable from expression. But expression does not consist in somehow pouring a thought related to the other into the mind of the other. We have known this—not since Heidegger, but since Socrates. Nor does expression consist in *articulating* the understanding I already have in common with the other. It consists, prior to any participation in a common content through understanding, in instituting sociality through a relationship that is, consequently, irreducible to understanding.

The relation to the other is therefore not ontology. This bond with the other which is not reducible to the representation of the other, but to his invocation, and in which invocation is not preceded by an understanding, I call *religion*. The essence of discourse is prayer. What distinguishes thought directed toward a thing from a bond with a person is that in the latter case a vocative is uttered: what is named is at the same time what is called.

In choosing the term religion—without uttering the word God or the word *sacred*—I had uppermost in mind the meaning given to it by Auguste Comte at the beginning of his *System of Positive Polity*. No theology, no mysticism is concealed behind the analysis I have just given of the meeting with the other, the formal structure of which I felt it was important to stress. The object of the meeting is at the same time given to us and *in society* with us, but without that event of sociality being reducible to any property whatsoever revealed in the given—without knowledge being able to take precedence over sociality. If the word religion is, however, to indicate that the relation between men, irreducible to understanding, is by that very fact distanced from the exercise of power, but in human faces joins the Infinite—I accept that ethical resonance of the word and all those Kantian reverberations.

"Religion" remains the relationship to a being as a being. It does not consist in *conceiving* of him as a being, an act in which the *being* is already assimilated—even if that assimilation ends in releasing him as a *being*—in *letting him be*. Nor does it consist in establishing I know not what *belonging*, or in overstepping the bounds of the rational in an effort to understand beings. Can the rational be reduced to having power over the object? Is reason domination, in which the resistance of the being as such is overcome not by an appeal to that resistance itself, but as if by a cunning trick of the hunter, who catches what is strong and irreducible in a being through its weaknesses, its renunciation of its particularity—through its place on the horizon of universal being? Can intelligence as cunning, the intelligence of struggle and violence, made for things, constitute a human order? Paradoxically, we have been trained to seek in struggle the manifestation of the mind itself and its reality. But is the order of reason not constituted rather in a situation in which things are "talked over," in which the resistance of beings *qua* beings is not broken, but pacified?

The concern of contemporary philosophy to free man from categories adapted solely to things, therefore, must not be content with the opposition between the static, inert, and determined nature of things, on one hand, and dynamism, *durée*, transcendence or freedom as the essence of man on the other. It is not so much a matter of opposing one essence to another, or of saying what human nature is. It is primarily a matter of our finding a vantage point from which man ceases to concern us in terms of the horizon of being, i.e., ceases to offer himself to our powers. The being as such (and not as an incarnation of universal being) can only be in a relation in which he is invoked. That being is man, and it is as a neighbor that man is accessible: as a face.

The Ethical Meaning of the Other

By relating to beings in the openness of being, understanding finds a meaning for them in terms of being. In this sense, understanding does not invoke them, but only names them. And thus, with regard to beings, understanding carries out an act of violence and of negation. A partial negation, which is violence. And this partialness can be described by the fact that, without disappearing, beings are in my power. The partial negation which is violence denies the independence of beings: they are mine. Possession is the mode by which a being, while existing, is partially denied. It is not merely the fact that the being is an instrument and a tool—that is to say, a means; it is also an end—consumable, it is food, and, in enjoyment, offers itself, gives itself, is mine. Vision certainly exercises power over the object, but vision is already enjoyment. The meeting with the other person consists in the fact that, despite the extent of my domination over him and his submission, I do not possess him. He does not enter entirely into the opening of being in which I already stand as in the field of my freedom. It is not in terms of being in general that he comes toward me. Everything from him that comes to me in terms of being in general certainly offers itself to my understanding and my possession. I understand him in terms of his history, his environment, his habits. What escapes understanding in him is himself, the being. I cannot deny him partially, in violence, by grasping him in terms of being in general, and by possessing him. The other is the only being whose negation can be declared only as total: a murder. The other is the only being I can want to kill.

I can want to. Yet this power is the complete opposite of power. The triumph of this power is its defeat as power. At the very moment when my power to kill is realized, the other has escaped. In killing, I can certainly *attain* a goal, I can kill the way I hunt, or cut down trees, or slaughter animals—but then I have grasped the other in the opening of being in general, as an element of the world in which I stand. I have seen him on the horizon. I have not looked straight at him. I have not looked him in the face. The temptation of total negation, which spans the infinity of that attempt and its impossibility—is the presence of the face. To be in relation with the other face to face—is to be unable to kill. This is also the situation of discourse.

If things are only things, it is because the relation with them is established as understanding: as beings, they let themselves be taken by surprise in terms of being, in terms of a totality that gives them meaning. The immediate is not an object of understanding. An immediate datum of consciousness is a contradiction in terms. To be given is to be exposed to the ruse of understanding, to be grasped by the mediation of the concept, by the light of being in general, indirectly, in a roundabout way; to be given is to mean in terms of what one is not. The relationship to the face, an event of the collectivity—speech—is a relationship to a being itself, as a pure being.

The fact that the relationship with a *being* is an invocation of a face and already speech, a relation with a depth rather than with a horizon—a gap in the horizon—the fact that my fellow man is the being par excellence, all this may appear rather surprising if we limit ourselves to the conception of a being, insignificant in itself, a silhouette on the luminous horizon, acquiring a meaning only by virtue of that presence on the horizon. The face *signifies* otherwise. In it, the infinite resistance of a being to our power is affirmed precisely in opposition to the will to murder that it defies, because, being completely naked—and the nakedness of the face is not a figure of speech—it means by itself. We cannot even say that the face is an opening; that would make it relative to a surrounding plenitude.

Can things take on a face? Isn't art an activity that gives things a face? Isn't the facade of a house a house that is looking at us? The analysis conducted thus far is not enough to give the answer. Yet, we wonder whether rhythm's impersonal gait—fascinating, magic—is not art's substitute for sociality, the face, and speech.

I set the signifying of the face in opposition to understanding and meaning grasped on the basis of the horizon. Will my brief remarks introducing this notion afford a glimpse of its role in understanding itself and all its conditions, which delineate a sphere of relations barely suspected? What I catch sight of in that sphere seems suggested by the practical philosophy of Kant, to which I feel particularly close.

How is the vision of the face no longer vision, but hearing and speech? How can the meeting of the face—that is to say, moral consciousness—be described as a condition for consciousness *tout court* and for disclosure? How does consciousness assert itself as an impossibility of murder? What are the conditions of the appearance of the face, that is to say, of the temptation and impossibility of murder? How can I appear to myself as a face? Finally, to what extent is the relation with the other or the collectivity—which cannot be reduced to understanding—a relation with the infinite? Such are the themes that arise from this first challenge to the primacy of ontology. In any case, philosophical research cannot be content with reflection on itself or on existence. Reflection gives us only the narrative of a personal adventure, a private soul, incessantly returning to itself, even when it seems to flee itself. The human gives itself only to a relationship that is not a being able.

The *I* and the Totality

two

entre nous

The Problem: The *I* in the Totality, or Innocence

A particular being can take itself for a totality only if it is unthinking. Not that it is wrong or thinks badly or foolishly—it simply does not think. Now we do observe freedom or violence in individuals: for us thinking beings who are aware of the totality, who situate every particular being relative to it and seek a meaning in the spontaneity of violence, this freedom seems to denote individuals who confuse their particularity with the totality. In individuals, this confusion is not thought, but life. That which lives in the totality exists as totality, as if it occupied the center of being and were its source, as if it drew everything from the here and now, but in which it is in fact placed or created. To it, the forces that traverse it are already assumed—it experiences them as already integrated into its needs and enjoyment. What is perceived by the thinking being as exteriority inviting it to labor and assume ownership is experienced by the living being as its substance, co-substantial with it, essentially immediate, an element and an environment. This behavior of the living being (which is *cynical*[1] in the philosophical sense of the term) can also be found in man; by abstraction, to be sure, since thought has already transfigured life in the concrete man. It appears as a relation to food—food in that very general sense in which all enjoyment enjoys something, a "something" stripped of its independence. Being that is assumed by that which lives—the assimilable—is food.

What simply lives is thus ignorant of the exterior world. Not with an ignorance constituting the outer limits of the known, but an absolute ignorance, through an absence of thought. The senses bring it nothing, or only sensations. It is its sensations: the "statue is a rose smell."[2] Sensibility as the very consciousness of what lives is not thought that is simply confused, it is not thought at all. Therein lies the great truth of sensualist philosophies, the criticism of the Husserlians notwithstanding; sensation is not a sensation of a sense-datum. Perhaps this is why Husserl himself remained loyal to that recollection of sensualism, stubbornly preserving the notion of "hyletic datum" at the core of intentional analysis. Therein lies the eternal truth of the Cartesian thesis as well, which posits the purely utilitarian character of sensibility, the radical relativity of sense data to the subject. The useful is being that has been sensed, taken up by life. The confusion and obscurity of sensibility are specifically contrasted with the clarity in which a horizon is opened. The adventure of living being is told in it—if the term "to tell" can still have a meaning here—in terms of intimacy. In the film, *The Gold Rush*, Charlie Chaplin's cabin is about to be hurled into an abyss by a blizzard. For Chaplin, closed up inside the cabin without any opening onto the world, the blizzard is reduced to the concerns of inside balance. If, stretched out on the floor, already a physicist, he gropes about, studying the elementary laws of those disorderly ups and downs and rejoins the world, it is precisely because he thinks.

The living being per se, then, is not without consciousness, but has a consciousness without problems, that is, without exteriority, an interior world whose center it occupies, a consciousness not concerned with situating itself in relation to an exteriority, which does not comprehend itself as part of a whole (for it precedes all comprehension), consciousness without consciousness to which the term unconscious (which hides no fewer contradictions) or instinct corresponds. The interiority that, to thinking being, is opposed to exteriority, plays itself out in the living being as an absence of exteriority. The identity of a living being throughout its history contains nothing mysterious: the living being is essentially the Same, the Same determining every Other, without the Other ever determining the Same. If the Other did determine it—if exteriority collided with what lives—it would kill instinctive being. The living being lives beneath the sign of liberty or death.

Thought begins the very moment consciousness becomes consciousness of its particularity, that is to say, when it conceives of the exteriority, beyond its nature as a living being, that encloses it; when thought becomes conscious of itself and at the same time conscious of the exteriority that goes beyond its nature, when it becomes metaphysical. Thought establishes a relationship with an unassumed exteriority. As thinking being, man is the one for whom the exterior world exists. From now on, his so-called biological life, his strictly interior life, is illuminated by thought. The object of need, henceforth an exterior object, goes beyond utility. Desire recognizes the desirable in an exotic world. Whatever one makes of Bergson's theory of reason, his formula, "instinct enlightened by intelligence," (considered separately from his theory of reason) suggests a transformation, brought about by the consciousness of self, in biological consciousness, which is blind to exteriority. This central existence, welcoming all exteriority in terms of its interiority, though capable of thinking an exteriority as foreign to the interior system, capable of representing to itself a not yet assumed exteriority, would make a life of labor possible. Thought does not spring forth from labor and will, is not the same thing as labor interrupted, a neutralized will: labor and will rest on thought. The position of man, a reasonable animal, in being, is accomplished as will and labor. A reasonable animal cannot mean an animal that reason rides on as if on horseback: the interpenetration of terms delineates an original structure.

The interior system of instinct can collide with exteriority as with an absolutely unassimilable object which makes the system capsize in death. In this sense, death would be a radical transcendence. But exteriority cannot have any meaning for instinct, since exteriority's entrance into that system implies the disappearance of vital consciousness itself. The relationship of instinct with exteriority is not a knowing, but a death. Through death, the living being enters the totality, but no longer thinks anything at all. In thinking, the being situated within the totality is not absorbed by it. It exists in relation to a totality, but remains here, separated from the totality: me.

But how then is this simultaneity of a position in totality and a reserve or separation with regard to it achieved? What is the meaning of the relationship with an exteriority which remains unassumed in this relationship? This is the problem of the *I* and the totality that I am raising. It is the problem of innocence itself. It is a problem that is not resolved by the simple affirmation of the separation between free beings—since innocence entails a relationship between beings and engagement in a totality. Innocence is not a sovereign interior state. For exteriority to present itself to me, it must, qua exteriority, exceed the "terms" of vital consciousness, yet at the same time, qua *present*, it must not be fatal to consciousness. This penetration of a total system into a partial one that cannot assimilate it is miracle. The possibility of thought is the consciousness of miracle, or wonder. The miracle ruptures biological consciousness; it possesses an intermediary ontological status between the lived and the thought. It is the *beginning* of thought, or *experience*. Thought at its beginning finds itself before the miracle of fact. The structure of the fact as distinct from the idea resides in the miracle. Hence, thought is not simply reminiscence, but always consciousness of the new.

But the miracle does not explain the beginning of thought; it already presupposes it. Thought cannot be *deduced* from biological consciousness. For the miraculous to hold the attention of vital consciousness— for an event like attention even to appear in that consciousness—consciousness must already have been in relation with the whole without that relationship having been reduced to absorption by the whole, or death. The *a posteriori* of the fact refers back to the *a priori* of a thought. The latter cannot be a foreknowledge of the fact itself. For the thinking individual, it must consist in positing himself, on the one hand, within the totality in such a way as to be part of it—in defining himself, that is, situating himself in relation to the other parts, and deriving his identity from what distinguishes him from the other parts with which he compromises himself; but at the same time it consists in remaining outside—in not coinciding with his concept—in deriving his identity not from his place in the whole (from his character, his work, his heritage), but from *himself*—from being *me*. The individuality of the *I* is distinct from any given individuality in that its identity is not constituted by what distinguishes it from others, but by its reference to itself. The totality in which a thinking being is situated is not a pure and simple addition of beings, but the addition of beings who do not make up one number with one another. This is the whole originality of society. The simultaneity of participation and non-participation is precisely an existence that moves between guilt and innocence, between ascendancy over others, betrayal of the self and return to the self. The relationship of the individual to the totality, which thought is, in which the *I* takes into account what is not itself and yet is not dissolved in it, assumes that the totality is manifested not as a milieu brushing against the skin, so to speak, of living being as an element in which it is immersed, but as a face in which being *faces* me. This relationship of both participation and separation, which marks the advent and the *a priori* of a thought—in which the bonds between the parts are constituted only by the freedom of the parts—is a society, beings who speak, who face one another. Thought begins with the possibility of conceiving a freedom exterior to my own. To think a freedom exterior to my own is the first thought. It marks my very presence in the world. The world of perception shows a face; things affect us as *possessed* by the other person. When pure nature does not testify to the glory of God, when it does not belong to anyone, being indifferent and inhuman nature, it is located on the margin of this human world, and is not comprehended as such except on the level of the human world of property. Things as things derive their original independence from the fact that they do not belong to me—and they do not belong to me because I am in relation to the men they come from. Hence, the relationship of the *I* with the totality is a relationship with human beings whose face I recognize. Before them, I am guilty or innocent. The condition of thought is a moral consciousness.

The problem of the relationship between the *I* and the totality, then, comes down to describing the moral conditions for thought. Our thesis is that these are realized in the work of economic justice. We want to show that the work of economic justice is not an enterprise determined by the contingencies of a history that has turned out badly, but articulates relationships that make possible a totality of beings exterior to the totality, the capacity of these beings for innocence and their presence to one another. Thus, the work of economic justice does not serve as a prelude to spiritual existence, but already achieves it. But first we must show why love does not fulfill this condition and how the impersonal and coherent discourse substituted for it destroys the singularity and life of spiritual beings.

The Third Man

Guilt and innocence presuppose a being—that does not coincide with the totality of being, since it is guilty or innocent with regard to the other or, at least, with regard to a principle that transcends the *I*; but they also presuppose a free me that, consequently, is equivalent to the totality or is radically separated from a totality of which it is a part. Also, guilt and innocence presuppose that a free being can injure a free being and suffer the repercussions of the wrong it has caused and, consequently, that the separation between free beings within the totality remains incomplete.

The ontological schema offered by revealed religions—a me in relation with a transcendent God—reconciles these contradictions. It maintains the insufficiency of human beings as well as their character of totality or freedom. Guilt or innocence can be conceived only with respect to God, who is exterior to this world, in which man is everything. The transcendence of a condescending God assures both separation and relation. Moreover, divine pardon restores to the *I* at fault its initial integrity, and guarantees its sovereignty, which is thus unchangeable.

But religions have lost their guiding role in modern consciousness. They have lost it not because of their mysterious dogmas, eroded by reason, or their incomprehensible an shocking practices, such as magic. Neither the "mystification of the priests" nor the moral ineffectiveness of rites denounced by the Age of the Enlightenment sufficiently shook the religiosity of souls. By a path some call mysterious, but which obeys, if not logic, at least a psychological necessity, pious souls are returning to historically constituted religions. When they create an individual religion for themselves, they are living on the flotsam and jetsam of shipwrecked churches, like Robinson Crusoe who achieved independence on his island only thanks to the barrels of gunpowder and the rifles he brought from his lost ship.

Yet does modern consciousness recognize itself in the pious soul? A large portion of humanity no longer finds the path to the spiritual life in religion or in religiosity. Not that these people feel less guilty than past generations. They feel guilty in a different way. The fault that oppresses them is not forgiven by piety; or, more precisely, the evil that weighs on them does not belong to the order of forgiveness. Hence, what does the existence or non-existence of God, the interest or indifference of God, matter with respect to men? The goodness toward which religion beckons does not achieve the Good and the purification it proposes does not cleanse.

The forgivable transgression, apart from its magical significance, is either intentional or is revealed by analysis to be such. Hence the primordial value placed upon the examination of consciousness. But forgiveness assumes especially that he who is wronged has borne the whole evil of the wrong and, consequently, disposes entirely of the right to pardon. Compared to the mystical transgression committed by the unwitting violation of a taboo, the idea of an intentional one, open to forgiveness, marks a definite spiritual progress. But the conditions of a legitimate forgiveness are realized only in a society of beings totally present to one another, in an *intimate society*; a society of beings who have chosen one other, but in such a way as to control every facet of that society; an intimate society in truth, quite similar in its autarchy to the false totality of the *I*. In fact, such a society consists of two people, I and thou. We are among ourselves. Third parties are excluded. The third man disturbs this intimacy essentially: my wrong with regard to you, which I can recognize entirely in terms of my intentions, is objectively falsified through your relations with *him*, which remain secret to me, since I, in turn, am excluded from the unique privilege of your intimacy. If I recognize my wrongs with regard to you, I may be wronging the third one through my repentance itself.

Hence, my intention no longer exactly measures the meaning of my act. Limited to the intimate society, faced with the only freedom concerned by the act, I was able, in dialogue, to receive absolution for it. Thus, the *I* recovered in dialogue—if only after the fact—its solitary sovereignty through forgiveness. The *I* capable of forgetting its past and renewing itself but which, through the act, creates the irreparable, freed itself through forgiveness of that last shackle to freedom, since the only victim of the act consented or was able to consent to forget it. Absolved, it again became absolute. But the violence experienced by a victim capable of annulling it is not violence, properly speaking; it does not encroach upon the offended freedom, which, as an almost divine freedom, fully preserves its power of absolution. Violence in intimate society offends, but does not wound. It is either beyond or on the hither side of justice and injustice. These latter, assuming a violence exercised on a freedom, a real wound, reside in work and not in thoughts, be they pious or impious—in power exerted over a freedom and not in respect or lack of it. The intimate society that makes forgiveness possible frees the will from the weight of acts that both escape and commit it—acts through which, in a real society, every will risks becoming alien to itself.

Posited in a configuration of wills which concern each other through their works, but who look one another in the face—in a true society— I act in a sense that escapes me. The objective meaning of my action prevails over its intentional meaning: I am no longer a me, properly speaking; I am at fault for something not reflected in my intentions. I am objectively guilty and my piety cannot purify me of it. "I didn't want that"—a ridiculous excuse by which the "I," which lingers in the "intimate society" where it was fully free, continues to exculpate itself for a wrong that is unforgivable, not because it is beyond forgiveness, but because it does not belong to the order of forgiveness. The pious soul can, to be sure, suffer from its social guilt, but as the latter differs from the wrong an *I* commits with regard to a *thou*, it is reconciled with a "good conscience." It tortures the pious conscience only with a second-order torture. One is cured of it, as best one can be, by charity, love of one's fellow man who knocks at the door, alms given to the pauper, philanthropy, a favorable act toward the first person who comes along.

One could only accept forgiveness legitimately if the other is God or a saint. Within society, the emotion that establishes a society that is master of all that it involves is love. To love is to exist as if the lover and the loved one were alone in the world. The intersubjective relation of love is not the beginning of society, but its negation. And that is certainly an indication of its essence. Love is the *I* satisfied by the *thou*, grasping in the other the justification of its being. The presence of the other exhausts the content of such a society. The affective warmth of love is the fulfillment of the consciousness of that satisfaction, that contentment, that fullness found outside the self, eccentric to it. The society of love is a society of two, a society of solitudes, resisting universality. Its universality can be constructed only in time, by successive infidelities, by the change of friends. This is the love of one's neighbor, determined by chance proximity, and, consequently, a love of one being to the detriment of another; always privilege, even if it is not preference. The morality of respect presupposes the morality of love. Love blinds respect which, impossible without blindness with regard to the third party, is but a pious intention oblivious to real evil.

Clearly we cannot act on a daily basis in approaching our fellow man as if he were the only person in the world. The cobbler makes shoes without asking his customer where he is going, the physician treats the patient who comes to him, and the priest comforts the soul in distress who asks him for help. And we do not invest our sense of justice in this activity; unless we are convinced that the general laws of society are fair and that all impact of our action on third parties has been taken into account by the conditions in which our daily action will take place. Respect and love for one's fellow man, as they are imposed in terms of religion, belong to our private activities and do not make innocence, in the etymological sense of the term, possible.

Thus, the love that contemporary religious thought, cleared of magical notions, has promoted to the rank of the essential situation of religious existence, does not contain social reality. The latter inevitably entails the existence of the third party. The real "thou" is not the loved one, detached from others: he presents himself in another situation. The crisis of religion in contemporary spiritual life stems from the awareness that society goes beyond love, that a third party listens, wounded, to the amorous dialogue, and that with regard to him, the society of love itself is in the wrong. The lack of universality here does not come from a lack of generosity, but from the intimate essence of love. All love—unless it becomes judgment and justice—is the love of the couple. The closed society is the couple.

Thus, the crisis of religion results from the impossibility of isolating oneself with God and forgetting all those who remain outside the amorous dialogue. The true dialogue is elsewhere. One can, to be sure, conceive isolation with God as including the totality, but unless a mystical or sacramental sense is given to this affirmation, the notion of God and worship of him would have to be developed in terms of the unavoidable necessities of a society that entails third parties. (It is not certain that this has never been attempted.) God would then appear not at all as the correlate of the *I* in an amorous and exclusive intimacy, not at all as a Presence in which the universe would be engulfed, and from which an infinite source of forgiveness would spring. He would be the fixed point exterior to Society, from which the Law would come: nowise an allegorical personification of my moral consciousness. Is there "moral consciousness" before "We" has been uttered? Is it certain that "moral consciousness" can be separated from a "received commandment," from a certain heteronomy, from a relation with the Other, with exteriority? The Other, Exteriority, do not necessarily imply tyranny and violence. *An exteriority without violence is the exteriority of discourse.* The absolute that upholds justice is the absolute of the interlocutor. Its mode of being and of making its presence known consists in turning its face toward me, in being a face. This is why the absolute is a person. To isolate one being among others, to be isolated with him or her in the secret ambiguity of the *between-us* does not guarantee the radical exteriority of the Absolute. Only the unimpeachable and stern witness inserting himself "between us," making our private clandestinity public with his speech, a demanding mediator between one man and another, is face to face, is *thou*. A thesis which is not at all theological, but God could not be God without having been first and foremost that interlocutor.

In any event, we have strayed far from the royal road of traditional piety. The latter smarts from the wound inflicted on man as if it were convertible into an outrage against God and, hence, eradicable in a sociality of love, in which the *I*, master of its intentions, is content with forgiveness. The social wrong is committed without my knowledge, with respect to a multiplicity of third parties whom I will never look at directly, whom I will not find in the face of God, and for whom God cannot answer. The intention cannot accompany the act to its ultimate prolongations, and yet the *I* knows it is responsible for these ultimate prolongations.

Thus the multiplicity in which the relation with the third party is placed does not constitute a contingent fact, a simple empirical multiplicity, the fact that a substance characterized as me is produced in the world in multiple copies, creating for the autonomous me one practical problem among others: the relationship with a third party—responsibility extending beyond intention's "range of action"—characterizes the subjective existence capable of discourse *essentially*. The *I* is in relationship with a human totality. Hence the strong sense of the notion of earthly morality: it does not consist in enclosing life in the world here below and in the pure and simple contempt for supernatural destinies. It does not limit the horizon; it moves in a horizon that is different from that of supernatural salvation, which is adumbrated in a love disengaged from all those who are absent. Earthly morality invites us to take the difficult turn leading toward third parties who remain outside of love. Only justice satisfies its need for purity. As we have in a sense just said, dialogue is called to play a privileged role in the work of social justice, but dialogue cannot resemble the intimate society and it is not the emotion of love that constitutes it. Law takes precedence over charity. In this sense, too, man is a political animal.

A paradoxical outcome. The certainty that the relation with the third party resembles neither my intimacy with myself nor the love of a neighbor compromises, as we shall see, the very status of man as an irreplaceable singularity—which is nonetheless presupposed in any aspiration to innocence. Did we not begin by affirming the singularity of man in an absolute fashion, to the point of denying anyone the right to answer and forgive in the place of another? But if fault is now outside the realm of what can be assessed by an examination of conscience, man as an interiority loses all importance. Fault is determined on the basis of a universal law, and consists in the wrong caused rather than in the disrespect. Hence, we are not what we are conscious of being, but are the role we play in a drama of which we are no longer the authors: characters or instruments of an order alien to the level of our intimate society—an order which is perhaps guided by an intelligence, but an intelligence which is revealed to consciousnesses only by its cunning. No longer can anyone find the law of his action in the depths of his heart. The impasse of liberalism resides in this exteriority of my consciousness to myself. The subject at fault awaits the meaning of his being from outside; he is no longer the man confessing his sins, but the one acquiescing to accusations. The distrust of introspection, of self-analysis, in our psychology, is perhaps only a consequence of the crisis of love and religion; it derives from the discovery of the true nature of the social.

Consciousness of self outside of self confers a primordial function to the language that links us with the outside. It also leads to the destruction of language. We can no longer speak. Not because we do not know our interlocutor, but because we can no longer take his words seriously, for his interiority is purely epiphenomenal. We are not satisfied with his revelations, which we take to be superficial data, a deceitful appearance unaware that it is lying. No one is identical to himself. Beings have no identity. Faces are masks. Behind the faces that speak to us and to whom we speak, we look for the clockwork and microscopic springs of souls. As sociologists, we seek social laws which behave like interstellar influences, governing the other's winks and smiles; as philologists and historians, we will even deny that anyone can be the author of his discourse. It is not only speech which is thereby demolished by psychoanalysis and history. Psychoanalysis and history really culminate with the destruction of the *I*, identifying itself from within. The reflection of the *cogito* can no longer arise to ensure the certainty of what I am; it barely guarantees the certainty of my existence itself. That existence—dependent on the recognition by the other, without which, insignificant, it grasps itself as a reality without reality—becomes purely phenomenal. Psychoanalysis casts a fundamental suspicion on the most unimpeachable testimony of self-consciousness. What makes the return of the *cogito* null and void is that the clear and distinct consciousness of what was formerly called a psychological fact is only the symbolism of a reality totally inaccessible to itself, and that it expresses a social reality or an historical influence totally distinct from its own intention. So the distinction between phenomenon and noumenon can be introduced even into the domain of self-consciousness! The cogito thus loses its value as foundation. Reality can no longer be reconstructed in terms of elements which, independent of any point of view and incapable of being deformed by consciousness, would make a philosophical knowledge possible.

I am as if enclosed in my portrait. It is characteristic of contemporary polemics to draw the portrait of the adversary instead of struggling against his or her arguments. To philology, whose abuses Plato denounced as early as in the *Phaedrus*, and which, confronted with one who speaks, asks itself only "Who is he?," "What country does he come from?,"[3] there is now added the art of the painter who reduces the other's words and deeds to a mute, immobile image. When, in a movement of sincerity, one rises up against an abuse or an injustice, one runs the risk of resembling the portrait of a chronic protester. The process is infinite: we must also draw the portrait of the portraitist and psychoanalyze the psychoanalyst. The real world is transformed into a poetic world—that is, into a world without beginning where one thinks without *knowing* what one *thinks*.

As opposed to a "person-to-person" discourse, which is impossible, since it is always determined by the condition of the interlocutors, we now have a discourse taking account of its conditions, absolutely coherent, supplying the condition of conditions. It is a discourse without interlocutors, for the interlocutors themselves represent "moments" of it. Bound to the universality of an impersonal reason, it would suppress the otherness of the interlocutor (who is irrational insofar as he is other) and the otherness of the *I* who is speaking (who, in his ipseity, also distinguishes himself as other from the discourse in which he is engaging). A reason cannot be other for a reason.

But such a discourse, expressing the coherence of concepts, assumes that the existence of the interlocutors can be reduced to concepts. It is only at this price that man can become a "moment" of his own discourse. Such is, in fact, man reduced to his accomplishments, reflected in his works, man past and dead who is totally reflected in that discourse. Impersonal discourse is a necrological discourse. Man is reduced to the legacy of man, absorbed by a totality of the common patrimony. The power he exercised over his work while living (and not only through the mediation of his work)—the essentially cynical man—is annulled. Man becomes—not, to be sure, a thing—but a dead soul. This is not reification; this is history. History which is determined by posterity, by those who are absent, with a judgment that can no longer change anything—the judgment by those who are not born of those who are dead. To seek the *I* as a singularity within a totality made up of relationships between singularities that cannot be subsumed under a concept is to ask whether a living person does not have the power to judge the history in which he is involved; that is, whether the thinker as me—beyond everything he does with what he possesses, creates and leaves behind—does not have the substance of a cynic.

The *I* as a Singularity

Language, as the manifestation of a reason, awakens in me and in the other what we have in common. But it assumes, in its expressive intention, our alterity and our duality. It is practiced between beings, between substances who do not enter into their words, but who proffer them. The transcendence of the interlocutor and the access to the other through language show that man is a singularity—a singularity other than that of the individuals who are subsumed under a concept or who articulate moments of it. The *I* is ineffable because it is speaking par excellence; respondent, responsible. The other as pure interlocutor is not a known, qualified content, apprehensible on the basis of some general idea, and subject to that idea. He faces things, in reference only to himself. Only with speech between singular beings is the interindividual meaning of beings and things, that is, universality, constituted.

No concept corresponds to the *I* as a being. That is why the very framework of the "experience" of the other cannot be sketched out by a labor of abstraction applied to oneself and that would end up with the "concept" of the *I*. The philosophers of *Einfühlung* at least knew that the "experience" of the other cannot be obtained by simple "variation" of oneself and the projection of one of those variants outside of oneself. They sought the irreducible approach leading to the thou, and when they placed it in sympathy and love—they eventually maintained that each encounter is the beginning of a new amorous adventure. Don Juan never repeated the same experience. Thus, the singularity of the *I* or the *thou* does not resemble the singularity of a sense datum. The particularity of the *I*—its personality—is not just its individuation in space and time. Its individuation *here* and *now* first allows space and time to assume a meaning on the basis of here and now. It locates and is located at the same time, without being reducible to the *knowing* of a situation. Its work of individuation coincides with its subjectivity as an individual. Ipseity consists in this coincidence. Knowing would already suppose the *I*. All knowing of the *here* is already a knowing for me, for I who am here. Knowing is based on ipseity; it does not constitute it. True, the self-referentiality in this prereflexive knowing is configured as a universal structure of the *I*, but, with Jean Wahl, I will say that if intention is common to all "me's," the *intentum* of that intention is absolutely particular. The *I* does know itself as reflected in all the objective reality that has constituted it or with which it has collaborated; hence, it knows itself in terms of a conceptual reality. But if this conceptual reality exhausted his being, a living man would not differ from a dead one. Generalization is death; it inserts the *I* into, and dissolves it in, the generality of its work. The irreplaceable singularity of the *I* comes from its life.

The totality that includes the *I* detached from amorous dialogue cannot be interpreted, then, as a universal order in which the ipseity of beings is absorbed or consumed or sublimated (almost in the sense physics gives this term) into their social position. Neither a simple addition of individuals belonging to the extension of a concept, nor a configuration of moments constituting or realizing the comprehension of the concept man, the totality cannot be reduced to a kingdom of ends. How could reasons constitute a kingdom? How could even their multiplicity be possible? How can we speak of their equality or their inequality, where the word identity alone is suitable? The totality, insofar as it implies multiplicity, is not established between reasons, but between substantial beings who are capable of maintaining relationships. What can this relationship be, since no conceptual link exists prior to this multiplicity? And what can injustice or justice mean in this relationship when individuals, like the different meanings of being in Aristotle, do not have the unity of a concept, and when the standard of justice cannot be obtained by simply comparing individuals? The totality rests on a relationship between individuals, other than the respect of reason. This is precisely what we must bring out. The ontological status of the *I* as a third party affords us to glimpse it.

The Status of the Third Party and Economy

Between the conception in which the *I* reaches the other in pure respect (based on sympathy and love) but is detached from the third party, and the one that transforms us into a singularization of the concept of man, an individual in the extension of this concept subject to the legislation of an impersonal reason—a third way emerges, in which we can understand the totality as a totality of me's, at once without conceptual unity and in relationship with one another.

This totality demands that one free being have control over another. If the violation of one free being by another is injustice, totality can be constituted only by injustice. But injustice cannot be achieved in the society of love, where forgiveness annuls it. There is no real—that is, unforgivable—injustice, except in relation to a third party. The third party is the free being whom I can harm by exerting coercion on his freedom. The totality is constituted by means of the other as third party.

But injustice entails a metaphysical paradox: it can only be directed toward a free being who, as such, does not lay himself open to violence. What meaning, then, can freedom have, such that the third party, injustice, and the totality are possible?

In a first analysis, freedom appears as a will impervious to all influence.

In courage, in accepting death, the will finds its total independence. He who has accepted death resists an alien will to the end—unless the other wills that very death. Therefore the acceptance of death does not make a successful resistance to the other's homicidal will a certainty. Absolute disagreement with an alien will does not bar the fulfillment of his intentions. My refusal of the other, my will that, severing all ties with the outside, is resolved to die, cannot prevent its work from being entered into that alien ledger which my will, by its supreme courage, both defies and recognizes. Thus, even in the extreme case in which it resolves on death, my will is enlisted in the designs of an outside will. Through its result, my will finds itself at the mercy of an outside will.

Thus, the will does not hold all the meaning of its own willing. Though it be the free subject of this willing, it exists as a plaything of a fate that reaches beyond it. Through its work, it implies an unforeseeable meaning which is given it by others, who situate the work, detached from its author, in a new context. Fate does not precede this decision, but is posterior to it: fate is history. The will enters history because *it exists in separating itself from itself*: while willing for itself, it finds itself having willed for others, too. It is an alienation which owes nothing to history, which institutes history—an ontological alienation. It is also the first injustice. Because of this injustice, persons form, around works that are fought over, the totality. To exist in producing works whose productive will is absent constitutes the very status of a being who, as it were, does not hold in his own hands the whole meaning of his being. Freedom, as a will productive of works, without being limited in its willing, enters into a history of which it is a plaything. The limitation of will is not interior here (will in man is infinite as in God)—is not in the willing of the will, but in its situation. We can recognize, in that situation in which, without abdicating anything, a freedom receives a meaning that remains foreign to it, the creature. The multiplicity of me's is not chance, but the structure of the creature. The possibility of injustice is the unique possibility of the limitation of freedom, and the condition of the totality.

The manifest injustice of that history lies in the possibility of depriving the will of its work. The will, in each of its products, without completely dying, without compliantly entering the history that the historians—that is, the survivors—will tell of it, is separated from its work and is misjudged by its contemporaries. In this sense, every work is a failed act. Thus, work differs from expression in which the other presents himself personally. The work presents its author in the absence of the author. It presents itself as being not only his result, but also as his possession. We must take account of the worker if we are to take over the work; it must be taken by force or bought from him. By means of steel and gold, things among things, I wield power over the freedom of the other, while recognizing that freedom that, *qua* freedom, precludes any passivity on which another's power might take hold. The will productive of works is a freedom that betrays itself. Through betrayal, society—a totality of freedoms, both maintained in their singularity and engaged in a totality—is possible. The *I*'s relationship with a totality, then, is essentially economic. "Earthly morality" correctly distrusts any relationship between beings that has not first been economic. The relationship between freedoms is based in the last resort on the ambiguity of the will, which is at once being and having: self-possessed being, exterior to its possession, yet enmeshed in its possession and betraying itself through it.

This amounts to saying that the ontological structure of the third party is delineated as a body: both the "I can" of the will—the body *qua* one's own—and at the same time its vulnerability—a physiological body. The simultaneity of these two moments—the turning of the "I can" into a thing—constitutes the mode of existence of the third party. Its existence is health and sickness. It reveals itself concretely in suffering, which is incapable of mastering itself from within, and inflected toward external medication. Ever since the first meditations of the Greek sages, the physician's practice of medicine has belied the autarchy of will. In the presence of the physician, the latter is stripped of its "for-itself" [*pour-soi*] in a strange confession of pure thinghood, and returns to the immediacy of nature. Injustice is not reducible to the offending of the will, wounded in its dignity. The will mistreats itself, violates itself, compels itself—to the point of making itself forget its for-itself—to the point of making it experience the force that bends it as its own inclination. One can do anything with man. The essentially violable will can emancipate itself only by constructing a world in which it eliminates the occasions for betrayal.

But the violence of the sword lets the will it seeks to dominate escape. True violence preserves the freedom it coerces. Its instrument is gold; violence is corruption. Without yet having recourse to justice, the path of peaceful violence, of exploitation, of slow death is substituted for the passion of war.

The third party, apprehensible in his work, is present and absent at the same time; his third person presence exactly indicates the simultaneity of that presence and that absence. He is given over to my power *qua* outside my grasp. He is accessible in injustice. And this is why injustice—which is at once recognition and non-recognition—becomes possible through the gold that compels and tempts; an instrument of guile. The injustice through which the *I* lives in a totality is always economic.

Discourse and Ethics

But if the totality begins in injustice (which is not unaware of the other's freedom, but, in the economic transaction, leads this freedom to betrayal), injustice is not ipso facto known as injustice. In the sphere of history itself, there is a level of innocent injustice in which evil is done naively. In order to hear justice crying out in the plaintive voice of poverty—or, if you will, in order to hear the voice of conscience—it is not sufficient, nor is it relevant, to be in relation with a freedom and to perceive it in the other, since we recognize that freedom in the transaction itself. This freedom is already presented to me when I buy or exploit. For me to realize my injustice—for me to glimpse the possibility of justice—a new situation is required: someone must ask me for an accounting. Justice does not result from the normal play of injustice. It comes from outside, "through the door," above the fray; it appears as a principle exterior to history. Even in the theories of justice forged in social struggle, in which moral ideas seem to reflect the needs of a society or a class, there is an appeal made to an ideal moral consciousness, an ideal justice, in which one seeks an ultimate justification, and the right to hold up those needs, relative though they are, as an access to the absolute. Though an expression of the objective relations of society, those ideas must also satisfy a living conscience, which judges those objective relations. The human world is a world in which we can judge history. Not a necessarily reasonable world, but one in which we can judge. What is inhuman is to be judged without anyone who judges.

The assertion of man as a power to judge history is the assertion of rationalism. It begins by denouncing the simply poetic thought that thinks without knowing what it thinks—that thinks as one dreams. It begins with reflection on oneself, in order to situate poetic thought in relation to an absolute. But reflection does not let us stop—since the position of the reflecting subject is as poetic as that of the thinker thinking objects, since all thought is poetic, pure *doing*, without any connection with principle, without any beginning. Questioning the position of the thinker suggests a psychoanalysis. Psychoanalysis is, in its philosophical essence, the end result of rationalism: it places the same demands on reflection that reflection placed on naively thinking thought. The non-philosophical end result of psychoanalysis consists in a predilection for some fundamental, but elementary, fables—the libido, sadism, or masochism, the Oedipus complex, repression of the origin, aggressivity—which, incomprehensibly, would alone be unequivocal, alone in not translating (or masking or symbolizing) a reality more profound than themselves: the end terms of psychological intelligibility. The fact of their having been collected from among the debris of the most diverse civilizations and called myths adds nothing to their worth as clarifying ideas, and at most evinces a return to the mythologies, which is even more amazing since forty centuries of monotheism have had no other goal than to liberate humanity from their obsessive grip. Still, the petrifying effect of myths must be distinguished from the comfort they are thought to offer the intelligence.

If self-knowledge rests on conditions, no knowledge, even reflective, even psychoanalytic, has a beginning.

One could, to be sure, invoke the unconditioned nature of that formal truth itself, as in the classical refutation of skepticism. But in reality that refutation derives its force only from the existence of language, i.e., from the existence of the interlocutor, whose presence is invoked by words. To be sure, words are deceptive: as the product of history, of society, of the unconscious, they disguise lies from everyone, even from the liar himself. And we are irremediably deceived when, in an expressed thought, we do not seek the background thoughts—when we take what is said to us literally. But we cannot find our way out of that whole phantasmagoria—we do not begin the work of criticism itself—except in terms of a fixed point. That fixed point can be no incontestable truth, no "certain" statement, which would always be subject to psychoanalysis; but the absolute of an interlocutor, of a being, and not that of a truth about beings. He is not affirmed as a truth, but is believed. Faith or trust—which does not mean here a second source of knowledge, but which is assumed by every theoretical statement. Faith is not the knowledge of a truth about which one might be doubtful or certain. Beyond these modalities, it is the face to face encounter with a substantial interlocutor—who is self-originating, already dominating the powers that constitute and stir it—a thou, springing up inevitably, solid and noumenal, behind the man known in that bit of absolutely decent skin that is the face, closing over the nocturnal chaos, opening onto what it can take up and answer for.

Language, in its expressive function, addresses and invokes the other. It does not, to be sure, consist in invoking him as represented and thought, but that is precisely why the *écart* between the same and the other, the gap in which language stands, cannot be reduced to a relation between concepts, one limiting the other, but describes the transcendence in which the *other* does not weigh on the *same*, but only obligates him, makes him responsible, that is, articulate. The relation of language is not reducible to the relation that obtains between thought and an object that is given to it. Language cannot encompass the other: the other, the concept of whom we are using at this very moment, is not invoked as a concept, but as a person. In speech, we do not just think of the interlocutor, we speak to him; we tell him the very concept we can have of him as "interlocutor in general." The one to whom I speak stands farther back, behind the concept I communicate to him. The absence of a common plane—transcendence—characterizes speech; the communicated content is, to be sure, common—or, more precisely, it becomes so through language. Invocation is prior to commonality. It is a relation with a being who, in a certain sense, is not in relation to me—or, if you like, who is in relation with me only inasmuch as he is entirely in relation to himself. He is a being beyond all attributes, which would have the effect of qualifying him, that is, of reducing him to what he has in common with other beings, of making a concept of him. It is this presence for me of a being identical to itself that I call the presence of the face. The face is the very identity of a being; it manifests itself in it in terms of itself, without a concept. The sensible presence of this chaste bit of skin with brow, nose, eyes, and mouth, is neither a sign allowing us to approach a signified, nor a mask hiding it. The sensible presence, here, de-sensibilizes itself in order to let the one who refers only to himself, the identical, break through directly. As an interlocutor, he faces me; and, properly speaking, only the interlocutor can face, without "facing" meaning hostility or friendship. The face as de-sensibilization, as de-materialization of the sense datum, completes the still encumbered movement in the figures of mythological monsters in which the body, or the animal half-body, allows the evanescent expression on the face of the human head they bear to break through. The particularity of the other in language, far from representing his animality or the remains of an animality of it, constitutes the total humanization of the Other.

The interlocutor does not always face us. Pure language emerges from a relation in which the other person plays the role of a third party. Immediate speech is ruse. We watch and spy on the interlocutor as he speaks and answers questions. But even thus he has an irreducible status which the speech addressed to him recognizes in its originality. Speech treats the freedom of the other with affection, diplomacy, eloquence and propaganda; it threatens and flatters a freedom in order to make the latter the accomplice to intrigues which must result in its own abdication. This speech is still a mode of violence, if violence means ascendancy over a freedom and not just over an inert being with respect to which freedom remains as detached as Plato's exiled soul remains alien to its body. The doctor who hears the patient's confession surprises freedom in the act of reverting to its existence as thing, and speaks to that distorted face of the body that manifests itself in it. The psychoanalyst apprehends the person in the illness itself and accedes to the other as to a third party: the interlocutor is the very person whom one wins over in speaking, since the full trust one solicits is a full betrayal, since all speech of the doctor here is ingenuity and ruse. The judge speaking to the accused is not yet speaking. It is true that the accused has a right to speak. But it is a speaking that precedes speaking; the accused speaks only to acquire a right to true speech. He is listened to, but also observed as he speaks. He is the accused—that is, already in a category. He is not an interlocutor in reciprocity.

To dominate the totality and rise to consciousness of justice, one must get out of the equivocal discourse of psychoanalysis, which is inevitable as long as thought is a part of the system it must encompass. This encompassing itself dissolves into relations that constitute the system; so that the sense of a truth is not in the realized intention of the thought, but in the ontological event of which that truth itself is but an epiphenomenon. It is not through psychoanalysis, leading back to myths, that I can dominate the totality of which I am a part—but by encountering a being who is not in the system, a transcendent being. If no proffered truth could, without dupery, impose itself as first truth, the interlocutor as being and our relationship with the being of the interlocutor—that is to say, language—places us above the totality, and allows us to seek, if not uncover, the very dupery of proffered truths.

Transcendence is what turns its face towards us. The face breaks the system. The ontology of being and truth may not ignore this face to face structure, that is, this structure of faith. The condition for propositional truth resides not in the revelation of a being or of the being of beings, but in the expression of the interlocutor to whom I *say* both the being he is and the being of his being. One must be face to face with the identical. The interlocutor appears as without a history, as outside the system. I can neither fail nor vindicate him; he remains transcendent in expression. Free in this very precise sense, how does he affect me?

I recognize him, that is, I believe in him. But if that recognition were my submission to him, that submission would deprive my recognition of all value: recognition by submission would annul my dignity through which recognition has value. The face that looks at me affirms me. But, face to face, I can no longer deny the other: it is only the noumenal glory of the other that makes the face to face situation possible. The face to face situation is thus an impossibility of denying, a negation of negation. The double articulation of this formula means concretely: the "thou shalt not murder" is inscribed on the face and constitutes its very otherness. Speech, then, is a relationship between freedoms who neither limit nor deny one another, but reciprocally affirm one another. They are transcendent in relation to one another. Neither hostile nor friendly, all hostility, all affection would already change the pure vis-à-vis of the interlocutor. The term respect can be taken up again here; provided we emphasize that the reciprocity of this respect is not an indifferent relationship, such as a serene contemplation, and that it is not the result, but the condition of ethics. It is language, that is, responsibility. Respect attaches the just man to his associates in justice before attaching him to the man who demands justice.

The face to face of language admits of a more radical phenomenological analysis. To respect cannot mean to subject oneself, and yet the other commands me. I am commanded, that is, recognized as capable of a work.[4] To respect is to bow down not before the law, but before a being who commands a work from me. But, for this commandment to entail no humiliation—which would deprive me of the very possibility of respecting—the commandment I receive must also be the commandment to command the one who commands me. It consists in commanding a being to command me. This reference of a commandment for a commandment is the fact of saying We, of constituting a party. By reason of this reference of one commandment to the other, We is not the plural of I.

But respect thus described is not the result of justice, since the commanded man is outside the realm of justice and injustice. The respected one is not the one to whom, but with whom justice is done. Respect is a relationship between equals. Justice assumes that original equality. Love, essentially, is established between unequals, lives from inequality. The interlocutor before whom reciprocity is initiated is not the empirical individual with his individual history; continuing a past, a family, hardships great and small, soliciting pity and compassion. As Saint-Exupéry saw in *Night Flight*, all the slackening, all the femininity of the world filters through "sympathetic" faces as soon as the relation of mutual responsibility is suspended. I wanted to describe the relation of man to man. Justice does not constitute it; it is what makes justice possible. One renders justice to the totality.

We are we because, commanding from identity to identity, we are disengaged from the totality and from history. But we are *we* in that we command each other to a work through which we recognize each other. To be disengaged from the totality while at the same time accomplishing a work in it is not to stand against the totality, but for it—that is, in its service. To serve the totality is to fight for justice. The totality is constituted by violence and corruption. The work consists in introducing equality into a world turned over to the interplay and the mortal strife of freedoms. Justice can have no other object than economic equality. It is not born of the playing out of injustice itself—it comes from outside. But it is illusion or hypocrisy to assume that, while born outside of economic relations, justice can be maintained outside, in the kingdom of pure respect.

Money

The relations between the *I* and the totality do not correspond to those that a study of formal logic would establish between the part and the whole, or between the individual and its concept. The *I* enters a whole without drawing its identity from its place in that whole, without coinciding with its situation, its fortune, or its work, through which it nonetheless combines with the universal order. Very different structures—some of which I have brought out in this study—henceforth replace those of a "formal ontology" in the Husserlian sense. They are not simply grafted onto the latter.

In economy—an element in which one will can have control over another will without destroying it as a will—there occurs the totalization of absolutely singular beings of which there are no concepts and which, by reason of their singularity itself, resist addition. In the transaction, the action of one freedom over another is achieved. Money, whose *metaphysical* meaning has perhaps not yet been measured[5] (despite the plethora of economic and sociological studies that have been devoted to it), corrupting the will by the power it offers it, is the middle term par excellence. It keeps individuals outside the totality since they dispose of it; and, at the same time, it includes them in the totality, since in commerce and transaction the man himself is bought or sold: money is always wages to some extent. As an exchange value of a product it acts on the will it flatters and takes possession of the person. It is thus the abstract element in which the generalization of that which has no concept, the equating of that which has no quantity, is brought about. It is an ambiguous milieu in which persons are integrated into the order of merchandise, but at the same time, remain persons, since the order of merchandise (which is not equivalent to the order of nature) assumes persons, who, consequently, remain inalienable in the very transaction in which they sell themselves. Even when he is a mere object of transaction, the slave tacitly gives his consent to the masters who buy or sell him.

Thus money is not purely and simply the indication of the reification of man. It is an element in which the personal is maintained while being quantified—and there precisely is where the originality of money and, as it were, its worth as a philosophical category, reside. It is not a simply contingent form taken on by the relation between persons. Being a universal power of acquisition and not a thing one enjoys, it creates relationships that last beyond the satisfaction of needs through products exchanged. It is the mark of men capable of postponing their needs and desires. What is possessed in money is not the object, but the possession of objects. As the possession of possession, money presupposes men disposing of time, present in a world that lasts beyond momentary contacts—men who credit one another, who form a society.

But the quantification of man—such as the ambiguity of money makes possible—heralds a new justice. If the radical difference between men (that which does not derive from differences of character or social position, but from their personal identity, irreducible to the concept— from their ipseity itself, as we say today) were not overcome by the quantitative equality of an economy measurable by money, human violence could be rectified only through vengeance or forgiveness. Such a rectification does not put an end to violence: evil engenders evil and infinite forgiveness encourages it. Such is the march of history. But justice interrupts that history. We have insisted on this interruption of history in which the *We* is constituted. Money lets us catch sight of a justice of redemption, replacing the infernal or vicious circle of vengeance or forgiveness. We cannot diminish the condemnation which, from Amos 2:6 to the *Communist Manifesto*, has fallen upon money, precisely because of its power to buy man. But the justice which is supposed to save us from money cannot deny the superior form of economy—that is, of the human totality—in which the quantification of man appears: the common measure between men for which money—whatever its empirical form—provides the *category*. It is certainly quite shocking to see in the quantification of man one of the essential conditions of justice. But can we conceive of a justice without quantity and without reparation?

three

Lévy-Bruhl and Contemporary Philosophy

Whether accepted or challenged, have not Lévy-Bruhl's well-known ideas on primitive mentality marked the orientation of contemporary philosophy?

We raise this issue not in regard to sociology or psychology, to which Lévy-Bruhl's work brings a hypothesis and tables of facts, and whose value we do not intend to examine. We raise it in regard to philosophy in the strict sense of the word.

Lévy-Bruhl himself attributed great importance to the scientific problem to which his work is a response. His hypothesis accounts for more facts[1] than does classical psychology's implicit hypothesis on the unity of the human mind. He goes beyond the psychology of the "healthy adult white male." But this research is governed by a philosophy. The one Lévy-Bruhl professes explicitly is connected with empiricism—very close to positivism—but an intellectualist empiricism. A work that has so many ties to the eighteenth and nineteenth centuries recognizes no dignity superior to that of intellect, which turns out to be manifested in science—if only as a faithful reading of the facts. The fundamental concepts of all thought, whether metaphysical or primitive, are placed under the jurisdiction of science. Primitive mentality is incomparably inferior—that is, can serve only as an object and topic—to the mentality that has broken free of it. Only the latter possesses the marvelous efficacy which was associated in the eighteenth century with "enlightenment."

Lévy-Bruhl's intellectualist empiricism is not without a philosophy of being—less explicit, of course—underlying it. Its concept of being is structured as nature and correlative with a type of knowledge, the only authentic access to reality, an *a priori* access, dominating experience. The existence of a primitive mentality challenges the notion of reason qua legislator of the world and older than it. The unity of mind and subject, according to Bruhl, prefigures an ideal toward which history tends; it could not possibly be its point of departure—he writes at the end of *How Natives Think* [*Fonctions mentales dans les sociétes primitives*].

Even though, through the five volumes that follow, including the *Notebooks* [*Carnets*],[2] the unity of the human mind is asserted progressively and the term *pre-logic* is dropped, a form of thought insensitive to formal contradiction turns out to be simply insensitive to the incompatibilities of facts,[3] and the difference between primitive mentality and modern mentality is seen to distinguish two depths of the soul rather than two souls—Lévy-Bruhl nonetheless has the sense that he is abandoning something essential to his thesis in the course of this evolution. Hence the moving tones of the *Carnets* ("down the slope on which I now find myself"[4]). Thus it is clear that the problem of the unity or diversity of thought and the positivist solution he gave it were very important to him.

We may be less sensitive to it in our time. We may even believe that the impact and novelty of Lévy-Bruhl's works do not suffer at all from the abandonment of the pre-logic. For the most striking feature of that intellectualism was not only an empiricist critique of rationalism, but an opposition to intellectualism itself. This opposition remains. An investigation that borrows its method from the natural sciences to study ethnographic facts results precisely in notions that explode the constitutive categories of natural reality.

This explosion of categories breaks with the *representation* that grounded all psychological life, and with the substance that supported being. Lévy-Bruhl's analyses do not describe experience as cast in the categories that, from Aristotle to Kant—all nuances aside—claimed to condition experience, but in which, with a bit of inconsistency, magic and miracle are also accommodated. Lévy-Bruhl questions precisely the supposed necessity of those categories for the possibility of experience. He describes an experience which makes light of causality, substance, reciprocity—of space and time—of those conditions of "every possible object." The problem of categories themselves is thus raised. We know the role it plays in the speculation of contemporaries. Hence, despite their conceptual framework which is a legacy of the eighteenth and nineteenth centuries, the works of Lévy-Bruhl go beyond psychology or social psychology, and attack the framework of intellectualist naturalism. Of course it is not a question of returning to the beliefs of the primitives themselves, but of highlighting the structures of mind that make such beliefs possible and, eventually, the modes of being—an ontology—that make such structures possible. Lévy-Bruhl's fundamental notions, familiar to the intellectual audience of the world since 1910, taken up again and developed in 1921, and later studied more thoroughly in four new volumes, echo—as we see more clearly now— Bergsonian anti-intellectualism on many points. They have certainly prepared or encouraged some advances characteristic of contemporary thought, and muffled the shock of their paradoxes in advance (or afterward). To a large extent, they have marked the formation of our contemporaries' fundamental concepts. It is the *specific shaping* of those concepts rather than the system they serve which we shall consider, relying especially on the early works, and on the *Carnets*, in which the entire work is reconsidered.

The Downfall of Representation

Representation guaranteed the philosophical tradition contact with the real. At the beginning of the century, in *Logical Investigations*, Husserl, while preparing the downfall of representation, still supported the thesis according to which all psychological fact is representation or based on representation.

Representation is to be understood as the theoretical, contemplative attitude; a knowing, even if of experimental origin, resting on sensations. The sensation has always been taken to be an atom of representation. The correlative of representation is a solid, fixed being, indifferent to the appearance it presents, endowed with a nature and consequently eternal, even if it changes, for the formula of its change is immutable. The relationships that bind such beings, the configurations of such beings, also give themselves to representation. Before acting, before feeling, one must *represent* to oneself the being that will receive the action or that stimulates the feeling. Affectivity in itself encompasses only internal states. It does not reveal anything of the world to us. Philosophers were not unaware of the influence exercised by feelings and passions on our intellectual life, nor of the repercussions of thought on our affectivity. There is a logic of feelings and an emotive charge in ideas. But emotion and representation remain separate. Some truths can manifest themselves in a premonition—but the premonition is then nothing but a confused representation.

The philosophy of our time no longer recognizes this privilege of representation. Bergsonian intuition, for example, is not a knowing about duration [durée], not even a knowing that itself takes time and in which coincidence with duration would still be a kind of limit of representation approaching its object. Intuition is no longer representation in any way, but duration: duration does not delineate a formal dimension in which being flows, but is at the same time being and experience of being. Being actualizes itself in creative efforts in which its being and its presence for the soul coincide. Similarly, in the phenomenological movement, the intentionality of feeling, which Husserl and Scheler still talked about—and in which feeling retained the structure of a *noesis*, although its correlative was value—is replaced by a feeling without support in representation. The poignancy of feeling is no longer interpreted as a reverberation of a knowing about an affectivity enclosed in itself, but as contact with being, more direct than sensation. Precisely what passed for the blindest and deafest in us goes the *farthest*. This is because the very existing of being does not flow forth as the calm subsistence of substance, but as control and possession, as a field of forces in which human existence stands, in which it is engaged, and in which, as we may say already in Lévy-Bruhl's terms, it participates. The poignancy of feeling is the exact measure of such an event. Representation retains only its congealed and superficial forms. Thus, in contemporary philosophy, objective reality is located on the surface of a more profound reality of which it is neither sign nor phenomenon (as it was in the classical distinction between object and being). Sign and phenomenon certainly do not have the dignity of the signified or the noumenon; the structure of *the represented* is common to them, however. Profound reality displays its existing in dimensions that can be defined by no category of representation, but to which, contrary to

Kantian formalism, we have direct access, although by modes of our existence distinct from theory.

From the beginning of *How Natives Think*, Lévy-Bruhl describes a representation in which emotional elements are not only mixed, but oriented in a new way.

> It is very difficult for us to realize by an effort of imagination more complex states in which emotional and motor elements are integral parts of representations. It seems to us that these states are not truly representations. And if we are to retain this term its meaning must be modified. This form of mental activity in primitives must be understood not as a purely or almost purely intellectual or cognitive element, but a more complex phenomenon in which what, for us, is properly "representation" is still blended with other elements of an emotive or motor nature, colored and penetrated by them, and consequently implying a different attitude toward the represented objects. . . . The objects of these representations are not simply grasped by the mind in the form of ideas or images: according to the circumstances of the case, fear, hope, religious awe, the need and the ardent desire to be merged into one common essence, the passionate appeal to a protecting power—these are the soul of these representations and make them at once cherished, formidable, and truly *sacred* to the initiated. . . . Never will that object appear . . . in the form of a colorless or indifferent image.[5]

Emotion, which, according to classical psychology, shuts us up within ourself, thus acquires a certain transcendence. The originality of this notion resides in the extension, the "intentionality" of emotion, as we would say today. Lévy-Bruhl does not limit himself to insisting on the emotional intensity of primitive representations: soon he will use emotion to designate a category of being, that of the supernatural and the mystical.

> Emotion does not follow the representation of the object; it precedes it. Before perception distinguishes the properties of the object, a synthesis, which is in fact emotional, organizes the world.

Syntheses appear primitive in it and . . . almost always unde-composed and undecomposable . . . Collective representations are not presented in it in isolation. They are not analyzed in it to be then arranged in a logical order. They are always involved in pre-perceptions, pre-occupations and pre-conceptions, pre-liaisons, we could almost say pre-reasonings, and it is thus that this men-tality, because it is mystical, is also pre-logical.[6]

Let us leave aside the notion of the prelogical which, from the start, as we see here, rests on the mystical. Mystical experience is not defined negatively. It does not have "a deficient or negative reason."[7] Mysticism is not obscurity or confusion or any imperfection whatever of logical thought. It has access to a completely different sphere, of which the object is but an extension and in which, between different fingers, a kin-ship is established which cannot be translated into thoughts, but is directly accessible to emotion.[8]

This "metaphysical" world is not later than the physical one, but is felt more directly and earlier than sensation. It rests on an emotion which is not tributary to representations, yet opens on being, a concept of emotion common to Lévy-Bruhl and contemporary metaphysicians. The *primeval* character of the structure it outlines is expressed very vig-orously in one of the last pages of the *Carnets*. It should not be taken for granted, he writes,

> that things are *given* first and that afterwards they enter into par-ticipations. In order that they shall be given, that they shall exist, it is already necessary to have participations. A participation is not only a mysterious and inexplicable fusion of things that lose and preserve their identity simultaneously. . . . Without participation, they would not be *given* in experience: they would not exist.

For the individual, participation "is a *condition of his existence*, perhaps the most important, the most essential. . . . For this mentality, to exist is to participate in a mystical force, essence and reality."[9]

The Metaphysics of Anonymity

Ever since Aristotle's metaphysics, substance has represented the ulti-mate and intimate structure of being; it is the term of the "analogy of being." It not only bears an idea of permanence and solidity—but also of a "polarization" of experience and a mastery exercised by substance over attributes and actions. Being can be thematized by thought and, in this sense, it can be conceived, grasped. One approaches it with the question: What? or Who? A name answers this question. Substance is a substantive noun. The denunciation of substantialism, the reduction of substances to relations and the setting aside of man from among things—all these innovations due to the advance of the exact and human sciences—have not shaken the logical and grammatical priority of the substantive. On the other hand, the promotion in modern philosophy of affective experience emancipated from representation introduces structures of being which no longer have anything of the substantive.

Action, which is expressed by the verb, and the *how*, which is translated by the adverb, precede the noun. Being, for example—in Heidegger and the Heideggerians—is not a being, but the being of beings, the source of a "chiaroscuro" which reveals beings, present participles of being. The condition of every entity, the first revealed one, is not an entity. Beings appear in a "world" which is not a totality of singular beings that can be expressed in substantive nouns, but a field or atmosphere. The modern novel, for its part, tends in this direction; and modern painting re-immerses things in a non-figurative reality. In a profusion of monstrous forms, it seeks the compossibility of the incompossible. No longer does anything impose choice, and imagination discovers its independence from perception, whose categories it shatters. Religious psychology—like that of Rudolf Otto (1917!), for example, so rich in influence—presents an experience in relation to the numinous or the sacred which is neither an object nor a person who speaks. Thus the very notion of form and nature which, since the Greeks, has seemed inseparable from ideas of being and the metaphysical, is destroyed.

Lévy-Bruhl analyzes primitive mentality, fully aware that he is risking a disruption of categories. "The causal connections which, to us, are the very framework of nature, the very basis of its reality and stability, are of very little interest in their (the primitives') eyes."[10] "Here we have a kind of *a priori* over which experience has no control."[11]

"To be is to participate."[12] The participation that comes into play in the affective category of the supernatural in no way leads from an imprecise physical phenomenon toward metaphysical being, but from the given thing toward a power that no longer has the solid framework of being, toward the diffuse presence of an occult influence. We are dealing here with anonymous realities. "As visitants from an inaccessible region, they float around, they radiate, so to speak."[13] These powers are not inscribed in a substantial form, nor are they the wills of subjects which reveal themselves. On the contrary, to a certain extent things exist as fetishes: they are borne by powers which are not their attributes. As "tools" which, in the Heideggerian analysis of the world, are not things first and usable afterwards, but are from the outset "objects of use," resulting from a world which is not a sum of entities, but a practical conjunction—fetishes derive their being from a conjunction of powers that cannot be reduced to a nature. The most perfected tools belong to this category. "The most important thing is not that the instruments be well made, but that they be successful."[14] Powers cannot be reduced to nature, not because they are part of the beyond, but because the beyond is never separated from this world. "The primitive makes no distinction between this world and the other."[15] Hence, to express being, there are formulas like "to be both,"[16] "duality-unity," "consubstantiality,"[17] and "interpenetration"[18].

This ambiguity "desubstantializes" substance. The confusion of the visible and the invisible is reducible neither to a relation of causality nor to symbolism (the relation of the sign to the signified) which, for a non-primitive mentality, connect the supernatural and the natural. If participation opens a dimension leading to the supernatural, this supernatural is not a simple replica, in the superlative, of this world, or a sublimation of objects, structured like them and separated only by the purely formal abyss of transcendence; its supernaturalness is directly accessible through emotional experience, through an "experience-belief" as Lévy-Bruhl says later.[19] From the outset, this supernatural is feared, hoped for, respected, already implicating our security,[20] "a 'perpetual possibility' of sorcery"[21] an experience of what is diametrically opposed to nature and the world. Hence the fluidity of that anti-universe. Things transform themselves into one another because their forms count for little next to the nameless powers that command them.

The *sensing* [*sentir*] with which Lévy-Bruhl characterizes participation is not simply an immediate and still uncertain relation with a form. Sensing is neither a lame *thinking* nor a shortcut—it works in another dimension. It is a way of subjecting oneself to a force. Mystical reality is given in the feeling "of an existence that is present although most often invisible and imperceptible to the senses, and acting. It is an ultimate given."[22] No contemplated image forms a screen between that force and man: "At the very moment when he perceives what is given to his senses, the primitive represents to himself the mystical force that is thus manifesting itself."[23] Sensing is not an empty form of knowledge, but a magic spell, an exposure to a diffuse threat of sorcery, a presence in a climate, in the darkness of being that is lurking and frightening, and not a presence of things, confronting us *face to face*.

Existence

In modern philosophy, the destruction of substance (or, more precisely, of the "substantiality" of beings)—correlative to the downfall of representation—has marked the end of a certain notion of exteriority; of that exteriority already very close to the subject, which made idealist philosophy possible. Since the primary experience of being is situated at the level of emotion, exterior being is stripped of the form that guaranteed thought a familiarity with it. The subject thus finds himself before an exteriority to which it is delivered up, for it is absolutely foreign to him, that is to say, unpredictable, and hence, peculiar. The unique, genus-free character of situations and moments, their bare existence, is thus the great theme of the moderns. As for the *I*, thus delivered up to being, it is thrown out of its abode into an eternal exile, losing its mastery over itself, overwhelmed by its own being. Henceforth, it is a prey to events that have already determined it. Whereas in a represented world engagement also signified a disengagement, a distance, a time lag, a freedom, a possession of self despite history—being-in-the-world is the exemplary *fait accompli*. The being that is about to be is already a being that has traversed you through and through. And, at the same time, this determination and this influence are not causality—since the *I* that is in their grasp decides, is engaged, takes responsibility. The structure is that of a future already sensed in the present, but still leaving a pretext for decision.

Lévy-Bruhl appears to have seen that structure in participation, and to have developed it in the analyses of omens, in which the sign is cause, and prediction is production,[24] and in which, at the same time, the power that manifests itself and determines is also beseeched.[25] "The field of action of mystical powers constitutes a kind of category of the real that dominates those of time and space, into which facts are necessarily arranged for us."[26] As in the language of the philosophers of existence, in which one *is* his future instead of representing it to himself— primitives who observe the results of a divinatory practice "personally feel at stake," and the aspect that concerns them in the ordeal "is not simply theirs, it is they themselves."[27]

But if the subject is replaced by existence, the idea of being assumes a new meaning. It used to be the case that only substantial forms conferred diversity and reality to an *existing* that was colorless and neutral without them. Henceforth bare existing, shorn of these forms, manifests itself not as a very general and empty term, but as deployment, as effectiveness, influence, control, and transitivity. This is certainly the meaning that being assumes in Bergsonism, in which neither being nor time, of which being is the unfolding, are formal anymore but in which, in duration [*la durée*], form and content merge totally—the contents being, as it were, the very modalities of form. This is also the meaning assumed by being in contemporary ontology. It loses the unequivocal nature it drew from its orientation, in the analogy of being, toward the term substance. Existents no longer differ because of their qualities or their nature, but because of their mode of existing.

Both the subject as existent and the verb to be appear in the primitive mentality as active and transitive. For the primitive, the world is never given, but is like an anonymous sphere which greatly resembles the agonizing anonymity of existence not yet assumed by a subject.

The being of the primitive mentality is not general. "Each of those participations is felt qualitatively. . . . Each among them is *separate*."[28] Time qua pure form is unknown to primitives;[29] every instant has a different potential, contrary to the homogeneity of form time. This potential comes from being itself that fills the instant—from the power of that naked being. The efficacy of the event is inherent in its actuality, its facticity, as we would say today. It acts as a precedent. Henceforth, the past has a special format, it is mystical as past; it still acts by virtue of the fact that it was. And, conversely, the fact of being is not an empty notion, accomplished identically in indifferent landscapes. This landscape and all that fills it are the stuff of that *existing* and its very exercise. To any given individual, to be alive means to be currently involved in a complex network of mystic "participations" in common with the other members, living or dead, of his social group, with the animal and vegetable groups born of the same soil, with the earth itself.[30]

The white man who saves a dying primitive compromises his life, "in the indigenous and mystical sense of the word."[31] To live, to be, has several lived and felt meanings. "Their experience . . . is not homogeneous and on a single plane, as we imagine it."[32] "It's 'reality' is not univocal."[33]

The Idea of Mentality

We are not at the level of representations, even the most elementary ones, but at another, situated in the depths of the individual, where the phenomena which occur are undoubtedly psychic but essentially affective, although eventually *the possibility of representations is not excluded: in that they are properly human.*[34]

The world of primitives is not a deformed representation of the universe. It is not a representation at all, even though the emotion that reveals it is "intentionality." But if Lévy-Bruhl wants less and less to demonstrate that Western thought results from a conjunction of circumstances which could have produced a different thought, he nevertheless questions, even by his abandoning of the term *prelogical*, the privilege of theoretical thought. In reality, this privilege results neither from the certainty of the *cogito* nor from the immutable laws of logic, but from the independence that representation, as such, retains in relation to all history—like Minerva, who emerged fully armed from Jupiter's head. The relativism of truth in the minds of the empiricists, who discover the variation of mental habits through the ages of man and humanity, does not diminish the absoluteness of the cognitive attitude, which is already entire in the sensation, that elementary piece of information, that illumination that reveals to the soul its homeland in the world of ideas. Lévy-Bruhl destroys this absolute precisely by showing that representation is not the original gesture of the human soul, but a choice, and that the supposedly sovereign *mens* rests on a *mentality.*

The term mentality is new; it designates a modern idea. People formerly thought that reason could be overcome by external causes, and they connected to those causes, which were external to the mind, the captivity of minds insensitive to reason. But, it was thought, a sound method could activate the good sense so miraculously common to all men. Reason is in possession of the key to the method; it can liberate itself by itself, for it is already itself from the start. The notion of mentality consists in affirming that the human mind does not depend solely on an exterior situation—climate, race, institution, or even contracted mental habits that would pervert the natural illumination.

Mentality is *in itself* dependence; it emerges from an ambivalent possibility of turning toward conceptual relations or of remaining in relationships of participation. *Prior* to representation it is strikingly engaged in being; it *orients* itself in being. Mentality is that orientation prior to the choice of knowledge [*savoir*], which is a modality of that orientation. Movement toward the object rests on a deeper movement that, in the mentality of the primitive, is more visible than in ours.[35] And thus a perspective is opened on this new type of events which are played out below the level of representation, but nonetheless remain in relation with being.

This is, in particular, the perspective glimpsed by philosophies of existence. Their contribution has been to uncover an event and a problem in the apparently tautological relation which binds the *man who is* to his being. Contrary to classical psychology, where existence was innocently possessed by the existent, and where conflict and struggle were played out only with beings and by the intervention of representations—the philosophy of existence sees the "pre-representative" engagement in being as a drama, where to exist becomes both a transitive verb like "to take" or "to seize," and a reflexive verb like "to feel" [*se sentir*] or "to stand" [*se tenir*]. The reflectivity conveyed by this verb is not a theoretical vision, but already an event of existing itself; not a consciousness, but already engagement, a *way* of being, qualified by all the circumstances one would have been tempted to take for settings. Doesn't the notion of an *existing* that participates in the ground, penetrated by protective or hostile forces, which we spoke of earlier, break with the traditional and very formal concept of being along the same lines?

In the crucial pages of the *Carnets*, this way of existing—in which the existent is both separated from everything and engaged in this everything—is associated with the social experience in which the autonomy of personal existence is not separated from belonging to the group.[36] "The participation of the individual in the social body is an immediate datum, contained in the feeling he has of his own existence."[37] This theory of participation is not without value in explaining the modern feeling of existence or even in its partial justification. Perhaps we belong to a philosophical era in which the conception of being, which had been conceived on the model of the living being, and then identified with the being of mechanistic matter, has been replaced by social experience as the primary intuition of being. But if Lévy-Bruhl's analyses have helped to forge the concepts of emotional experience and participation, of existence and being which are effective because of their existence itself (beyond any notion of substantial form, since content and form are inseparable)—concepts in which modern thought, both atheistic and religious, has found inspiration and the possibility of a broadening of the notion of Reason itself—it is also true that they have nourished a nostalgia for outdated and retrograde forms. The renewal of mythology, the elevation of myth to the rank of superior thought by secular thinkers, the struggle in the domain of religion with what has recently been called the spiritualizing of dogma and morality, conveys not a broadening of reason, but a reversion to primitive mentality pure and simple. This is a nostalgia which is perhaps explained by the insufficiency of technical reason and the catastrophes it has unleashed. But is monotheistic civilization incapable of responding to this crisis by an orientation liberated from the horrors of myths, the confusion of thought they produce, and the acts of cruelty they perpetuate in social customs?

A Man-God?

Philosophy is a bringing to light. According to a fashionable expression, invented as if to underline the indiscretion of the philosophical enterprise, it is an unveiling. How, then, can I deal philosophically with a notion that belongs to the intimate sphere of hundreds of millions of believers—the mystery of mysteries of their theology—that for nearly twenty centuries has united people whose fate I share along with most of their ideas, with the exception of the very belief in question here this evening?

I could of course have declined. But the request to participate in this meeting was so cordial that it made it impossible to refuse. Not that I would have been afraid of being impolite. But how could I turn away from the generous intentions of our times and forget the camaraderie of the tragic years?

I do not have the effrontery to enter an area forbidden to those who do not share the faith, and the ultimate dimensions of which no doubt escape me. I want to reflect on two of the multiple meanings suggested by the notion of Man-God, which, followed as it is by a question mark on the programs of this colloquium, is recognized as a problem.

On the one hand, the problem of the Man-God includes the idea of a self-inflicted humiliation on the part of the Supreme Being, of a descent of the Creator to the level of the Creature; that is to say, an absorption of the most active activity into the most passive passivity.

On the other hand the problem includes, as if brought about by this passivity pushed to its ultimate degree in the Passion, the idea of expiation for others, that is, of a substitution. The identical par excellence, the noninterchangeable, the unique par excellence, would be substitution itself.

These ideas, at first blush theological, overturn the categories of our representation. So I want to ask myself to what extent these ideas, which have unconditional value for the Christian faith, have philosophical value, and to what extent they can appear in phenomenology. True, it is a phenomenology that is already the beneficiary of Judeo-Christian wisdom. That is no doubt the case—but consciousness does not assimilate everything in the various wisdoms. It supplies phenomenology only with what has been able to nourish it. Hence I ask myself to what extent the new categories we have just described are philosophical. I am certain that this extent will be judged insufficient by the believing Christian. But it may not be a waste of time to show the points beyond which nothing can replace religion.

I think that the humility of God, up to a certain point, allows for conceiving the relationship with transcendence in terms other than those of naiveté or pantheism; and that the idea of substitution—in a certain modality—is indispensable to the comprehension of subjectivity.

The appearance of man-gods, sharing the passions and joys of men who are purely men, is certainly a common characteristic of pagan poems. But in paganism, as the price for this manifestation, the gods lose their divinity. Hence philosophers expel poets from the City to preserve the divinity of the gods in men's minds. But divinity thus saved lacks all condescension. Plato's God is the impersonal Idea of the Good; Aristotle's God is a thought that thinks itself. And it is with this divinity which is indifferent to the world of men that Hegel's *Encyclopedia*, that is to say, perhaps, philosophy, ends. As the world absorbed the gods in the works of the poets, so in the works of the philosophers the world is sublimated into the Absolute. Infinity then manifests itself *in* the finite, but it does not manifest itself *to* the finite. Man is no longer *coram Deo*. The extra-ordinary surplus of the proximity between finite and Infinite falls back into the order. Men, their misery and despair, their wars and sacrifices, the horrible and the sublime are all resolved and summed up in an impassive order of the absolute and the totality. It is true that, if we are to believe the philosophers, the real meaning of our lives appears in an uninterrupted discourse capable of articulating even its own interruption, ever reviving in immortal intersubjectivity. It never has the meaning it has in our lives.

But this impossibility for the philosopher of thinking the face to face, the proximity and the uncanniness of God and the strange fecundity of the encounter does not derive from some aberration of logical thought—it results from the irrefutable formalism of logic itself. If the absolutely Other appears to me, is its truth not integrated by that very fact into the context of my thoughts, there to find a meaning, and into my time, there to becoming contemporary? Every disturbance ends up falling back into the order, allowing a broader and more complex order to appear. That is not a purely theoretical view: it is the great experience of our time. The historian finds a natural meaning in all strange out-breaks. How can we maintain the communication of two orders against a universe in which everything is God, in which everything is world? How is the extravagant movement toward God possible without under-lining, as in an interplanetary flight, the unity of the order that makes it possible?

The idea of a truth whose manifestation is not glorious or bursting with light, the idea of a truth that manifests itself in its humility, like the still small voice in the biblical expression[1]—the idea of a persecuted truth—is that not henceforth the only possible modality of transcen-dence? Not because of the moral quality of humility which I do not wish to challenge in any way, but because of its *way of being* which is perhaps the source of its moral value. To manifest itself as humble, as allied with the vanquished, the poor, the persecuted—is precisely not to return to the order. In this defeatism, in this timidity that does not dare to dare, through this asking that does not have the impudence to ask and that is non-audacity itself, through this solicitation of the beggar, and of the homeless without a place to lay his head—at the mercy of the bid-ding of the one who welcomes—humility disturbs absolutely; it is not of the world. Humility and poverty are a bearing within being—an ontological (or meontological)[2] mode—and not a social condition. To present oneself in this poverty of the exile is to interrupt the coherence of the universe. To pierce immanence without thereby taking one's place within it.

Obviously such an opening can only be an ambiguity. But the appearing of an ambiguity in the seamless texture of the world is not a looseness in its weave or a failure of the intelligence that examines it, but precisely the proximity of God which can only occur in humility. The ambiguity of transcendence—and consequently the alternation of the soul moving from atheism to belief and from belief to atheism, and consequently the solecism that would result in the use the first person singular of the present indicative of the verb to believe—is not the feeble faith surviving the death of God, but the original mode of the presence of God, the original mode of communication. Communication does not mean certainty's presence of self to self, that is, an uninterrupted sojourn in the same—but the risk and danger of transcendence. Living dangerously is not despair, but the positive generosity of Uncertainty. The idea of persecuted truth thus allows us to put an end to the game of unveiling in which immanence always wins out over transcendence; for, once being is unveiled, even partially, even in mystery, it becomes immanent.

It is doubtless Kierkegaard who best understood the philosophical notion of transcendence contributed by the biblical theme of God's humility. For him, persecuted truth is not simply truth approached in a bad way. The persecution and humiliation par excellence to which it is exposed are modalities of the true. The force of transcendent truth is in its humility. It manifests itself as if it did not dare say its name; it does not come to take its place in the world with which it would be confused immediately, as if it did not come from beyond. Reading Kierkegaard, one may even wonder whether the Revelation that says its origin is not contrary to the essence of the transcendent truth which thus would again affirm its impotent authority against the world. One may wonder whether the true God can ever discard His incognito, whether the truth which is said should not immediately appear as not said, in order to escape the sobriety and objectivity of historians, philologists, and sociologists who will deck it out in all the names of history, reducing its still small voice to the din of battlefields and marketplaces, or to the structured configuration of meaningless elements. One may wonder whether the first word of revelation must not come from man, as in the ancient prayer of the Jewish liturgy in which the faithful gives thanks not for what he receives, but for the very fact of giving thanks.

But the opening of ambiguity into which transcendence slips may demand a supplementary analysis. Can the God who humbles Himself to "dwell with the contrite and the humble" (Isaiah 57:15), the God "of the stranger, the widow, and the orphan," the God manifesting Himself in the world through His covenant with that which is excluded from the world—can He, in His excessiveness, become a *present* in the time of the world? Isn't that too much for His poverty? Is it not too little for His glory without which His poverty is not a humiliation? In order for the alterity that upsets the order not to become at once *participation* in the order, in order for the horizon of the beyond to remain open, the humility of the manifestation must already be a distancing. In order that the extirpation from the order not be ipso facto a participation in the order, this extirpation—by a supreme anachronism—must precede its entrance into the order. It requires the inscription of a retreat in the advance and, as it were, a past that was never present. The conceptual figure delineated by the ambiguity—or the enigma—of this anachronism in which an entrance follows the withdrawal and which, consequently, has never been contained in my time and is thus immemorial— is what we call trace. But the trace is not just one more word: it is the proximity of God in the countenance of my fellowman.

The nakedness of the face is an extirpation from the context of the world, from the world signifying as a context. The face is precisely that through which the exceptional event of the *facing* [*en-face*] is produced, which the facade of the building and of things can only imitate. But this relation of the *coram* is also the most naked nakedness, the "defenseless" and "without resources" itself, the destitution and poverty of absence that constitutes the proximity of God—the trace. For if the face is *facing* per se, the proximity interrupting the series, it is because it comes enigmatically from the Infinite and its immemorial past, and because this covenant between the poverty of the face and the Infinite is inscribed in the force with which my fellowman is imposed for my responsibility before all engagement on my part—the covenant between God and the pauper is inscribed within our brotherhood. The infinite is unassimilable otherness, absolute difference in relation to everything that can be shown, symbolized, announced, and recalled— in relation to everything that is presented and represented, and hence "contemporized" with the finite and the Same. He is He, Illeity. His immemorial past is not an extrapolation from human duration, but the original anteriority or the original ultimacy of God in relation to a world which cannot accommodate Him. The relation with the Infinite is not a knowledge, but a proximity, preserving the excessiveness of the uncontainable which grazes the surface; it is Desire, that is, precisely a thought thinking infinitely more than it thinks. To solicit a thought thinking more than it thinks, the Infinite cannot incarnate itself in a Desirable, cannot, being infinite, enclose itself in an end. It solicits through a face. A Thou is inserted between the I and the absolute He. It is not history's present that is the enigmatic interval of a humiliated and transcendent God, but the face of the Other. And we will then understand the unusual meaning—or the meaning that becomes unusual and surprising again as soon as we forget the murmur of our sermons—we will understand the amazing meaning of Jeremiah 22:16: "He judged the cause of the poor and needy; . . . Was not this to know me? saith the Lord."

But, in this transubstantiation of the Creator into the creature, the notion of Man-God affirms the idea of substitution. Hasn't this blow to the principle of identity expressed the secret of subjectivity to some extent? But it is necessary to see precisely to what extent. In a philosophy that, in our time, credits the mind with no other practice than theory, and which leads to the pure mirror of objective structures—the humanity of man reduced to consciousness—does not the idea of substitution allow for a rehabilitation of the subject, which naturalist humanism, quickly losing in naturalism the privileges of the human, does not always achieve?

Human subjectivity, interpreted as consciousness, is always activity. I can always assume what is imposed on me. I always have the capacity to consent to what I submit to and to put a good face on a bad situation. Thus, everything happens as if I were at the beginning; except at the approach of my fellowman. I am recalled to a responsibility never contracted, inscribed in the face of an Other. Nothing is more passive than this prior questioning of all freedom. It must be thought through with acuity. Proximity is not a consciousness of proximity. It is an obsession which is not an overenlarged consciousness, but counterconsciousness, reversing consciousness. It is an event that strips consciousness of its initiative, that undoes me and puts me before an Other in a state of guilt; an event that puts me in accusation—a persecuting indictment, for it is prior to all wrongdoing—and that leads me to the *self*, to the accusative that is not preceded by any nominative.

The oneself is not a representation of the self by the self—not a consciousness of self—but a prior recurrence which alone makes possible all return of consciousness to itself. Oneself, passivity or patience, the "inability to take a distance toward oneself." *I* is in itself, up against itself, inescapably in his skin—ill at ease in its own skin—that incarnation having no metaphorical meaning, but being the most literal expression of an absolute recurrence, which any other wording would say only approximately. The oneself is not an incarnated me *in addition* to its expulsion into itself—that incarnation is already its expulsion into itself, exposure to offense, to accusation, to grief.

An unlimited passivity? Does not the identity of the self set a limit to the passivity of submitting, the final resistance that even matter opposes to its form? But the passivity of the self is not matter. Pushed to the end, it consists in inverting its identity, in getting rid of it.

If such a desertion of identity, such a reversal is possible without turning into alienation pure and simple, what else can it be if not a responsibility for others, for what others do, even to the point of being made responsible for the very persecution it undergoes. According to Lamentations 4:30, "He giveth his cheek to him that smiteth him; he is filled full with reproach." Not because suffering has any supernatural power whatever; but because it is still I who am responsible for the persecution I undergo. The self is the passivity on the hither side of identity, that of the hostage.

Absolute passivity transforming itself into absolute undeclinability: accused beyond freedom, but precisely dedicated to the initiative of response. There is in this a strange reversal of patience into activity and of the singular into the universal, and the outline of an order and a meaning in being which depends neither on a cultural work nor on a simple structure. Modern antihumanism, denying the primacy of the person, an end in itself, in being, consequently seeking that meaning in a pure and simple configuration of elements, may have left a place for subjectivity as substitution. It is not that the self is just a being endowed with certain qualities called moral, which it would bear as attributes. It is the infinite passivity or passion or patience of the me—its self—the exceptional uniqueness to which it is reduced that is that incessant event of substitution, the fact for being of emptying itself of *its* being.

But the analysis that has led to my conclusions took as its point of departure neither a God nor a mind nor a person nor a soul nor an *animal rationale*. Each of these terms is an identical substance. To unsay one's identity is a matter of the *I*. How can I expect another to sacrifice himself for me without requiring the sacrifice of others? How can I admit his responsibility for me without immediately finding myself, through my condition as hostage, responsible for his responsibility itself. To be me is always to have one more responsibility.

The idea of the hostage, of expiation of me for the Other, in which relations based on the exact proportionality between wrongdoing and punishment, between freedom and responsibility (relations which transform collectivities into societies with limited responsibility) are overturned, cannot be extended outside me. The fact of exposing oneself to the charge imposed by the suffering and wrongdoing of others posits the oneself of the *I*. I alone can, without cruelty, be designated as victim. The *I* is the one who, before all decision, is elected to bear all the responsibility for the World. Messianism is that apogee in Being—a reversal of being "persevering in his being"—which begins in me.

A New Rationality: On Gabriel Marcel

During the twenty-five centuries in which our civilization has been chronicled, the impregnable Rock of God, the *fundamentum inconcussum* of the Cogito, and the star-studded sky of the world have, one after the other, resisted the fluidity of time's passage and guaranteed a presence to the present. Since then, we have been taught successively the death of God and the contingency of the human and of humanism in human thought. And now the end of the world is approaching, the broken world of which Marcel already speaks.

Is all this the decadence of writing and the hallucinations of jaded intellectuals? I don't think so. Something is happening or has happened. And it is not to comfort myself with the memory of the philosophy of the good old days that I evoke Gabriel Marcel. In this disintegration, I already divine positive modalities of the mind, new signifying of meaning. Amid these ruins, Gabriel Marcel himself conceived this end and the beginnings it contains.

Ruin of the world. In a world still going about its business, it manifests itself in language admitting its inability to synchronize the life of things, playing the game of signifiers without signified. As if there were no longer any room for *durée* in the simultaneity of propositions, as if the Platonic anamnesis that maintained the unity of representation were becoming amnesia. Anti-Bergsonism in the heart of Bergsonism: all disorder is no longer another order.[1] It is the end of the Book, which Blanchot speaks of, and the problems with teaching *ex cathedra*.[2] But ever since Nietzsche's aphoristic language, it is the whole distance that separates Hegel's (and Diderot's) *Encyclopedia* from a *Metaphysical Journal*[3] publishable in its chronology of a journal, without seeking, in the guise of material or posthumous reliquary, any synthesis at all. Like the work of Jean Wahl—a companion and friend of Marcel's, a witness to the same endings and initiator of the same beginnings—where the most highly informed philosophy espouses the new rhythms of free verse and the diachrony of time, freed from any imperative of scansion. It is the disaffection with positional significations, with the meaningful as belief, the denunciation of the rigors of the logical proposition and the repressive verdict of judgment, and the disaffection with the dogma rather than with the God it posits. An obsession with the inexpressible, the ineffable, the unsaid, though it may be badly said or a *lapsus linguae*, an obsession with the genealogy and etymology of words: modernity is also that.

It is not mysticism. Mysticism still remains loyal to the order established by logic, to the absolute as being, correlative to logic; loyalty to ontology, despite its audacity in reaching the absolute without the labor of the concept. Modern philosophical literature, on the contrary, prefers to play with verbal signs rather than to take seriously the system registered in their Said. But thus the end of a mode of signifying appears, the end of a rationality attached exclusively, in words, to being, to the Said of Saying, to the Said conveying fields of knowledge. Condillac saw in science a well-made language; language—even if it were badly made—is meaningful for the Western tradition by virtue of all it knows, by virtue of the truth of this knowing, that is to say, by virtue of the unchanging identity of *what is* or of the *being of what is*—capable of gloriously renewing its self-sufficiency—its perfection—through the very differences which seem to betray or limit it.

So there is an end; but a new wisdom, a new rationality begins, a new notion of spirit. It is Gabriel Marcel who tells us in the entry of October 21, 1919, of the *Metaphysical Journal*:

> There is no doubt that we need to react strongly against the classical idea of the eminent value of [*autarkia*] or personal self-sufficiency. The perfect is not perfect because it suffices for itself; or at least the perfection of self-sufficiency is that of a system, not that of a being . . . Under what conditions can the relationship binding

a being to what it needs have a spiritual value? It seems as though here there must be reciprocity, an awakening. The only relationship that can be said to be spiritual is that of a being with a being; . . . What really matters is spiritual commerce between beings, and that involves not respect but love.[4]

An essential text! It speaks a great deal about being, spirit and the spiritual, and love is mentioned at the end. But being here is not consciousness of self, it is relation with the other than self and awakening. And is not the other than self the Other Person? And love, above all, means welcoming the other person as *thou*, that is to say, not empty-handed. The spirit is not the Said, it is the Saying which goes from the Same to the Other, without suppressing the difference. It paves a way for itself where nothing is in common. Non-indifference of the one for the other! Under the spirituality of the *I* awakened by the *thou* in Marcel, in convergence with Buber, a new signifying is signified. Not a nonidentity of the identical and the nonidentical; nor their identity! Despite the continued use of so many set phrases and so many traditional institutions in Marcel's writings, from the time of the writing of the *Journal* on, his sublime work is obsessed with and inflamed by this new signifying of the meaningful.

It is rich enough to be relieved of its bad spiritualism without harm. What I call the non-indifference[5] of Saying is, in its double negation, the difference behind which no commonality arises in the guise of an entity. And thus there is both relation and rupture, and thus, awakening: awakening of Me by the other, of Me by the Stranger, of Me by the stateless person, that is, by the fellow human being who is but a fellow human being. Awakening which is neither reflection upon oneself nor universalization; an awakening that signifies a responsibility for the other who must be fed and clothed, my substitution for the other, my expiation for the suffering, and no doubt, for the wrongdoing of the other person. Expiation, assigned to me without any possible evasion and in which my own uniqueness is exalted, irreplaceable.

But in this rupture, and in this awakening, and in this expiation, and in this exaltation, the divine comedy of a transcendence beyond ontological positions unfolds.

Whether the thought awakened to God believes itself
to go *beyond* the world or to listen to a voice more
intimate than intimacy,[1] the hermeneutics that interprets that life or that religious psychism cannot assimilate it to an experience which that thought specifically thinks it is going beyond. That thought lays claim
to a *beyond*, a *deeper-than-self*—a transcendence different from the *outside-the-self* that intentional consciousness opens and traverses. What does this going
beyond mean? What does this difference mean?
Without making any decision of a metaphysical
character,[2] we would like here only to ask how, in its
noetic structure, this transcendence breaks with the
outside-the-self of intentionality. This demands a pre-
liminary reflection on the specific modality of intentionality in its reference to the world and to being.

WE will take the Husserlian phenomenology of consciousness as a point of departure. Its essential principle—which, to a large extent, can be considered as
the corollary of the formula "all consciousness is
consciousness of something"—states that being commands its ways of *being given*, that being orders the
forms of knowing which apprehend it, that an essential necessity attaches being to its ways of appearing
to consciousness. These formulas might certainly be
understood as affirming *a priori* or even empirically a
certain *state of things*, as one "eidetic" truth among
"eidetic" truths, if they did not concern that which
(bearing as they do on the correlation of
being/knowledge) guarantees the possibility of all

truth, all *empire*, and all eidetic, and that on which *appearing* as exposure and consciousness as knowing depend. The relation here between
consciousness and the reality of the real is no longer conceived as an
encounter of being with a consciousness that would be radically distinct
from it, subjugated to its own necessities, reflecting encountered
being—faithfully or otherwise—at the mercy of some "psychological
laws" or other, and arranging images into a coherent dream in a blind
soul. The possibility of such a psychologism is henceforth destroyed,
even if the difference between being and the subjectivity to which being
appears hypostatizes the psychism that is consciousness or knowing into
an *ipseity*.

HENCE, it is necessary to think the Husserlian formulas beyond their
formulations. Consciousness is promoted to the rank of an "event"
which somehow develops in *appearance*—in a manifestation—the energy or the ess*a*nce[3] of being which in this sense becomes psychism. The
ess*a*nce of being is equivalent to an ex-*position*. The ess*a*nce of being,
understood as ex-position, refers on the one hand to its position as an
entity, to a consolidation on an unshakable ground, which is the earth
beneath the firmament, that is to say, to the *positivity* of the here and
now, the positivity of presence: to the positivity of presence, that is to
say, to the repose of the identical. Moreover, it is through this positivity—presence and identity, presence or identity—that the philosophical
tradition almost always understands the *ess*a*nce of being*. And it is to the
*ess*a*nce of being* in its identity that the intelligibility or the rationality of
the *founded* and the identical is reduced. On the other hand, exposition
refers being to exhibition, to appearing, to the phenomenon. From position or ess*a*nce to phenomenon, it is not simple degradation, but an
emphasis that is described.

Presence, becoming re-presentation, is exalted in this representation,
as if ess*a*nce, consolidation on a foundation, went as far as thetic affirmation in a consciousness, as if its "energy" of position, outside all
causality, brought about the activity of consciousness, an experience
proceeding from the me, developing as psychic life—exterior to this
energy—the very energy the entity expends in being. To recapitulate a
Hegelian formula (*Logic* II, p. 2), is the process of knowing not "the
movement of being itself"? Through synthetic and inclusive activity

(although marking its difference by its ipseity of a me, "transcendent in immanence"), transcendental apperception confirms presence: presence turns back upon itself in re-presentation and fulfills itself or, as Husserl says, identifies itself. This *life* of presence in re-presentation is certainly also *my* life, but in that life of consciousness, presence becomes an event or a duration of presence. A duration of presence or a duration as presence: in it every loss of time, every lapse, is retained or returns in memory, "finds itself again" or "reconstructs itself," adheres to a *whole* through memory or the writing of history. Consciousness as reminiscence glorifies the ultimate vigor of presence in representation. *The time of consciousness lending itself to representation is a synchrony stronger than diachrony.* Synchronization which is one of the functions of intentionality: representation.

This is the reason for the persistence of Brentano's famous formula through all of Husserl's phenomenology: the fundamental character of representation in intentionality. The psychic is representation or has representation as a foundation. In any case, in all its modalities, it is transformable into a doxic thesis. Consciousness makes and remakes *presence*—it is the *life* of presence. Consciousness which already allows itself to be forgotten for the benefit of *present entities*: it withdraws itself from appearing, to make room for them. The immediate, pre-reflexive, non-objectified, lived, and from the beginning anonymous or "mute" life of consciousness is this *allowing to appear* through its withdrawal, this disappearing in the allowing-to-appear. It is a consciousness in which identifying intentionality is teleologically turned toward the "constitution" of ess*a*nce in truth, but which is commanded by the energy or entelechy of ess*a*nce according to the latter's own modes—and truly *a priori*. The energy thus deploys itself as *turned back* in the working consciousness that fixes being in its theme and that, when lived, forgets itself in that fixation. The reference to consciousness disappears in its effect.

> Precisely because we are dealing with a *universal and necessary reference* to the subject that belongs to every object, to the extent to which, as an object, it is accessible to those who are experiencing, this reference to the subject *cannot enter into the terms themselves* of the object. Objective experience is an orientation of experience

toward the object. In an inevitable way, the subject is there, so to speak, anonymously. . . . All experience of an object leaves the ego behind it, does not have it in front of it.[4]

In consciousness, firmness, positivity, and presence of the *primordially* thematized entity are "lived" and identified; and it is in the guise of pre-reflexive consciousness, anonymous from the start, that consciousness dissimulates itself and remains in any case absent from the "objective sphere" it fixes.

The permanent effort of the transcendental reduction comes down to leading "mute consciousness" to speech and to not taking the exercise of constituent intentionality led to speech for a being placed in the positivity of the world. The life of consciousness is excluded from it and, precisely as excluded from the positivity of the world, as a "mute subject," it allows beings of the world to affirm themselves in their presence and in their numerical identity.

Thus, in the transcendental idealism of Husserlian phenomenology, we are beyond all doctrine in which the interpretation of being in terms of consciousness would still retain any restrictive meaning of the *esse-percipi*, and would signify that being *is only* a modality of perception, and in which the notion of the *in-itself* would claim a greater firmness than that which might ever proceed from an agreement between identifying thoughts. On the contrary, Husserl's entire work consists in understanding the notion of the *in-itself*, separated from the play of intentionality in which it is lived, as an abstraction.

BUT the affinity of presence and representation is even closer. The ess*a*nce appearing to the life of a me that, as a monadic ipseity, is distinguished from it, the ess*a*nce *gives* itself to life. The transcendence of things in relation to the lived intimacy of thought—in relation to thought as *Erlebnis*, in relation to the lived (which is not exhaustively expressed by the idea of a "still confused" and non-objectifying consciousness)—the transcendence of the object, of an environment, like the ideality of a thematized notion, is opened, but is also traversed by intentionality. It signifies distance as well as accessibility. It is a way for the distant to give itself. *Perception* already grasps; the concept—*Begriff*—retains that sense of seizure. Whatever effort may be required for the appropriation and utilization of things and notions, their transcendence promises possession and enjoyment that consecrates the lived equality of thought to its object in thought, the identification of the Same, satisfaction. Astonishment—a disproportion between *cogitatio* and *cogitatum*—in which knowing seeks itself, is dulled in knowledge. This way for the real to exist in intentional transcendence "on the same scale" as the lived, and for thought to think on its own level and thus to enjoy, signifies immanence. Intentional transcendence seems to delineate a map on which the adequacy of the thing to the intellect is produced. This map is the phenomenon of the world.

Intentionality, identification of the identical as stable, is aim taking aim, straight as a beam, at the target. It is a spirituality granted to terminal points, to entities, to their position on a firm ground; it is a spirituality granted to the founding firmness of the earth, to the foundation as essance. "In evidence . . . we have an *experience* of a being and of its manner of being."[5] Position and positivity confirming themselves in the doxic thesis of logic. A presence of the retrievable which the finger points to, the hand grasps, "manifestation"[6] or present where thought thinking on its level *joins* what it thinks. Thought and psychism of immanence and satisfaction.

Is the psychism exhausted in deploying the "energy" of the essance, of the positing of entities?

To state such a question is not to expect that the *in-itself* of entities has a stronger meaning than the one received from the identifying consciousness. It is to ask whether the psychism does not signify *otherwise* than through that "epic" of essance that is exalted in the psychism and *lived*; whether the positivity of *being*, identity, presence—and consequently knowing—are the ultimate concern of the soul. Not that there is reason to expect that affectivity or will are more significant than knowing. Axiology and practice, Husserl teaches, still rest on re-presentation. Hence they concern entities and the being of entities, and do not compromise but presuppose the priority of knowing. To ask whether the psychism is limited to the confirmation of entities in their position is to suggest that consciousness—finding itself to be the *same*, identifying itself even in the exteriority of its intentional object, remaining immanent even in its transcendences—breaks that balance of an *even mind*[7] and a mind thinking on its own level, to understand more than its capacity. It is to suggest that its desires, its questions, its research, instead of being indications of its voids and its finitude, are awakenings to the Excessive—that in its temporality that scatters it in successive moments (which however synchronize themselves in retention and protention, in memory and anticipation, and in historical narrative and foresight) an otherness can destroy that simultaneity and that gathering of the successive in the presence of re-presentation, and that it is affected by the Immemorial.

Our wisdom pushes us to take seriously only the transcendence of intentionality, which, however, is converted into immanence in the world. Thought awakened to God—or eventually devoted to God—is interpreted spontaneously in terms—and according to articulations—of the noetico-noematic parallelism of the perception of significance and of its fulfillment. The idea of God and even the enigma of the word God—which we find fallen into our midst without our knowing whence or how, and already circulating, e-normous, as a substantive noun, among the words of a language—is fitted, by current interpretation, into the order of intentionality. The de-ference to God which would insist on a difference other than that which separates the thematized or represented from the lived and would require of the psychism a different intrigue, is salvaged in intentionality. We have recourse to the notion of a horizontal religion, remaining on the earth of human beings, which is intended to replace the vertical one that mounts toward Heaven, in order to refer to the world, for it is in terms of the world that we continue to conceive of human beings themselves. This substitution may seem to be a simple confusion: by what right, after all, would the person perceived at my side come to take the place of the "intentional object" corresponding to the word God that names him or calls him? But, in its arbitrariness, perhaps this confusion of terms reflects the logical necessity of fixing the object of religion in keeping with the immanence of a thinking directed toward the world and that, in the order of thinking, would be ultimate and unsurpassable. To postulate a thinking structured otherwise would challenge logic and announce an arbitrariness of thought—or of the reflection on that thought—that would be more intolerable than that substitution of objects.

Philosophical atheism as well as philosophical theism refuse to admit even the originality[8] of a psychism claiming to go beyond the world, even the irreducibility of its noetic features. In expressions involving the term *the beyond*, they suspect the use of an emphatic metaphor for intentional distance. But in this suspicion they are in danger of forgetting that the "movement" beyond is metaphor and emphasis itself, that metaphor is language, and that the expression of a thought in discourse is equivalent neither to a reflection in the indifferent milieu of a mirror, nor to any vicissitude disdainfully called verbal, and that, in the lived experience of significance, saying presupposes relations other than those of intentionality, relations that, as it happens, concern in an unreformable manner the otherness of the other person. They risk forgetting that the elevation of meaning by metaphor in the *said* owes its height to the *transcendence* of the *saying* to the other person.

WHY is there saying? It is the first visible chink in the psychism of satisfaction. Of course we can reduce language to a teleology of being by invoking the necessity of communicating in order to succeed in human enterprises. We can take an interest, accordingly, in the *said*, in its various genres and in their various structures, and explore the birth of communicable meaning in words, and the means of communicating it most surely and effectively. We can thus attach language again to the world and to the being to which human enterprises refer, and thus attach language to intentionality. Nothing blocks this positivist interpretation. And the analysis of language in terms of the *said* is a respectable, considerable and difficult work.

It is nonetheless true that the very relationship of the *saying* cannot be reduced to intentionality, or that it rests, properly speaking, on an intentionality that fails. It is established with the other man whose monadic inwardness eludes my gaze and my control. But this *deficiency of re-presentation turns into a relation of a superior order*; or more exactly, into a relation in which just the faint outline of the meaning of the superior itself and of another order appears. The Husserlian "appresentation,"[9]—which does not reach satisfaction, the intuitive fulfillment of representation—is inverted from a failed experience into a *beyond of experience*, into a *transcendence*, whose rigorous *determination* is described by ethical attitudes and exigencies, and by responsibility, one of the modalities of which is language. The nearness of my neighbor, instead of being considered a limitation of the *I* by the other person or the aspiration for a unity still to be accomplished, becomes desire, nourishing itself on its hunger, or, to use a worn-out word, love, more precious to the soul than the full possession of self by self.

This is an incomprehensible transfiguration in an order in which every signified meaning goes back to the appearing of the world, that is, to the identification of the Same, that is, to Being—a new rationality, or perhaps we should say the most ancient one, prior to what coincides with the possibility of the world, and that consequently does not lead back to ontology. A different, or more profound rationality, that cannot be dragged into the adventure that, from Aristotle to Heidegger, has been pursued by a theology that has remained the thought of Identity and Being, and that has proved fatal to the God and the man of the Bible, or to their homonyms. Fatal to the One, if we are to believe Nietzsche; fatal to the other, according to contemporary antihumanism. Fatal to the homonyms, in any case. All thought that does not lead to installing an identical being in the absolute repose of the earth under the firmament would be subjective, the unhappiness of an unhappy consciousness.

Must nonrepose, the dissatisfaction in which the safety of the accomplished and the established are questioned, *always* be understood in terms of the positivity of the answer, the lucky find, *satisfaction?* Is the question *always*, as in functional language (or even scientific language, whose answers open onto new questions, but questions that aim only at answers), a knowledge in the process of constituting itself, a *still* insufficient thought of the *datum*, which latter might satisfy it by measuring up to the expectation? Is then the question that of the famous question/answer sequence in the soul's dialogue with itself in which Plato saw thought, initially solitary, moving toward a coinciding with itself—toward self-consciousness? Must we not admit, on the contrary, that the request and the prayer that cannot be dissimulated in the question attest to a *relation to the other person*, a relation that cannot be accommodated in the interiority of a solitary soul, and that is delineated in the question? A relation delineated in the question, not just as in any modality, but as in its originary one. A relationship to an Other that, precisely because of its irreducible difference, refuses to give itself to a thematizing knowing, and, thus, is always assimilative. A relationship that thus does not become a correlation. Hence a relationship that, properly speaking, cannot be called a relationship, since even the commonality of synchrony is lacking between its terms; a commonality that, being ultimate, no relationship could withhold from its terms. Yet to the Other—a relationship. A relationship and a nonrelationship. Is that not the meaning of the question? As the relationship to the absolutely other—to the nonlimited by the same—to the Infinite—would transcendence not be equivalent to an originary question? A relationship without simultaneity of terms: unless we are to say that time itself lasts in the guise of this relationship/nonrelationship, this question. Time being understood in its dia-chrony and not as a "pure form of sensibility." The soul in its dia-chronous temporality in which retention does not annul lapse, nor protention the absolutely new—the soul in the passive synthesis of aging and of the to-come [à-venir], in its life, would be the originary question, the to-God [à-Dieu] itself. Time as question: an unbalanced relationship with the Infinite, with what cannot be comprehended. Nor encompassed, nor touched. A rupture of the correlation—a rupture below the correlation and below the noetico-noematic parallelism and equilbrium, below the emptiness and the fullness of the signative—question or originary "insomnia," the very waking to psychism. *But also the way in which the Incomparable concerns the finite and that is, perhaps, what Descartes called the Idea of the Infinite in us.* Proximity and religion: all the newness entailed in love, as opposed to hunger, and in desire, as opposed to need. Proximity that to me is better than all interiorization and all symbiosis. A rent beneath the rectilinear straightness of the intentional aim that is assumed by the intention and from which it derives in its correspondence to its intentional object, although that originating *vigil*, that insomnia of psychism, lends itself to the moderation that its own derivatives make of it, and it, too, risks being expressed in terms of satisfaction and dissatisfaction. An ambiguity or enigma of the spiritual.

Is not transcendence to God—which is neither linear, like the intentional aim, nor teleological, tending toward an end in the punctuality of a pole and thus stopping at entities and substantives, nor even initially dialogual, naming a *thou*—already produced through ethical transcendence so that desire and love make themselves more perfect than satisfaction?[10] It would be appropriate, however, to ask at this point whether we are dealing with a transcendence to God or a transcendence in terms of which a word like God can only first reveal its meaning. The fact that that transcendence is produced from the (horizontal?) relationship with the other person means neither that the other person is God nor that God is a great Other Person.

Desire that turns into perfection? Satisfaction-oriented thinking has judged otherwise. And it is, certainly, good sense itself. Diotima discredited love by declaring it a demigod, on the pretext that, *qua* aspiration, it is neither attained nor perfect. This good sense is, certainly, infallible in relation to the world and to things of the world for eating and drinking. To challenge it in the order of the world is a sign of foolishness. From Plato to Hegel, who spoke ironically of the beautiful soul! But when Kierkegaard recognizes in dissatisfaction an access to the supreme, despite Hegel's warnings, he does not relapse into romanticism. His point of departure is no longer experience, but transcendence. He is the first philosopher who thinks God without thinking Him in terms of the world. The proximity of the other person is neither some sort of "separation of being in relation to self," nor a "degradation of coincidence," according to the Sartrean formulations. Desire here is not pure deprivation; the social relationship is worth more than the enjoyment of self. And the proximity of God that has fallen to the lot of mankind is, perhaps, a more divine fate than that of a God enjoying His divinity. Kierkegaard writes: "In the case of earthly goods, to the extent that man feels less need of them, he becomes more perfect. A pagan who could speak of earthly goods said that God was happy because He didn't need anything and that after Him came the sage because he needed little. But in the relationship between man and God, the principle is reversed: the more man feels the need for God, the more perfect he is." Or: "One must love God not because He is the most perfect, but because one needs Him." Or: "A need to love—supreme Good and supreme bliss."

There is the same reversal of absence into supreme presence in the order of knowing. Kierkegaard writes: "If I have faith, I cannot succeed in having an immediate certainty of it—for to believe is precisely that dialectical balance which, although incessantly in fear and trembling, never, however, despairs; faith is precisely that infinite preoccupation with the self that keeps you alert to risk everything, that internal preoccupation of knowing whether you really have faith.

A transcendence that is possible only through uncertainty! In the same spirit, a break with the "triumphalism" of common sense. In that which is a failure in relation to the world, a triumph is celebrated: "We will not say that the good man will triumph some day in another world or that his cause will some day win on earth; no, he triumphs in the midst of life, he triumphs in suffering in his living life, he triumphs in the day of his affliction."

According to the models of satisfaction, possession is superior to searching, joy better than need, triumph truer than failure, certainty more perfect than doubt, and the answer goes farther than the question. Searching, suffering, and the question would all be simply deficient modes of the felicitous find, enjoyment, happiness, the answer: insufficient thoughts of the identical and the present, indigent knowledge or knowledge in the condition of indigence. Once more, it is good sense itself. It is also common sense.

But can the hermeneutics of the religious do without thoughts that go off the deep end? And does not philosophy itself consist in treating "crazy" ideas with wisdom or in bringing wisdom to love? Knowledge, the answer, the result . . . would be from a psychism still incapable of thoughts in which the word *God* takes on meaning.

entre nou

THE independence or exteriority of being in relation
to the knowledge that it commands in truth, and the
possibility of this exteriority's being "internalized" in
knowledge, which is equally the *locus* of truth, is the
fact of the world, where the agreement between
thought and being takes place. This agreement is not
some mysterious adequation of the incomparable; it
is not an absurd equality of the "psychic fact" and the
spatial and "physical fact," which obviously have no
common measure. It is the feat of perception: the
original union of the open and the graspable in the
world, the given and the apprehended—or the comprehended. Hence the ideas of knowledge and being
are correlative and refer back to the world. To think
being and to think knowledge is to think on the basis
of the world. Furthermore, being and consciousness
are bound to presence and representation, to the graspable solid that is the primordial thing, to some *thing*,
to the identical to be identified through its multiple
aspects or, as one could say, to the Same. This is the
ontic wisdom of perception, the wisdom of everyday
life and the wisdom of nations, guaranteeing universality to the science born of perception, the wisdom
of truth and of the world.

Philosophy has maintained—in the way it is
taught, but already in the forms of its direct discourse—an ontic style. It seems to pertain to *beings*,
even when it wants to be ontological. To be sure, the
being of beings will no longer be a "something,"
since one cannot say that it *is*; the temptation remains
nonetheless (and it is not the effect of some clumsi-

ness or superficiality on the part of the writer) to speak about the truth of this verb-being and of the disclosure in which it manifests itself. Does it suffice to reduce this ontic style to the logic of a certain language that would have to be surpassed? Does it signify the truth of Kantianism: the impossibility of an intelligible thought that would not somehow be reducible to a datum, to the representation of being, to the world? In another Kantian register, does it signify a new transcendental appearance? There have been frequent denunciations of this language of representation in philosophy, in which truths are stated as if they were the truths of some sublime perception or some sublimated sensibility, in which they are understood as are those of the natural sciences or historical narrative, and as if, in their scholarly and even sophisticated texture, they still referred to the arrangement of some piece of being's delicate clockwork. For example, Jeanne Delhomme's effort from *Pensée Interrogative* and *La Pensée et le Réel* to *Impossible Interrogation* consists in finding in the language of philosophers another significance than that of an ontic or even ontological speech, in separating philosophy and ontology, and even, in a certain sense, in separating philosophy and truth. Which is not to say, let us add in passing, that philosophy is the reign of the lie, no more than it would be true to say that about art.

But taken as ontic knowledge, and compared to the coherent, communicable and universal results of scientific knowledge, philosophy today has lost all credence. For a long time it had already been compromised due to disagreement among philosophers. This disagreement is deplored in the *Discourse on Method*; it is one of the motivations of the *Critique of Pure Reason* and of Husserl's phenomenological research, as it was justified in 1910 in the well-known article "Philosophy as Rigorous Science." But, beneath the rubric of the end of metaphysics, that depreciation of philosophy means in our time, perhaps most clearly, an awareness of the misconception perpetuated by a philosophy bogged down in its language, and which hypostasizes, in the form of worlds-behind-the-world, the meaning of its thoughts, for which it is unable to find a meaning other than ontic. The rear-guard work of this philosophy in retreat consists in de-constructing this so-called metaphysical language, which, for all its onticality, is neither perception nor science, and in which one would like to uncover, through a psychoanalysis of deconstructed materials, at least a meaning of symptoms of some ideology.

EVEN before today's crisis, Hegel's philosophy appears to be acquainted with the hubris of philosophy speaking the language of perception or expressing the arrangement of the cosmic order or the connection of historical events. Philosophical truth would not be an opening onto something, but the intrinsic rule of a discourse, the logic of its logos. Perception, science, narration, in their ontic structure of correlation between a subject and an object to which the subject conforms, are no longer the model of truth; they constitute determined moments, vicissitudes of the dialectic. But discourse as logos is not, for its part, a discourse *about* being, but the very being of beings, or, if you will, their being *qua* being. Hegel's philosophy is coherent even to the point of already having broken with the realist prototype of truth in the statement of this rupture. It is already dialectical discourse when it is only on the verge of adopting dialectical discourse. It never uses metalanguage; properly speaking, it reveals itself without prefaces, although philosophers, while denouncing a particular language, still speak the language they are in the process of condemning.

It is a philosophy that retrieves the "truths" of the history of philosophy, despite their reciprocal contradictions and their apparent exclusivism. The truths of *Representation* occupy, in specific moments of the dialectical discourse, or in the movement of being *qua* being, the place that is logically theirs, but the process of thought and of being and its truth no longer fall within the province of *Representation*. Rationality consists in being able to pass from *Representation* to the *Concept*, which is no longer a modality of *Representation*.

Nonetheless, Hegel's philosophy preserves one element from representation that marks the rationality of our philosophical tradition, and that still belongs to the wisdom of perception and the narrative tending toward what is graspable. To arrive at the rational is to grasp. Knowledge is no longer perception, but it is still concept. The rational is syn-thesis, syn-chronization of the historical, that is, presence; that is, being: world and presence. The thought of rational animality is accomplished in the *Idea* in which history presents itself. It is toward the idea that the dialectic tends, the dialectic in which diachronically traversed moments are recovered, that is, identified, sublimated, and conserved. A philosophy of Presence, of Being, of the Same. The reconciliation of contradictions, the identity of the identical and the non-identical! It is still the philosophy of the intelligibility of the Same, beyond the tension of the Same and the Other.

The dialectical unfolding of rationality and the process of being as the logic of logos, in their Hegelian and neo-Hegelian form, doubtless remain even today a possibility (perhaps the ultimate possibility) of a proud philosophy that does not, in the face of the sciences, apologize for philosophizing—the possibility of a mature humanity, that is, one that does not yet forget or no longer forgets its past. But these memories can disregard neither the aftermath of the Hegelian system, nor the crises that have characterized the attempts, derived from this system, to transform the world; nor the paling of its rationality before the rationality that triumphs and is communicated to everyone in the development of the "exact" sciences and the techniques they inspire; nor the new disagreements between philosophers that the Hegelian message could not prevent; nor the discovery of the social and subconscious conditioning of human knowledge. Husserl's harsh statement on the arbitrariness of speculative constructions in his "Philosophy as Rigorous Science"—a critique disseminated throughout his work—is directed against Hegel.

While remaining totally external to Hegel's work in the detail of its execution, this critique testifies to an entire epoch's profoundly felt disaffection, which has not been dispelled during the sixty years—two thirds of a century—that separate us from this text of Husserl's. The influence of the phenomenology of *Logical Investigations*, returning "to the things themselves," to the truth of evidence in which things "show themselves in the original," attests not only to the difficulties of naturalist positivism, but to a distrust of dialectical discourse and also of language itself.

But did not the new promises of a scientific philosophy, Husserl's promises, prove to be just as fallacious? Being untenable in the effort to return naively, in the straightforwardness of spontaneous consciousness, to truth/opening, to truth/evidence-of-being-given, to being "in flesh and blood" right down to and including its categorial forms, Husserlian phenomenology corrected itself with a transcendental teaching in which being-given-in-the-original is constituted in immanence. The "beyond language" promised by the *Logical Investigations* does not spare those investigations themselves the necessity of stressing the irreducible role played by linguistic signs in the constitution of meaning; in the *Ideas*, Husserl affirms that doxic theses underlie all conscious life, which then is apophantic in its most intimate structure, at the point of becoming discourse in its mental articulation—though this discourse would reject the dialectic. On the other hand, one cannot ignore the uninterrupted reference, in Husserl, of consciousness to an identified being; consciousness as thought of the Same. The pre-predicative toward which analysis proceeds, as if to put logical thought into question, knots itself right away around *substrata* which are the support for all of the formal modifications of the logical. And thus the substantive, the nameable, the entity [*étant*] and the Same—so essential to the structure of re-presentation and of truth as the truth of presence—remain the privileged and primordial terms of consciousness. But above all, phenomenology itself isolates these structures by a reflection that is an inner perception and in which the descriptive process "synchronizes" the flux of consciousness into knowledge. Phenomenology, in its philosophical act of ultimate *Nachdenken*, ["thinking back" or reflection], thus remains faithful to the ontic model of truth. Perception, grasping, in its relation with the present, with the Same, with the entity, remains both the first movement of the naive soul in its prepredicative experience (precisely insofar as it is experience) and the ultimate gesture of the reflecting philosopher.

NONETHELESS, I think that phenomenology, despite its gnoseological expression (both ontic and ontological), calls attention to a sense of philosophy in which the latter is not reduced to a reflection on the relation between thought and the world, a relation that sustains the notions of being and the world. Husserlian phenomenology made it possible to show the importance of thought for reasons other than the elucidation of experience. The latter is always the experience of being or presence in the world; it is a thinking that, even if begun in wonder, remains an adequation of the given to the "signitive"; a thinking on the scale of the subject, and that, precisely as such, is experience, the act of a conscious subject, the act of a unity fixed in a firm position, such as the unity of *transcendental apperception*, in which the diverse comes to be unified under a stable rule. Now, this is not the only nor even the initial modality of the subjective in Husserl's analyses, which are always more surprising than the "system" and the programmatic discourse.

Although Husserl's phenomenology turns to intuition as to the principle of principles, in which being presents itself in the original and in its identity, and in which we are vouchsafed a glance at the origin of the notions of Being and of the Same, and although it appeals to this presence in evidence, and to the horizons of the Same in which this presence shows itself (or to the nostalgia for this presence) as the rationality of reason, it nonetheless *puts into question* even the very same formal logical-mathematical chains of reasoning whose objectivity the "Prolegomena" to the *Logical Investigations* had already secured against all psychologism. The appearance of presence is certainly not deceptive, but it is at the same time the obturation, as it were, of living thought. Signs borrowed from language and from the opinions it conveys, while useful in operations of calculation, replace the significations of living thought. The latter, in their objective essence, move on, and they do so under the open eye of the thinker, without his or her knowledge. Acquired knowledge, the result deposited in writings separated from living thought—and even the knowledge given in the theme of a thought absorbed by what it thinks and forgetting itself in the object—does not maintain itself in the plenitude of its meaning. Shifts and displacements of meaning (*Sinnverschiebungen*), enchanting or enchanted games, are played out at the heart of objectifying consciousness—good, clear and distinct consciousness—without, however, in the least jarring its spontaneous, naive, and rational gait. But everything happens as if, in its lucidity, the reason identifying being were moving forward like a sleepwalker or daydreamer, as if—despite its lucidity for the objective order, it were sleeping off, in broad daylight, the effects of some mysterious wine. The full intelligence of the undistorted, objective gaze remains defenseless against meaning's displacements. Nonetheless, the naiveté continues to guide scientific inquiry in its objective rectitude, according to common sense, which is the most evenly shared thing in the world. It is as if the self-evidence of the world as a state in which reason is contained paralyzed, Medusa-like, and petrified the reasonable life that *lives* that self-evidence! It is as if the naive look, in its ontic intention, found itself obstructed by its very object, and spontaneously underwent an inversion or somehow "embourgeoised" in its condition or, to use an expression from Deuteronomy, *waxed fat*.[1]

Consequently it is as if the adventure of knowledge—which is knowledge of the world—were not only light, but a drowsiness of the mind. It is as if the adventure of the mind required a rationality in another sense. It is not a matter of overcoming some limitation of the *seen*, of enlarging the horizons belonging to the dimension in which the seen—the thematized—appears; thus it is not a matter of being prompted to recover, through some dialectic, the totality from one of its parts. Examining in depth the objective horizon of the given within the theme in which it is presented would still be a naive procedure. There is a radical heterogeneity, a difference that blocks the dialectic, between the vision of the world and the life underlying this vision. We must change levels. But it is not a matter of adding an inner experience to an outer one. We must return from the world to life, which has already been betrayed by knowledge. The latter delights in its theme and is absorbed in the object to the point of losing its soul and its name and of becoming mute and anonymous. By a movement against nature—because against the world—we must return to a psychism other than that of the knowledge of the world. This is the revolution of the Phenomenological Reduction, a permanent revolution. The Reduction will reanimate or reactivate that life, forgotten or become anemic in knowledge; a Life henceforth termed absolute or apodictically known, as Husserl will say, thinking in terms of knowledge. Beneath the resting-within-itself of the Real which refers to itself in identification, beneath its presence, the Reduction raises up a life against which thematized being, in its sufficiency, has already kicked, and which it has repressed by its appearing. Drowsy intentions awakened to life will reopen vanished horizons, ever new, disturbing the theme in its identity *qua* result, awakening subjectivity from the identity in which it rests in its experience. The subject as intuitive reason in harmony, in the World, with being—reason in the adequation of knowledge—thus finds itself put into question. And the very style of Husserl's phenomenology—multiplying the gestures of reduction and tirelessly erasing every trace of subordination to the worldly in consciousness in order to lay bare what he calls pure consciousness—does not this style call attention to what is discovered *behind* the consciousness that is subject to its ontic destiny in the thought of the Same?

The Reduction signifies the passage from the natural to the transcendental attitude. The comparison with the Kantian position that this language recalls is well known. And yet it is also just as well known that for Husserl it is less a matter of fixing the subjective conditions for the validity of the science of the world, or of laying bare its logical presuppositions, than of bringing out, in all its scope, the subjective life, forgotten by thought turned toward the world. What is the specific interest of this transcendental life, and what rationality does it add to the rationality of natural consciousness focussed on the world? The passage to transcendental life, first carried out along the so-called Cartesian route, seems to seek certitude. This route leads back from the inadequate evidence of experience with the world to reflection upon the cogitations from which this experience is constituted, in order to measure its degree of certitude or incertitude. We are still in a philosophy of knowledge—knowledge of being and the Same—an epistemology. But one can also say that the Reduction, upheld by the certitude of reflection, frees reasoned thought from the world itself, from the norms of adequation, from obedience to the completed work of identification, from the being that can only be as a complete gathering into a theme, as the re-presentation of presence. Thus the Transcendental Reduction would not be a simple retreat back to the certitude of the *cogito*, as the standard of all true meaning in its evidence, adequate to thought, but the doctrine of a meaning *despite* the incompleteness of knowledge and identification, an incompleteness which contrasts with the norms that the identity of the Same commands. Nevertheless, if the Reduction does not complete the incompleteness of perception and of science bearing on the world, in which the perfect coinciding of the intended and the seen is impossible, it recognizes and measures this non-adequation in an adequate way and is thus called apodictic. Thus, in the adequation of reflection, there is the completion and closing in upon itself of a knowledge that is both knowledge and non-knowledge, but still a reasoning psychism.

AND now we see that in the *Cartesian Meditations* (sections 6 and 9), this apodictic rationality of reflection upon reduced consciousness is no longer the result of an adequation of intuition with the signitive it fulfills. Apodicticity is lodged in an inadequate intuition. The indubitable or founding character of the apodictic is not due to any new trait of the evidence or to any new light. It is due to a limited portion, a nucleus of the field of the consciousness called "properly adequate." And it is here that there appear, with an emphatic accent on the word *living*, expressions such as "this nucleus is the living presence of the ego to itself" (*die lebendige Selbstgegenwart*), and then "the living evidence of the *I am* (*während der lebendigen Gegenwart des* Ich bin). Does the living character of this evidence or this present reduce to an adequate coincidence? (One may well ask whether the exception of the Cartesian *cogito* itself is truly due, as Descartes says, to the clarity and distinction of his knowledge.) Must the vivacity of life be interpreted on the basis of consciousness? Is it, under the label *erleben* [to live (something)] just a confused or obscure consciousness, merely something preparatory to the distinction between subject and object, a pre-thematization, a pre-knowledge? Must we not affirm our psychism otherwise? Does not the adjective *living*, from the beginning of Husserl's work on, underscore the importance of the word *Erlebnis* as expressing the way of the subject? The *I*'s prereflective experience, designated by the term *Erlebnis*— the lived, is not just a moment of pre-objectification, like the *hulē* prior to the *Auffassen* [apprehending]. The "living present": we know the importance this term took on in Husserl's manuscripts on time. Its explosive and surprising character (similar to that of the present in the Bergsonian *durée*) is expressed in *The Phenomenology of Internal Time-Consciousness* as the *primal impression*. Unforeseeable, it is in no way prepared in some germinating seed that would bear the past. The absolute traumatism that is inseparable from the spontaneity of its upsurge is of as much importance as the sensible quality that it offers to the adequation of knowledge. The living present of the *cogito-sum* occurs not only on the model of self-consciousness, absolute knowledge; it is the rupture of the equanimity of the "even mind," the rupture of the Same of immanence; awakening and life.

In *Phenomenological Psychology*,[2] sensibility is lived prior to the *hulē* taking on the function of *Abschattung* (adumbration). Its immanence is the gathering of a presence to self within the passive synthesis of time. But this presence to self takes place in keeping with a certain rupture insofar as the lived is lived for a me that, in the inwardness of immanence, distinguishes itself from it, and that, as early as *Ideas I*, is recognized as "transcendence in immanence." In the identity of presence to self, in the silent tautology of the pre-reflexive, a difference between the same and the same takes shape—a dephasing, a difference at the heart of interiority. This difference is irreducible to adversity, which remains open to reconciliation and is surmountable by assimilation. Here the alleged self-consciousness is also a rupture, the other splits the same of consciousness which is thus lived; the other that calls it deeper than itself. *Waches ich*—myself awake. The slumbering self is asleep with respect to . . . without blending into. . . . Transcendent in immanence, the heart keeps watch without blending into what solicits it. "Sleep, on close inspection," Husserl writes, "has meaning only in relation to wakefulness, and in itself bears the potentiality for awakening."[3]

But the *I* that emerges and breaks up the identification of *hulē* with itself to differentiate itself from this immanence—is it not once again an identification of the Same? I think that the Reduction reveals its true meaning, and the meaning of the subjective that it allows to be signified, in its final phase: the Intersubjective Reduction. In it, the subjectivity of the subject shows itself in the traumatism of wakefulness, despite the gnoseological interpretation that, for Husserl, characterizes the element of mind [*esprit*] to the very end.

The Intersubjective Reduction is not leveled solely against the "solipsism" of the "primordial sphere" and the relativism of truth which would result from it, in order to ensure the objectivity of knowledge, which depends on the agreement between multiple subjectivities. The explication of the meaning that an *I* other than me has *for me*—primordial me—describes the way in which the Other Person tears me away from my hypostasis, from the *here*, at the heart of being or the center of the world in which, privileged, and in this sense primordial, I place myself. But the ultimate meaning of my "mineness" is revealed in this tearing away. In conferring the meaning of "*I*" to the other, and also in my alterity to myself through which I can confer onto the other the meaning of *I*, the *here* and the *there* come to be inverted into one another. It is not the homogenization of space that is thus constituted: I am the one—I so obviously primordial and hegemonic, so identical to myself, within my "own," ever so comfortably installed in my body, in my *hic et nunc*—who moves into the background. I see myself from the other's vantage point; I expose myself to the other person; I have things to account for.

It is this relation to the other *I*, in which the *I* is torn from its primordiality, that constitutes the non-gnoseological event necessary to reflection itself understood as knowledge, and consequently necessary to the egological Reduction itself. In the "secondariness" in which, facing the face of the other person (and all the expressivity of the other body of which Husserl speaks is the openness and ethical exigency of the face), the primordial sphere loses its priority, subjectivity awakens from the egological—from egotism and from egoism.

In opposition to the simple abstraction that, setting out from "the individual consciousness" rises to "consciousness in general," as a result of an ecstatic or angelic omission of its terrestrial weight and in the intoxication or idealism of an almost magical sublimation, Husserl's theory of the Intersubjective Reduction describes the astonishing or traumatizing (*trauma*, not *thauma*) possibility of a sobering up in which the *I*, facing the Other, is freed from itself, and awakens from dogmatic slumber. The Reduction, repeating as it were the disturbance of the Same by the Other who is not absorbed into the Same—and who does not hide himself from the other—describes the awakening, beyond knowledge, to an insomnia or watchfulness (*Wachen*) of which knowledge is but one modality. It is a fission of the subject, not shielded by the atomic consistency of the unity of transcendental apperception; an awakening coming from the other—whom the Other person is—that ceaselessly puts the priority of the same into question. Awakening as a sobering up, beyond the sobriety of the simple lucidity which, despite the anxiety and the movements of a possible dialectic, still remains consciousness of the Same—identity of the identical and the nonidentical in its completion and repose. Awakening and sobering up by the Other who does not leave the Same alone, and through which the Same, as living—and through its slumber—is from the beginning exacerbated [*excédé*]. It is not an *experience* of inequality posited within the theme of a knowledge, it is the very event of transcendence as life. It is the psychism of responsibility for the Other, which is the lineament of this transcendence and which is psychism *tout court*. A transcendence perhaps in which the distinction between transcendence toward the other man and transcendence toward God should not be made too quickly.

BUT all this is no longer in Husserl. To him, the Reduction remained to the last a passage from a less perfect to a more perfect knowledge. The

Reduction which the philosopher miraculously decided to perform was motivated solely by contradictions arising in naive knowledge. The psychism of the soul or the intellectuality of the mind remains knowledge—the crisis of the European spirit is a crisis of Western science. Never will the philosophy that begins with the presence of being,—equality of the mind with itself, the gathering of the diverse into the Same—express its revolutions or its awakenings in terms other than those of knowledge. It remains the case, however, that in Husserl, beyond the critique of technique, which comes from science, there is a critique of knowledge as knowledge, a critique of the civilization of science in the broad sense. The intelligibility of knowledge is found alienated through its very identity. The necessity for a reduction in Husserl's philosophy attests to a sort of closure at the heart of the opening onto the given, a drowsiness within spontaneous truth. This is what I have called "becoming bourgeois," rebelling against the anxiety of transcendence, a self-complacency.

In the identity of the Same, in its return to itself, in which identifiable Reason claims its fulfillment, in the identity of the Same to which thought itself aspires as to a place of repose, one should beware of a stupefaction, a petrification or a laziness. Is not the most reasonable reason the most awakened watchfulness, the awakening at the heart of the wakeful state, at the heart of wakefulness as a state? And is not ethical relation to the other that event in which this permanent revolution of sobering up is concrete life? Is not the vivacity of life an excession, the rupture of the container by the uncontainable, form ceasing to be its own content, already offering itself as experience? An awakening to consciousness, the truth of which is not the consciousness of that awakening? An awakening that remains a first movement toward the other, the traumatism of which is revealed in the Intersubjective Reduction, a traumatism secretly striking the very subjectivity of the subject? Transcendence: this term is used without any theological presupposition. It is, to the contrary, the excession of life that is presupposed by theologies. Transcendence like the dazzling of which Descartes speaks at the end of the Third Meditation.

But before I examine this matter with more care, and pass on to the consideration of other truths which may be derived from it, it seems right to me to pause for a while in order to contemplate God Himself, to ponder at leisure His marvelous attributes, to consider, and admire, and adore, the beauty of this light so resplendent, at least as far as the strength of my mind, which is in some measure dazzled by the sight, will allow me to do so."[4]

It is the suffering of the eye overtaxed by light, the Same disturbed and held in wakefulness by the other who exalts him. If *on the basis of this transcendence of life*, one thinks the idea of God, one can say that life is enthusiasm and that enthusiasm is not drunkenness but a sobering up. It is a sobering up always in need of sobering up, a wakefulness on the eve of a new awakening. Ethics.

The fact that this questioning of the Same by the Other, and what we have called "wakefulness" or "life," is, outside of knowledge, a part of philosophy, is not only verified by certain articulations of Husserl's thought that we have just shown, but appears at the heights of various philosophies. It is the beyond being in Plato; the entrance through the door of the agent intellect in Aristotle; the idea of God in us, going beyond our capacity as finite beings; the exaltation of theoretical reason in practical reason in Kant; the search for recognition by the Other in Hegel himself; the renewal of *durée* in Bergson; the sobering up of lucid reason in Heidegger—from whom the very notion of sobering up used in this essay is borrowed.

It is not as knowledge of the world, or of some world-behind-the-world, or as a *Weltanschauung* that we have tried to articulate the transcendence—wakefulness and sobering up—whence philosophies speak. Philosophies: permanent revolutions, and also necessary to knowledge, concerned with reducing the naiveté of its consciousness or extending itself into epistemology, inquiring about the meaning of the results. A transcendence that cannot be reduced to an experience of transcendence, for it is a seizure prior to all *positing* of a subject and to every perceived or assimilated content. Transcendence or awakening that is the very life of the human, already troubled by the Infinite. Whence philosophy: a language of transcendence and not the tale of experience: a language in which the teller is part of the tale, thus a necessarily personal language, to be understood beyond what it says, that is, to be interpreted. Philosophy is the philosophers in their intersubjective "plot," which no one unravels but in which no one is allowed a lapse of attention or a lack of strictness. This is not the place to delve into the perspectives which then open up, from the point of view of the ethical significance of keeping watch and transcending, particularly on time and its diachrony in connection with the Uncontainable.

Phenomenology

Suffering is, of course, a *datum* in consciousness, a certain "psychological content," similar to the lived experience of color, sound, contact, or any other sensation. But in this very "content" it is an in-spite-of-consciousness, the unassumable. The unassumable and "unassumability." "Unassumability" that does not result from the excessive intensity of a sensation, from just some quantitative "too much," surpassing the measure of our sensibility and our means of grasping and holding; but an excess, an unwelcome superfluity, that is inscribed in a sensorial content, penetrating, as suffering, the dimensions of meaning that seem to open themselves to it, or become grafted onto it. It is as if suffering were not just a *datum*, refractory to the synthesis of the Kantian "I think"—which is capable of reuniting and embracing the most heterogeneous and disparate data into order and meaning in its *a priori* forms—but the *way* in which the refusal, opposing the assemblage of data into a meaningful whole, rejects it; at once what disturbs order and this disturbance itself. It is not only the consciousness of rejection or a symptom of rejection, but this rejection itself: a backward consciousness, "operating" not as "grasp" but as revulsion. A modality. The categorial ambiguity of quality and modality. The denial, the refusal of meaning, thrusting itself forward as a sensible quality: that is, in the guise of "experienced" content, the *way* in which, within a consciousness, the unbearable is precisely not borne, the manner of this not-being-borne; which, paradoxically, is itself a sensation or a datum. A quasi-contradictory structure, but a contradiction that is not formal, like that of the dialectic tension between the affirmative and the negative that occurs for the intellect. Contradiction *qua* sensation: the ache of pain—woe.[1]

Suffering, in its woe, in its in-spite-of-consciousness, is passivity. In this case apprehension, a taking into the consciousness, is no longer, strictly speaking, a "taking," no longer *the performance of an act of consciousness*, but, in adversity, a submission—and even a submission to submission, since the "content" that suffering consciousness is conscious of is precisely this same adversity of suffering—its woe. But, here again, *passivity*—that is, a modality—signifies as a *quiddity*, and perhaps as the locus in which passivity signifies originally, independently of its conceptual opposition to activity. The passivity of suffering, in its pure phenomenology, abstracting from its psychophysical and psychophysiological conditions, is not the other side of any activity, as would be an effect correlative to its cause, or sensorial receptivity correlative to the "ob-stance" of the object that affects it and leaves its impression on it. The passivity of suffering is more profoundly passive than the receptivity of our senses, which is already active reception, immediately becoming perception. In suffering, sensibility is a vulnerability, more passive than receptivity; an encounter more passive than experience. It is precisely an evil. It is not, to tell the truth, through passivity that evil is described, but through evil that suffering is understood. Suffering is a pure undergoing. It is not a matter of a passivity that would degrade human beings by affecting their freedom, which would be curtailed to the point of compromising self-consciousness, thus leaving the human being, in the passivity of undergoing, the identity of a mere thing. The humanity of those who suffer is overwhelmed by the evil that rends it, otherwise than by non-freedom: violently and cruelly, more irremissibly than the negation that dominates or paralyzes the act in non-freedom. What counts in the non-freedom or the submission of suffering is the concreteness of the *not*, looming as an evil more negative than any apophantic *not*. This negativity of evil is probably the source or kernel of all apophantic negation. The *not* of evil, a negativity extending as far as to the realm of un-meaning. All evil relates back to suffering. It is the *impasse* of life and of being—their absurdity—in which pain does not just somehow innocently happen to "color" consciousness with affectivity. The evil of pain, the deleterious per se, is the outburst and deepest expression, so to speak, of absurdity.

Thus the least one can say about suffering is that, in its own phenomenality, intrinsically, it is useless: "for nothing." Doubtless this depth of meaninglessness that the analysis seems to suggest is confirmed by empirical situations of pain, in which pain remains undiluted, so to speak, and isolates itself in consciousness, or absorbs the rest of consciousness. It would suffice, for example, to take from the medical journals certain cases of persistent or obstinate pain, the neuralgias and intolerable lumbagos resulting from lesions of the peripheral nerves, and the tortures that are experienced by certain patients stricken with malignant tumors.[2] Pain can become the central phenomenon of the diseased state. These are the "pain-illnesses," to which the patient's other psychological states bring no relief but, on the contrary, anxiety and distress, adding to the cruelty of the pain. But we can go on—and doubtless thus arrive at the essential facts of pure pain—to consider the "pain-illnesses" of beings who are psychologically deprived, retarded, impoverished in their social life and impaired in their relation to the other person—that relation in which suffering, without losing anything of its savage malignancy, no longer eclipses the totality of the mental and moves into a new light, within new horizons. These horizons remain closed to the mentally deficient, except that the latter, in their "pure pain," are projected into them in exposing themselves *to me*, raising the fundamental ethical problem posed by pain "for nothing": the inevitable and preemptory ethical problem of medication, which is *my duty*. Is not the evil of suffering—extreme passivity, helplessness, abandonment and solitude—also the unassumable, whence the possibility of a half opening, and, more precisely, the half opening that a moan, a cry, a groan or a sigh slips through—the original call for aid, for curative help, help from the other[3] me whose alterity, whose exteriority promises salvation? Original opening toward merciful care, the point at which—through a demand for analgesia, more pressing, more urgent, in the groan, than a demand for consolation or the postponement of death—the anthropological category of the medical, a category that is primordial, irreducible and ethical, imposes itself. For pure suffering, which is intrinsically senseless and condemned to itself with no way out, a beyond appears in the form of the interhuman.[4] It is seen in the light of such situations, be it said in passing, that medicine as technique, and consequently the technology as a whole that it presupposes—technology, so easily exposed to the attacks of "right-thinking" rigor—does not derive solely from the so-called "will to power." That bad will is perhaps only the price that must sometimes be paid by the high-mindedness of a civilization called upon to feed human beings and to lighten their sufferings.

A high-mindedness that is the honor of a still uncertain, still vacillating modernity, emerging at the end of a century of unutterable suffering, but in which the suffering of suffering, the suffering for the useless suffering of the other, the just suffering in me for the unjustifiable suffering of the other, opens suffering to the ethical perspective of the inter-human. In this perspective there is a radical difference between *the suffering in the other*, where it is unforgivable to *me*, solicits me and calls me, and suffering *in me*,[5] my own experience of suffering, whose constitutional or congenital uselessness can take on a meaning, the only one of which suffering is capable, in becoming a suffering for the suffering (inexorable though it may be) of someone else. It is this attention to the suffering of the other that, through the cruelties of our century (despite these cruelties, because of these cruelties) can be affirmed as the very nexus of human subjectivity, to the point of being raised to the level of supreme ethical principle—the only one it is impossible to question—shaping the hopes and commanding the practical discipline of vast human groups. This attention and this action are so imperiously and directly incumbent on human beings (on their *I*'s) that it makes awaiting them from an all-powerful God impossible without our lowering ourselves. The consciousness of this inescapable obligation brings us close to God in a more difficult, but also a more spiritual, way than does confidence in any kind of theodicy.

Theodicy

In the ambiguity of suffering that the above phenomenological essay has shown, the modality averred itself also to be the content or sensation that consciousness "bears." That adversity-to-all-harmony, as a quiddity, enters into conjunction with other "contents" that it disturbs, to be sure, but with which it is rationalized or finds a way of justifying itself. Already within an isolated consciousness, the pain of suffering can take on the meaning of pain that wins merit and hopes for a reward, and so lose, it would appear, its modality of uselessness in various ways. Is it not meaningful as a means with an end in view, when it makes itself felt in the effort that goes into the preparation of a work, or in the fatigue resulting from it? One can see a biological finality in it: the role of an alarm signal manifesting itself for the preservation of life against the cunning dangers that threaten it in illness. "He that increaseth knowledge increaseth sorrow," says Ecclesiastes (1:18), where suffering appears at the very least as the price of reason and spiritual refinement. It is also thought to temper the individual's character. It is said to be necessary to the teleology of community life, when social discontent awakens a useful attention to the health of the collective body. Perhaps there is a social utility in the suffering necessary to the pedagogic function of Power in education, discipline and repression. Is not fear of punishment the beginning of wisdom? Do people not have the idea that suffering, undergone as punishment, regenerates the enemies of society and humankind? This political teleology is founded, to be sure, on the value of existence, on the perseverance in being of society and of the individual, on their health, taken as the supreme and ultimate end.

But the bad and gratuitous meaninglessness of pain already shows beneath the reasonable forms espoused by the social "uses" of suffering, which in any case do not diminish the outrage of the torture that strikes the psychically handicapped, isolating them in their pain. But behind the rational administration of pain in the penalties meted out by human courts, which immediately begin to look suspiciously like repression, the arbitrariness and strange failure of justice amidst wars, crimes and the oppression of the weak by the strong, rejoin, in a sort of fatality, the useless suffering that springs from natural plagues, as if they were the effects of an ontological perversion. Beyond the fundamental malignity of suffering itself, revealed in its phenomenology, does not human experience in history attest to a wickedness and an ill will?

Western humanity has nonetheless sought the meaning of this outrage by appealing to a meaning that would be peculiar to a metaphysical order and an ethics that are not visible in the immediate lessons of moral consciousness. This is the kingdom of transcendent ends, willed by a benevolent wisdom, by the absolute goodness of a God who is in a sense defined by that super-natural goodness; or a goodness invisibly disseminated in Nature and History, whose paths, indeed painful but leading to the Good, benevolent wisdom would direct. This is pain henceforth meaningful, subordinated in one way or another to the metaphysical finality glimpsed by faith or belief in progress. Beliefs presupposed by theodicy! That is the grand idea necessary to the inner peace of souls in our distressed world. It is called upon to make sufferings here below comprehensible. These will make sense within the framework of an original sin or the congenital finitude of human being. The evil that fills the earth would be explained by a "grand design"; it would be destined to the atonement of a sin, or announce, to the ontologically limited consciousness, compensation or recompense at the end of time. These supra-sensible perspectives are invoked in order to divine, in a suffering that is essentially gratuitous and absurd, and apparently arbitrary, a meaning and an order.

Certainly one may inquire into whether theodicy, in the broad and narrow senses of the term, effectively succeeds in making God innocent or in saving morality in the name of faith or in making suffering bearable, or into the true intent of the thought that has recourse to theodicy. It is impossible, in any case, to underestimate the temptation of theodicy, and to fail to recognize the profundity of the empire it exerts over humankind, and the *epochemachend* (or, as one says these days, the *historial*) character of its entry into thought. It has been, at least up to the trials of the twentieth century, a component of the self-consciousness of European humanity. It persisted in watered-down form at the core of atheist progressivism, which was confident of the efficacy of the Good that is immanent in being and destined to visible triumph by the simple play of the natural and historical laws of injustice, war, misery and illness. Providential Nature and History, which furnished the eighteenth and nineteenth centuries with the norms of moral consciousness, have many links to the Deism of the Enlightenment. But theodicy, although Leibniz did not give it its name until 1710, is as old as a certain reading of the Bible. It dominated the consciousness of believers who explained their misfortunes by reference to Sin, or at least to their sins. Alongside the Christians' major reference to Original Sin, this theodicy is in a certain sense implicit in the Old Testament, in which the drama of the Diaspora reflects the sins of Israel. The misconduct of the ancestors, still unexpiated by the sufferings of the exile, explained to the exiles themselves the length and harshness of that exile.

The End of Theodicy

Perhaps the most revolutionary fact of our twentieth-century consciousness—but it is also an event in Sacred History—is that of the destruction of all balance between Western thought's explicit and implicit theodicy and the forms that suffering and its evil are taking on in the very unfolding of this century. This is the century that in thirty years has known two world wars, the totalitarianisms of right and left, Hitlerism and Stalinism, Hiroshima, the Gulag, and the genocides of Auschwitz and Cambodia. This is the century that is drawing to a close in the obsessive fear of the return of everything these barbaric names stood for: suffering and evil inflicted deliberately, but in a manner no reason set limits to, in the exasperation[6] of a reason become political and detached from all ethics.

Among these events the Holocaust of the Jewish people under the reign of Hitler seems to me the paradigm of gratuitous human suffering, in which evil appears in its diabolical horror. This is perhaps not a subjective feeling. The disproportion between suffering and every theodicy was shown at Auschwitz with a glaring, obvious clarity. Its possibility puts into question the multimillennial traditional faith. Did not Nietzsche's saying about the death of God take on, in the extermination camps, the meaning of a quasi-empirical fact? Should it be a source of surprise, then, that this drama of Sacred History has had among its principal actors a people that has forever been associated with that history, whose collective soul and destiny would be wrongly understood as limited to any sort of nationalism, and whose historic deeds, in certain circumstances, still belong to the Revelation (be it as apocalypse) that gives philosophers "food for thought," or keeps them from being able to think?[7]

Here I wish to recall the analysis that the Canadian Jew, the philosopher Emil Fackenheim of Toronto, has made of this catastrophe of the human and the divine in his work, and particularly in his book *God's Presence in History*.

The Nazi Genocide of the Jewish people has no precedent within Jewish history. Nor . . . will one find a precedent outside Jewish history. . . . Even actual cases of genocide, however, still differ from the Nazi holocaust in at least two respects. Whole peoples have been killed for "rational" (however horrifying) ends such as power, territory, wealth. . . . The Nazi murder . . . was annihilation for the sake of annihilation, murder for the sake of murder, evil for the sake of evil. Still more incontestably unique than the crime itself is the situation of the victims. The Albigensians died for their faith, believing unto death that God needs martyrs. Negro Christians have been murdered for their race, able to find comfort in a faith not at issue. The more than one million Jewish children murdered in the Nazi holocaust died neither because of their faith, nor despite their faith, nor for reasons unrelated to the Jewish faith [but] because of the Jewish faith of their great-grandparents [who brought] up Jewish children.[8]

The inhabitants of the Eastern European Jewish communities constituted the majority of the six million tortured and massacred; they represented the human beings least corrupted by the ambiguities of our world, and the million children killed had the innocence of children. Theirs is the death of martyrs, a death inflicted in the torturers' unceasing destruction of the dignity that belongs to martyrs. The final act of this destruction is being accomplished today in the posthumous denial of the very fact of martyrdom by the would-be "revisionists of history." Pain in its undiluted malignity, suffering for nothing. It renders impossible and odious every proposal and every thought that would explain it by the sins of those who have suffered or are dead. But does not this end of theodicy, which imposes itself in the face of this century's inordinate trial, at the same time and in a more general way reveal the unjustifiable character of suffering in the other, the outrage it would be for me to justify my neighbor's suffering?

Thus the very phenomenon of suffering in its uselessness is, in principle, the pain of the other. For an ethical sensibility, confirming, in the

inhumanity of our time, its opposition to this inhumanity, the justification of the neighbor's pain is certainly the source of all immorality.
Accusing oneself in suffering is undoubtedly the very turning back of
the *I* to itself. It is perhaps thus that the for-the-other—the most upright
relation to the other—is the most profound adventure of subjectivity,
its ultimate intimacy. But this intimacy can only be discreetly. It cannot
give itself out as an example, or be narrated in an edifying discourse. It
cannot, without becoming perverted, be made into a preachment.

The philosophical problem, then, that is posed by the useless pain
that appears in its fundamental malignancy through the events of the
twentieth century, concerns the meaning that religiosity, but also the
human morality of goodness, can continue to have after the end of
theodicy. According to the philosopher we have just quoted, Auschwitz
would paradoxically entail a revelation from the very God who nevertheless was silent at Auschwitz: a commandment of faithfulness. To
renounce after Auschwitz this God absent from Auschwitz—no longer
to assure the continuation of Israel—would amount to finishing the
criminal enterprise of National Socialism, which aimed at the annihilation of Israel and the forgetting of the ethical message of the Bible,
which Judaism bears, and whose multimillennial history is concretely
prolonged by Israel's existence as a people. For if God was absent in the
extermination camps, the devil was very obviously present. Hence, in
Emil Fackenheim's view, the obligation for Jews to live and to remain
Jews, in order not to be made accomplices of a diabolical project. Jews,
after Auschwitz, are pledged to their faithfulness to Judaism and to the
material and even political conditions of its existence.

That final reflection of the philosopher from Toronto, formulated in
terms that make it relative to the destiny of the Jewish people, can be
given a universal meaning. The portion of humanity that, from
Sarajevo to Cambodia, witnessed a host of cruelties in the course of a
century in which its Europe, with its "human sciences," seemed to have
fully explored its subject—the humanity that, during all these horrors,
breathed—already or still—the smoke from the ovens of the "final
solution" crematoria where theodicy abruptly appeared impossible—
will it, in indifference, abandon the world to useless suffering, leaving it
to the political fatality—or drifting—of blind forces that inflict misfortune on the weak and conquered, while sparing the conquerors, with

whom the shrewd are not slow to align themselves? Or, incapable of adhering to an order—or a disorder—that it continues to think diabolical, must not humanity now, in a faith more difficult than before, in a faith without theodicy, continue to live out Sacred History; a history that now demands even more from the resources of the *I* in each one of us, and from its suffering inspired by the suffering of the other, from its compassion which is a non-useless suffering (or love), which is no longer suffering "for nothing," and immediately has meaning? At the end of the twentieth century and after the useless and unjustifiable pain which is exposed and displayed therein without any shadow of a consoling theodicy,[9] are we not all committed—like the Jewish people to their faithfulness—to the second term of this alternative? This is a new modality in the faith of today, and even in our moral certitudes; a modality most essential to the modernity that is dawning.

The Interhuman Order

To envisage suffering, as I have just attempted to do, in the interhuman perspective—that is, as meaningful in me, useless in the Other—does not consist in adopting a relative point of view on it, but in restoring it to the dimensions of meaning outside of which the immanent and savage concreteness of evil in a consciousness is but an abstraction. To think suffering in an interhuman perspective does not amount to seeing it in the coexistence of a multiplicity of consciousnesses, or in a social determinism, accompanied by a simple knowledge that people in society can have of their proximity or of their common destiny. The interhuman perspective can subsist, but can also be lost, in the political order of the City where the Law establishes mutual obligations between citizens. The interhuman, properly speaking, lies in a non-indifference of one to another, in a responsibility of one for another, but before the reciprocity of this responsibility, which will be inscribed in impersonal laws, comes to be superimposed on the pure altruism of this responsibility inscribed in the ethical position of the *I qua I*. It is prior to any contract that would specify precisely the moment of reciprocity—a point at which altruism and disinterestedness may, to be sure, continue, but at which they may also diminish or die out. The order of politics (post-ethical or pre-ethical) that inaugurates the "social contract" is neither the sufficient condition nor the necessary outcome of ethics. In its ethical position, the *I* is distinct both from the citizen born of the City, and from the individual who precedes all order in his natural egotism, but from whom political philosophy, since Hobbes, has tried to derive—or succeeded in deriving—the social or political order of the City.

The interhuman is also in the recourse that people have to one another for help, before the astonishing alterity of the other has been banalized or dimmed down to a simple exchange of courtesies that has become established as an "interpersonal commerce" of customs. I have spoken of this in the first section of this study. These are expressions of a properly ethical meaning, distinct from those acquired by *self* and *other* in what is called the state of Nature or civil society. It is in the interhuman perspective of *my* responsibility for the other, without concern for reciprocity, in my call for his or her disinterested help, in the asymmetry of the relation of *one* to the *other*, that I have tried to analyze the phenomenon of useless suffering.

QUESTION: *"The Face of the Other is perhaps the very beginning of philosophy." Do you mean to say that philosophy does not begin with and in the experience of finitude, but rather in that of the Infinite as the call of justice? Does philosophy begin before itself, in an experience prior to philosophical discourse?*

EMMANUEL LEVINAS: My main point in saying that was that the order of meaning, which seems to me primary, is precisely what comes to us from the interhuman relationship, so that the Face, with all its meaningfulness as brought out by analysis, is the beginning of intelligibility. Of course the whole perspective of ethics immediately emerges here; but we cannot say that it is already philosophy. Philosophy is a theoretical discourse; I thought that the theoretical presupposes more. It is inasmuch as I have not only to respond to the Face of the other, but alongside him to approach the third party, that the necessity for the theoretical attitude arises.

From the start, the encounter with the Other is my responsibility for him. That is the responsibility for my neighbor, which is, no doubt, the harsh name for what we call love of one's neighbor; love without Eros, charity, love in which the ethical aspect dominates the passionate aspect, love without concupiscence. I don't very much like the word love, which is worn-out and debased. Let us speak instead of the taking upon oneself of the fate of the other. That is the "vision" of the Face, and it applies to the first comer. If he were my only interlocutor, I would have had nothing but obligations! But I don't live in a world in which there is but one single "first comer"; there is always a third party in the world: he or she is also my other, my fellow. Hence, it is important to me to know which of the two takes precedence. Is the one not the persecutor of the other? Must not human beings, who are incomparable, be compared? Thus justice, here, takes precedence over the taking upon oneself of the fate of the other.

I must judge, where before I was to assume responsibilities. Here is the birth of the theoretical; here the concern for justice is born, which is the basis of the theoretical. But it is always starting out from the Face, from the responsibility for the other that justice appears, which calls for judgment and comparison, a comparison of what is in principle incomparable, for every being is unique; every other is unique. In that necessity of being concerned with justice that idea of equity appears, on which the idea of objectivity is based. At a certain moment, there is a necessity for a "weighing," a comparison, a pondering, and in this sense philosophy would be the appearance of wisdom from the depths of that initial charity; it would be—and I am not playing on words—the wisdom of that charity, the wisdom of love.

Q: *Would the experience of the death of the other, and in a sense, the experience of death itself, be alien to the ethical reception of one's neighbor?*

E.L.: Now you are posing the problem: "What is there in the Face?" In my analysis, the Face is definitely not a plastic form like a portrait; the relation to the Face is both the relation to the absolutely weak—to what is absolutely exposed, what is bare and destitute, the relation with bareness and consequently with what is alone and can undergo the supreme isolation we call death—and there is, consequently, in the Face of the Other always the death of the Other and thus, in some way, an incitement to murder, the temptation to go to the extreme, to completely neglect the other—and at the same time (and this is the paradoxical thing) the Face is also the "Thou Shalt not Kill." A Thou-Shalt-not-Kill that can also be explicated much further: it is the fact that I cannot let the other die alone, it is like a calling out to me. And you see (and this seems important to me), the relationship with the other is not symmetrical, it is not at all as in Martin Buber. When I say *Thou* to an *I*, to a me, according to Buber I would always have that me before me as the one who says Thou to me. Consequently, there would be a reciprocal relationship. According to my analysis, on the other hand, in the relation to the Face, it is asymmetry that is affirmed: at the outset I hardly care what the other is with respect to me, that is his own business; for me, he is above all the one I am responsible for.

Q: *Does the executioner have a Face?*

E.L.: You are posing the whole problem of evil. When I speak of Justice, I introduce the idea of the struggle with evil, I separate myself from the idea of nonresistance to evil. If self-defense is a problem, the "executioner" is the one who threatens my neighbor and, in this sense, calls for violence and no longer has a Face. But my central idea is what I called an "asymmetry of intersubjectivity": the exceptional situation of the *I*. I always recall Dostoyevsky on this subject. One of his characters says: "We are all guilty for everything and everyone, and I more than all the others." But to this idea—without contradicting it—I immediately add the concern for the third and, hence, justice. So the whole problematic of the executioner is opened here; in terms of justice and the defense of the other, my fellow, and not at all in terms of the threat that concerns me. If there were no order of Justice, there would be no limit to my responsibility. There is a certain measure of violence necessary in terms of justice; but if one speaks of justice, it is necessary to allow judges, it is necessary to allow institutions and the state; to live in a world of citizens, and not only in the order of the Face to Face.

But, on the other hand, it is in terms of the relation to the Face or of me before the other that we can speak of the legitimacy or illegitimacy of the state. A state in which the interpersonal relationship is impossible, in which it is directed in advance by the determinism proper to the state, is a totalitarian state. So there is a limit to the state. Whereas, in Hobbes's vision—in which the state emerges not from the limitation of charity, but from the limitation of violence—one cannot set a limit on the state.

Q: *So is the state always the acceptance of some level of violence?*

E.L.: There is an element of violence in the state, but the violence can involve justice. That does not mean violence must not be avoided as much as possible; everything that replaces it in the life between states, everything that can be left to negotiation, to speech, is absolutely essential; but one cannot say that there is no legitimate violence.

Q: *Would a form of speech such as prophetic speech be contrary to the state?*

E.L.: It is an extremely bold, audacious speech, since the prophet always speaks before the king; the prophet is not in hiding, he is not preparing an underground revelation. In the Bible—it's amazing—the king accepts this direct opposition. He's an odd kind of king! Isaiah and Jeremiah submit to violence. Let us not forget the perennial false prophets who flatter kings. Only the true prophet addresses the king and the people without truckling, and reminds them of ethics. In the Old Testament, there is certainly no denunciation of the state as such. There is a protest against the pure and simple assimilation of the state into the politics of the world . . . What shocks Samuel when they come to demand that he give them a king for Israel is wanting to have a king like *all the nations*! In Deuteronomy, there is a doctrine of royal power; the state is supposed to be in conformity with the Law. The idea of an ethical state is biblical.

Q: *Is it seen as the lesser of two evils?*

E.L.: No, it is the wisdom of the nations. The other concerns you even when a third does him harm, and consequently you are there before the necessity of justice and a certain violence. The third party isn't there by accident. In a certain sense, all the others [*autres*] are present in the face of the other [*autrui*]. If there were two of us in the world, there wouldn't be any problem: it is the other who goes before me. And to a certain extent (may God keep me from being reduced to it as a rule of daily usage) I am responsible for the other even when he bothers me, even when he persecutes me. There is in the Lamentations of Jeremiah— since we're talking a lot about prophets today—this not very long text, which says: "Offering my cheek to him that smiteth . . ."[1] But I am responsible for the persecution of my neighbors [*prochains*]. If I belong to a people, that people and my relatives [*proches*] are also my neighbors. They have a right to defense, just as do those who are not my relatives.

Q: *You spoke of the asymmetry that differs from Buber's relationship of reciprocity . . . .*

E.L.: As citizens we are reciprocal, but it is a more complex structure than the Face to Face.

Q: *Yes, but in the initial, interhuman domain, wouldn't there be the risk that the dimension of gentleness might be absent in a relation in which there would not be reciprocity? Are justice and gentleness dimensions alien to one another?*

E.L.: They are very close. I have tried to make this deduction: justice itself is born of charity. They can seem alien when they are presented as successive stages; in reality, they are inseparable and simultaneous, unless one is on a desert island, without humanity, without a third.

Q: *Might one not think that the experience of justice assumes the experience of love which is indulgent toward the suffering of the other? Schopenhauer identified love with compassion and made justice an aspect of love. What is your thought on that subject?*

E.L.: Certainly. Except that for me the suffering of compassion, suffering because the other suffers, is only one aspect of a relationship that is much more complex and much more complete at the same time: that of responsibility for the other. I am in reality responsible for the other even when he or she commits crimes, even when others commit crimes. This is for me the essence of the Jewish conscience. But I also think that it is the essence of the human conscience: All men are responsible for one another, and "I more than anyone else." One of the most important things for me is that asymmetry and that formula: All men are responsible for one another and I more than anyone else. It is Dostoyevsky's formula which, as you see, I quote again.

Q: *And the relation between justice and love?*

E.L.: Justice comes from love. That definitely doesn't mean to say that the rigor of justice can't be turned against love understood in terms of responsibility. Politics, left to itself, has its own determinism. Love must always watch over justice. In Jewish theology—I am not guided by that theology explicitly—God is the God of justice, but his principal attribute is mercy. In talmudic language, God is always called *Rachmanah*, the Merciful: this whole topic is studied in rabbinic exegesis. Why are there two accounts of creation? Because the Eternal—called *Elohim* in the first account—wanted at first (all that is only a fable, of course) to create a world sustained solely by justice. It didn't hold up. The second account, in which the Tetragrammaton appears, attests to the intervention of mercy.

Q: *So, love is originary?*

E.L.: Love is originary. I'm not speaking theologically at all; I myself don't use it much, the word love, it is a worn-out and ambiguous word. And then, too, there is something severe in this love; this love is commanded. In my last book, which is called *De Dieu qui vient à l'idée*,[2] there is an attempt (outside all theology) to ask at what moment the word of God is heard. It is inscribed in the Face of the Other, in the encounter with the Other: a double expression of weakness and strict, urgent requirement. Is that the word of God? A word that requires me as the one responsible for the Other; and there is an election there, because that responsibility is inalienable. A responsibility you yield to someone is no longer a responsibility. I substitute myself for every man and no one can substitute for me, and in that sense I am chosen. Let us think again of my quotation from Dostoyevsky. I have always thought that election is definitely not a privilege; it is the fundamental characteristic of the human person as morally responsible. Responsibility is an individuation, a principle of individuation. On the famous problem: "Is man individuated by matter, or individuated by form," I support individuation by responsibility for the other. It also is hard; I leave the whole consoling side of this ethics to religion.

Q: *Does gentleness belong to religion?*

E.L.: What responsibility lacks as a principle of human individuation is that God perhaps helps you to be responsible; that is gentleness. But to deserve the help of God, it is necessary to want to do what must be done without his help. I am not getting into that question theologically. I am describing ethics: it is the human *qua* human. I think that ethics is not an invention of the white race, of a humanity which has read the Greek authors in school and gone through a specific evolution. The only absolute value is the human possibility of giving the other priority over oneself. I don't think that there is a human group that can take exception to that ideal, even if it is declared an ideal of holiness. I am not saying that the human being is a saint, I'm saying that he or she is the one who has understood that holiness is indisputable. This is the beginning of philosophy, this is the rational, the intelligible. In saying that, it sounds as if we are getting away from reality. But we forget our relation to *books*—that is, to inspired language—which speaks of nothing else. The book of books, and all literature, which is perhaps only a premonition or recollection of the Bible. One is easily led to suspect pure bookishness and the hypocrisy of bookishness in our books, forgetting the depth of our relationship to the book. All humanity has books, be they but books before books: the inspired language of proverbs, fables, and even folklore. The human being is not only in the world, not only an *in-der-Welt-Sein*, but also *zum-Buch-Sein* [being-toward-the-book] in relationship to the inspired Word, an ambiance as important for our existence as streets, houses, and clothing. The book is wrongly interpreted as pure *Zuhandenes*, as what is at hand, a manual. My relation to the book is definitely not pure use; it doesn't have the same meaning as the one I have with the hammer or the telephone.

Q: *On this relation between philosophy and religion, don't you think that, at the origin of philosophizing, there is an intuition of being that would be close to religion?*

E.L.: I would say, yes, insofar as I say that the relation to the other is the beginning of the intelligible. I cannot describe the relation to God without speaking of my concern for the other. When I speak to a Christian, I always quote Matthew 25; the relation to God is presented there as a relation to another person. It is not a metaphor: in the other, there is a real presence of God. In my relation to the other, I hear the Word of God. It is not a metaphor; it is not only extremely important, it is literally true. I'm not saying that the other is God, but that in his or her Face I hear the Word of God.

Q: *It is a mediator between God and us?*

E.L.: Oh, no, not at all, it is not mediation—it is the way the word of God reverberates.

Q: *There is no difference?*

E.L.: Now hold on a minute. Now we're getting into theology!

Q: *What is the relationship between the Other [*l'Autre*] and the Other Person [*Autrui*]?*

E.L.: To me, the Other Person [*Autrui*] is the other human being. Shall we do a bit of theology? In the Old Testament, you know, God also comes down to mankind. God the Father descends, for example, in Genesis 9,5,15 [sic][3] and Numbers 11:17, Exodus 19:18. There is no separation between the Father and the Word; it is in the form of speech, in the form of an ethical order, an order to love, that the descent of God takes place. It is in the Face of the Other [*Autre*] that the commandment comes which interrupts the progress of the world. Why would I feel responsible in the presence of the Face? That is Cain's answer when someone says to him: "Where is your brother?" He answers: "Am I my brother's keeper?" That is the Face of the Other taken as an image among images, and when the Word of God it bears is not recognized. We must not take Cain's answer as if he were mocking God or as if he were answering as a little boy: "It isn't me, it's the other one." Cain's answer is sincere. Ethics is the only thing lacking in his answer; there is only ontology: I am I, and he is he. We are separate ontological beings.

Q: *In this relation to the Other, as you said, consciousness loses its first place . . .?*

E.L.: Yes, subjectivity, as responsible, is a subjectivity which is commanded at the outset; heteronomy is somehow stronger than autonomy here, except that this heteronomy is not slavery, is not bondage. As if certain purely formal relationships, when they are filled with content, could have a stronger content than the formal necessity they signify. *A* commanding *B* is a formula of *B*'s non-freedom; but if *B* is the human being and *A* is God, the subordination is not servitude; on the contrary, it is an appeal to the human being. We must not always formalize: Nietzsche thought that if God exists, the *I* is impossible. That can be very convincing. If *A* commands *B*, *B* is no longer autonomous, no longer has subjectivity; but when, in thinking, you do not remain on the level of form, when you think in terms of content, a situation called heteronomy has a completely different signification. The consciousness of responsibility immediately imposed is certainly not in the nominative, it is rather in the accusative. It is "ordered," and the word "to order" is very good in French: when you become a priest, you are ordained, you take orders; but in reality, you receive powers. The word "*ordonné*" in French means both having received orders and having been consecrated. It is in that sense that I can say that consciousness, subjectivity, no longer have first place in their relationship to the other.

My view is opposed to the tendency of one whole portion of contemporary philosophy that prefers to see in man a simple articulation or a simple aspect of a rational, ontological system that has nothing human about it; even in Heidegger, the *Dasein* is ultimately a structure of being in general, bound to its profession of being, "its historic deeds of being," its event of being. The human is not the entire meaning of being; man is a being who comprehends being and, in that sense, is the manifestation of it, and only thus does he concern philosophy.

Similarly, in certain trends in structuralist research, rules, pure forms, universal structures, combinations which have a legality as cold as mathematical legality are isolated. And then that dominates the human. In Merleau-Ponty, you have a very beautiful passage in which he analyzes the way one hand touches the other.[4] One hand touches the other, the other hand touches the first; the hand, consequently, is touched and touches the touching—one hand touches the touching. A reflexive structure: it is as if space were touching itself through man. What is pleasing here is, perhaps, that nonhuman—nonhumanist, right?—structure in which man is only an aspect. In the same distrust with regard to humanism according to contemporary philosophy there is a battle against the notion of the subject. What they want is a principle of intelligibility that is no longer enveloped by the human; they want the subject to appeal to a principle that would not be enveloped by concern for human fate.

On the contrary, when I say that consciousness in the relationship with the other loses its first place, it is not in that sense; I mean to say that, in consciousness thus conceived, there is the awakening to humanity. The humanity of consciousness is definitely not in its powers, but in its responsibility: in passivity, in reception, in obligation with regard to the other. It is the other who is first, and there the question of my sovereign consciousness is no longer the first question. I advocate, as in the title of one of my books, the humanism of the other man.[5]

One last thing that is very close to my heart. In this whole priority of the relationship to the other, there is a break with a great traditional idea of the excellence of unity. The relation would already be a deprivation of this unity. That is the Plotinian tradition. My idea consists in conceiving sociality as independent of the "lost" unity.

Q: *Is that the origin of your criticism of Western philosophy as egology?*

E.L.: As egology, yes. If you read the *Enneads*, the One doesn't even have consciousness of self; if it did have consciousness of self, it would already be multiple, as a loss of perfection. In knowledge, one is two, even when one is alone. Even when one assumes consciousness of self, there is already a split. The various relations that can exist in man and in being are always judged according to their proximity or distance from unity. What is relation? What is time? A fall from unity, a fall from eternity. There are many theologians in all religions who say that the good life is a coincidence with God; coincidence, that is, the return to unity. Whereas in the insistence on the relation to the other in responsibility for him or her the excellence of sociality itself is affirmed; in theological terms, proximity to God, society with God.

Q: *This is the excellence of multiplicity?*

E.L.: This is the excellence of the multiple, which evidently can be thought as a degradation of the one. To cite another verse, created man is blessed with a command to "multiply." In ethical and religious terms: you will have someone to love, you will have someone for whom to exist, you cannot be just for yourself. He created them man and woman at the outset, "man and woman created He them." While at every moment, for us Europeans, for me and for you, the essential thing is to approach unity. The essential thing is fusion. We say that love is a fusion, that it triumphs in fusion. Diotima, in Plato's *Symposium*, says that love as such is a demigod, precisely because he is only separation and desire for the other.

Q: *In this perspective, what, according to you, would be the difference between Eros and Agape?*

E.L.: I am definitely not a Freudian; consequently I don't think that Agape comes from Eros. But I don't deny that sexuality is also an important philosophical problem; the meaning of the division of the human into man and woman is not reduced to a biological problem. I used to think that otherness began in the feminine. That is, in fact, a very strange otherness: woman is neither the contradictory nor the opposite of man, nor like other differences. It is not like the opposition between light and darkness. It is a distinction that is not contingent, and whose place must be sought in relation to love.

I can say no more about it now; I think in any case that Eros is definitely not Agape, that Agape is neither a derivative nor the extinction of love-Eros. Before Eros there was the Face; Eros itself is possible only between Faces. The problem of Eros is philosophical and concerns otherness. Thirty years ago I wrote a book called *Le temps et l'autre* [*Time and the Other*][6]—in which I thought that the feminine was otherness itself; and I do not retract that, but I have never been a Freudian. In *Totalité et Infini* [*Totality and Infinity*],[7] there is a chapter on Eros, which is described as love that becomes enjoyment, whereas I have a grave view of Agape in terms of responsibility for the other.

Q: *You say that "the responsibility for the other comes from the hither side of my freedom." It is the problematic of the awakening-reawakening. To reawaken is to discover oneself responsible for the other; it is to discover oneself always-in-debt, on the hither side of freedom itself. To wake up and to respond: are they the same thing? To discover oneself-in-debt: is that already to respond? Or, between "discovering oneself" and "responding," is there not freedom? (A possibility of bad faith, of nonresponse.)*

E.L.: What is important is that the relation to the other is awakening and sobering up—that awakening is obligation. You say to me: Isn't that obligation preceded by a free decision? What matters to me is, in the responsibility for the other, something like an older involvement than any rememberable deliberation constitutive of the human. It is evident that there is in man the possibility of not awakening to the other; there is the possibility of evil. Evil is the order of being pure and simple—and, on the contrary, to go toward the other is the penetration of the human into being, an "otherwise than being."

I am not at all certain that the "otherwise than being" is guaranteed to triumph. There can be periods during which the human is completely extinguished, but the ideal of holiness is what humanity has introduced into being. An ideal of holiness contrary to the laws of being. Reciprocal actions and reactions, compensation for forces expended, the regaining of an equilibrium, whatever the wars, whatever the "cruelties" that take cover in that indifferent language that passes for justice: such is the law of being. Without illness, without exception, without disorder—that is the order of being.

I have no illusions; most of the time, things happen that way and it will probably recur. Humanity attains friendship, even when it seems to be broken off, but also constructs a political order in which the determinism of being can reappear. I have no illusions about it and I have no optimistic philosophy for the end of history. Perhaps the religions have a deeper insight into such things. But the human consists in acting without letting yourself be guided by these menacing possibilities. That is what the awakening to the human is. And there have been just men and saints in history.

Q: *Is being also inertia, the fact of not responding, of not awakening to another?*

E.L.: Inertia is certainly the great law of being; but the human looms up in it and can disturb it. For a long time? For a moment? The human is a scandal in being, a "sickness" of being for the realists, but not evil.

Q: *The madness of the Cross?*

E.L.: Yes, certainly, if you like, that suits the idea I just expressed, and there are equivalent ideas in Jewish thought. There is the history of the Jewish people itself. This idea of the crisis of being describes for me something which is specifically human and certainly corresponds to its prophetic instants. In the very structure of prophecy, a temporality is opened up, breaking with the "rigor" of being, with eternity understood as presence which does not pass away.

Q: *Is it the opening up of time?*

E.L.: Yes, there is the time that one can understand in terms of presence and the present, and in which the past is only a retained present and the future a present to come. Re-presentation would be the fundamental modality of mental life. But, in terms of the ethical relationship with the other, I glimpse a temporality in which the dimensions of the past and the future have their own signification. In my responsibility for the other, the past of the other, which has never been my present, "concerns me": it is not a re-presentation for me. The past of the other and, in a sense, the history of humanity in which I have never participated, in which I have never been present, is my past. As for the future—it is not my anticipation of a present which is already waiting for me, all ready, and like the imperturbable order of being, "as if it had already arrived," as if temporality were a synchrony. The future is the time of pro-phecy, which is also an imperative, a moral order, herald of an inspiration. I have tried to present the essence of these ideas in a study that will soon appear: a future that is not a simple to-come [*à-venir*]. The infinity of time doesn't frighten me; I think that it is the very movement of the to-God, and that time is better than eternity which is an exasperation of the "present," an idealization of the present.

Q: *You see Heidegger as a continuator of Western philosophy who maintains the primacy of the Same over the Other . . . .*

E.L.: For me, Heidegger is the greatest philosopher of the century, perhaps one of the very great philosophers of the millennium; but I am very pained by that because I can never forget what he was in 1933, even if he was that for only a short period. What I admire in his work is *Sein und Zeit*. It is a peak of phenomenology. The analyses are brilliant. As for the later Heidegger, I am much less familiar with him. What scares me a little is also the development of a discourse in which the human becomes an articulation of an anonymous or neutral intelligibility, to which the revelation of God is subordinated. In the *Geviert*,[8] there are gods in the plural.

Q: *In terms of the ontological difference Heidegger establishes between beings and being, might one not think that Heideggerian being would correspond to a certain extent to the "other than being?"*

E.L.: No, I don't think so. Besides, otherwise than being isn't a "something." It is the relation to the other, the ethical relation. In Heidegger, the ethical relation, the *Miteinandersein*, the being-with-another-person, is only one moment of our presence in the world. It does not have the central place. *Mit* is always being next to . . . it is not in the first instance the Face, it is *ʒusammensein* [being-together], perhaps *ʒusammenmarschieren* [marching-together].

Q: *True, it is a moment; but might one not also say that, at the same time, it is an essential structure of the Dasein?*

E.L.: Yes, certainly, but we have always known that man is a social animal. That is definitely not the meaning I'm looking for. . . . They say that in my view—I am often criticized for this—there is an underestimation of the world. In Heidegger, the world is very important. In the *Feldwege*, there is a tree; you don't find men there.

Q: *And a structure or a moment such as the Fürsorge, the assistance to the other?*

E.L.: Yes, but I don't believe he thinks that giving, feeding the hungry and clothing the naked is the meaning of being or that it is above the task of being.

Q: *It is an open question . . . .*

E.L.: Yes, it is open. Don't worry; I'm not a fool. I could not fail to recognize Heidegger's speculative greatness. But the emphasis in his analyses is elsewhere. I repeat, they are brilliant analyses. But what does fear for the other mean in his theory of *Befindlichkeit?* To me, it is an essential moment; I even think that fearing God primarily means fearing for the other. Fear for the other doesn't enter into the Heideggerian analysis of *Befindlichkeit* because in that theory—a very admirable theory of double intentionality—all emotion, all fear is finally emotion for self, fear for self, fear of the dog but anguish *for* self.

But then what of fear for the other? Obviously that fear could be interpreted as fear for self, on the pretext that in fearing for the other I may be afraid of being in the same situation as the other. But that is not what fear for the other really is. The mother who fears for the child, or even, each of us who fears for a friend, is afraid for the other. (But every "other man" is a friend. Do you see what I mean?)

As if by chance, in chapter 19 of Leviticus, certain verses that end with "And thou shalt fear God" concern prohibitions of bad acts concerning the other man. Doesn't the theory of *Befindlichkeit* come up short here?

Q: *Do you think that Heidegger would make a kind of sacralization of the world, and that his thought represents a culmination of paganism?*

E.L.: Whatever the case may be, he has a very great sense for everything that is part of the landscape; not the artistic landscape, but the place in which man is enrooted. It is absolutely not a philosophy of the émigré! I would even say that it is not a philosophy of the emigrant. To me, being a migrant is not being a nomad. Nothing is more enrooted than the nomad. But he or she who emigrates is fully human: the migration of man does not destroy, does not demolish the meaning of being.

Q: *Do you think that, in Heidegger, it is a question of geographical enrootedness? For example, reading your text in* Difficile Liberté *on Heidegger and Gagarin,*[9] *one has the impression that enrootedness in Heidegger, as you interpret it, is a local enrootedness, on a geographical space. Is that what Heidegger has in mind, or is it not rather an enrootedness in the world?*

E.L.: But the human is lived, is described, always in the same landscape. When you have been on the moon a bit, you certainly return to the world as to your village. But Heidegger said that one cannot live in geometrical space. Gagarin didn't settle in geometrical space since he returned to earth, but he was able to make geometrical space his place and the place of his professional activity.

Q: *Is the world in Heidegger in fact something other than the terrestrial world, other than identification with a landscape?*

E.L.: They say that my article on Gagarin and Heidegger went too far. There are texts in Heidegger on the place of man in Central Europe. Europe and the German West are central to him. There is a whole geopolitics in Heidegger.

Q: *What is the influence of Rosenzweig on your thought?*

E.L.: It is his critique of totality, his critique of Hegel that has given me the most, and I have been very appreciative of the idea that initial intelligibility—Rosenzweig's great idea—is the juncture of Creation, Revelation, and Redemption. These are not late and derived notions (it hardly matters at what moment they appear in history) but the source of all meaning. I reiterated this in the preface I wrote for Stéphane Mosès's book on Rosenzweig.[10] In Rosenzweig's work, the abstract aspects of time—past, present, future—are deformalized; it is no longer a question of time, an empty form in which there are three formal dimensions. The past is Creation. It is as if Rosenzweig were saying: to think the past concretely, you have to think Creation. Or, the future is Redemption; the present is Revelation. What I retain is definitely not that second or third identification, but that very precocious idea that certain formal notions are not fully intelligible except in a concrete event, which seems even more irrational than they are, but in which they are truly thought. This is also certainly one of the ideas presented by Husserlian phenomenology, which Rosenzweig never knew.

Q: *And the influence of Buber and Marcel?*

E.L.: I read Buber very late, and Marcel too; but I said in a little article soon to be published[11] that whoever has walked on Buber's ground owes allegiance to Buber, even if he didn't know where he was. It is as if you were about to cross the frontier without knowing it; you owe obedience to the country where you are. It is Buber who identified that ground, saw the theme of The Other, the *Du*, the *Thou*. Marcel is also very close to me; but I find that, in Marcel, dialogue is finally overwhelmed by ontology. There is in Marcel the concern to prolong traditional ontology: God is Being. The idea that God is something other than being, beyond being, as Marion says (Have you read Marion's book, *Dieu sans l'Etre?*),[12] must have frightened him.

Q: *Various attempts have been made, notably in Latin America, to establish a synthesis of your philosophy and Marxism. What do you think of that?*

E.L.: I knew Dussel, who used to quote me a lot, and who is now much closer to political, even geopolitical thought. Moreover, I have gotten to know a very sympathetic South American group that is working out a "liberation philosophy" —Scannone in particular. We had a meeting here, with Bernhard Casper, a friend of mine who is a professor of theology at Freiburg, and some Catholic philosophers from South America. There is a very interesting attempt there to return to the spirit of the people in South America, along with a great influence of Heidegger in the manner—the rhythm—of developing topics, and in the radicalism of the questioning. I am very happy, very proud even, when I find reflections of my work in this group. It is a fundamental approval. It means that some people have also seen "the same thing."

Q: *Can your thought, which is a thought of love, be reconciled with a philosophy of conquest, such as Marxism?*

E.L.: No, in Marxism, there is not just conquest; there is recognition of the other. True enough, it consists in saying: We can save the other if he himself demands his due. Marxism invites humanity to demand what it is my duty to give it. That is a bit different from my radical distinction between me and others, but Marxism cannot be condemned for that.

Not because it succeeded so well, but because it took the Other serious-ly.

Q: *As a political philosophy, Marxism is nevertheless a philosophy of power, which preaches the conquest of power by violence.*

E.L.: That is true of all political ideologies . . . But in principle those who preach Marxism hoped to make political power useless. That is the idea of some of the most sublime phrases, when Lenin said for example that the day would come when the woman cook would be able to lead a state. That really doesn't mean that she will lead the state, but that the political problem will no longer be posed in today's terms. There is a messianism there. As for what it has become in practice. . . . For me, one of the great disappointments of the history of the twentieth century has been that a movement like that produced Stalinism. That is finitude!

Q: *In the nineteenth century, there was already that schism between anarchist socialism and Marxist socialism . . . .*

E.L.: Of course. But the degeneration of generosity into Stalinism is infinitely more serious.

Q: *In modern Marxism, the idea of a withering away, which was dear to ini-tial Marxism, has disappeared. . . .*

E.L.: Perhaps, but there is room for a just state in what I say of the rela-tionship to the other. Our conversation began with that subject.

Q: *Do you think that state could exist?*

E.L.: Yes, there is a possible harmony between ethics and the state. The just state will come from just men and women and saints rather than from propaganda and preaching.

Q: *This love might make the very existence of the state unnecessary, as Aristotle says in the treatise On Friendship.*

E.L.: I think rather, as I said at the beginning, that charity is impossible without justice, and that justice is warped without charity.

ten

The Method

The meaning of a philosophical journey varies, for the traveler, according to the moment or the place from which he or she tries to give an account of it. It is only from outside that such an unfolding process can be encompassed and judged. All that the investigator himself can do is describe the themes that are uppermost when he pauses to give his account.

Doubtless it is Husserl who is at the origin of my writings. It is to him that I owe the concept of intentionality animating consciousness, and especially the idea of the *horizons of meaning* which grow blurred when thought [*la pensée*] is absorbed in *what it thinks* [*le pensé*], which always has the meaning of being. *Horizons of meaning*, which "intentional" analysis rediscovers when it focuses on the *thought* [*la pensée*] that "has forgotten," in reflection, and revives those horizons of the *entity* [*l'étant*] and of *being* [*l'être*]. Above all, I owe to Husserl—but also to Heidegger—the principles of such analyses, the examples and models that have taught me how to get at those horizons and how to look for them. For me, that is the essential contribution of phenomenology, to which must be added the great principle on which everything depends: The thought [*le pensé*]—object, theme, meaning—refers back to the thought [*la pensée*] that thinks it, but also determines the subjective articulation of its appearing: being determines its phenomena.

All this determines a new mode of concreteness. For phenomenology, this concreteness encompasses and sustains the naive abstractions of everyday consciousness, but also those of scientific consciousness, absorbed in the object, bogged down in the object. Hence a new way of developing concepts and of passing from one concept to another—a new way that is reducible neither to an empirical process nor to analytic, synthetic, or dialectic deduction.

However, in the phenomenological analysis of that concreteness of mind, there appears in Husserl—in conformity with a venerable Western tradition—a privilege of the theoretical, a privilege of representation, of knowing; and, hence, of the ontological meaning of being. And this is the case despite all the opposing suggestions one can also get from his work: non-theoretical intentionality, a theory of *Lebenswelt* (the life world), the role of the lived body, the importance of which Merleau-Ponty has succeeded in demonstrating. That is the reason (but also because of the events that took place from 1933 to 1945, events that conceptual knowledge has been able neither to avoid nor understand) why my reflection deviates from the last positions of Husserl's transcendental philosophy, or at least from its formulations.

Those are the points to which I would like to draw attention at the outset, in order to go on to point out the perspectives opened up to me by the affirmation of the priority of the *relation to the other person*, a theme that has preoccupied me for several years, and which does not involve the knowledge structures contoured by *intentionality* that Husserl calls into play in the study of intersubjectivity. I will end on a notion of *meaning* that, proceeding from that basis, imposes itself on thought in a radically different way.

Phenomenology and Knowing

It is in the psyche *qua* knowledge—even including self-consciousness—that traditional philosophy locates the origin or natural place of the meaningful and recognizes mind. Does not everything that occurs in the human psyche, all that happens there, end up being known? Secrecy and the unconscious, repressed or altered, are still assessed or healed by the consciousness that they have lost, or that has lost them. Everything lived is legitimately called *experience*. It is converted into "lessons

learned" which converge in a unity of knowing, whatever its dimensions and modalities: contemplation, will, affectivity; or sensibility and
understanding; or external perception, consciousness of self and reflection on self; or objectifying thematization and familiarity with what is
not explicitly set forth; or primary and secondary qualities, kinesthetic
and coenesthetic sensations. Relations with one's neighbor, the social
group, and God would also be collective and religious *experiences*. Even
reduced to the indetermination of *living* and to the formality of pure
existing, pure being, the psyche *lives* this or that, in the mode of *seeing*,
of feeling, as if *to live* and *to be* were transitive verbs, and *this* and *that*
their objects. It is no doubt this implicit knowing which justifies the
broad use Descartes makes of the term *cogito* in the *Meditations*. And
this verb in the first person clearly expresses the *unity* of the *I*, in which
all knowing is self-sufficient.

As knowing, thought focuses on the thinkable; the thinkable called
being. Focusing on being, it is outside itself, but remains marvelously
within itself, or returns to itself. The exteriority or otherness of the self
is recaptured in immanence. What thought knows or what it learns in its
experience is both the *other* and thought's *self.* One learns only what one
already knows and what can be put into the interiority of thought in the
guise of recallable, re-presentable memory. Reminiscence and imagination lend a kind of synchrony and unity to what, in experience that is
subjected to time, is lost or is only in the future.

We find in Husserl a privilege of presence, of the present, and of
representation.

The dia-chrony of time is almost always interpreted as a privation of
synchrony. The coming to be of the future is understood in terms of
protention, as if the temporality of the future were only a kind of taking in hand, an attempt at recuperation, as if the coming to be of the
future were only the entrance of a present.

Thought, *qua* learning [*apprendre*], requires a taking [*prendre*], a
seizure, a *grip* on what is learned, and a possession. The "seizing" of
learning is not purely metaphorical. Even before technological interestedness, it is already the adumbration of an embodied practice, already
"seizure of property" [*mainmise*]. Presence is now "at hand."[1] Does
even the most abstract lesson dispense with all hold on the things of the
"life-world," the famous *Lebenswelt?* The being that appears to the

knowing subject not only instructs it, but ipso facto *gives* itself to it. Perception already grasps; and the term *Begriff* echoes that connotation of prehension. The *"being given"*—whatever efforts may be required to overcome the distance "from cup to lip"—is already on the scale of thinking, promising it, through its "transcendence," a possession and an enjoyment, a satisfaction. It is as if thinking thought on its own scale by virtue of being able—incarnate—to rejoin what it thinks. The thought and psyche of immanence: self-sufficiency. The phenomenon of the world is precisely that: the fact that there is a guaranteed harmony, in the act of grasping, between the thinkable and the thinking, that the appearing of the world is also a *giving of itself*, and that the knowledge of it is a satisfaction, as if it fulfilled a need. Perhaps that is what Husserl expresses when he states a correlation—which is *the* correlation— between thought and world. Husserl describes theoretical knowledge in its most accomplished forms—objectifying and thematizing knowledge—as fulfilling the intention—empty intentionality fulfilling itself.

Hegel's work, into which all the tributaries of the Western spirit flow, and in which all its levels are manifested, is a philosophy of both absolute knowledge and the satisfied man. The psyche of theoretical knowledge constitutes a thought that thinks in its own terms, and in its adequacy to the thinkable, is equal to itself, and will be consciousness of self. It is the Same that rediscovers itself in the Other.

The activity of thought *triumphs over* [*a raison de*] all otherness and it is therin, ultimately, that its very rationality resides. Conceptual synthesis and synopsis are stronger than the dispersion and incompatibility of what gives itself as an other, as *before* and as *after*. They refer to the unity of the subject and of the transcendental aperception of the *I think*. Hegel writes:

> Among the profoundest and most correct discoveries of the *Critique of Pure Reason* is this, that the unity which constitutes the essence of the Notion is recognized to be the original and synthetic unity of the "I think" or of self-consciousness.[2]

The unity of the *I think* is the ultimate form of the mind as knowledge. And all things lead back to this unity of the *I think* in constituting a system. The system of the intelligible is, ultimately, a consciousness of self.

A question may be asked at this point: Isn't a thought on the scale of the thinker a truism? Unless it signifies a thought incapable of God.

I ask: Is intentionality always based on a representation—as Husserl and Brentano affirm? Or: Is intentionality the only mode of the "gift of meaning?" Is the meaningful always correlative to a thematization and a representation? Does it always result from the assembling of a multiplicity and a temporal dispersion? Is thought devoted from the start to adequation and truth? Is it only a grasping of the given in its ideal identity? Is thought essentially a relation to what is equal to it, that is to say, essentially atheistic?

Bad Conscience and the Inexorable

IN terms of *intentionality*, consciousness must be understood as a modality of the voluntary. The word intention suggests this; and thus the use of the term "acts" to designate the unities of intentional consciousness is justified. Moreover, the intentional structure of consciousness is characterized by representation, which would appear to be fundamental to all theoretical or nontheoretical consciousness. This thesis of Brentano's remains valid for Husserl, despite the refinements the latter brought to it, and the precautions in which he enveloped it, namely his notion of objectifying acts.

Consciousness implies presence, a positing vis-à-vis the self, that is, "worldliness," the fact of being given. An exposure to the grasp, to taking: com-prehension, appropriation.

Is intentional consciousness not, in being, an active intervention on the stage where the being of beings is played out, gathers and shows itself? Consciousness as the very scenario of the incessant effort of the *esse* with respect to that *esse* itself,[3] a quasi-tautological exercise of the *conatus*, which is what the formal meaning of that privileged verb—summarily termed "auxiliary"—comes down to.

But a consciousness directed at the world and at objects, structured as intentionality, is also *indirectly*, and supplementarily, as it were, consciousness of itself: consciousness of the active self that represents the world and objects to itself, as well as consciousness of its very acts of representation, consciousness of mental activity. But it would be an indirect consciousness: immediate, but without an intentional aim;

implicit and purely of accompaniment. Nonintentional, to be distinguished from the inner perception into which it would be apt to be converted. The latter, reflective consciousness, takes the self, its states, and its mental acts *as objects*: reflective consciousness, in which consciousness directed toward the world seeks help in overcoming the inevitable naiveté of its intentional rectilinearity, forgetful of the indirect *vécu*[4] of the nonintentional and its horizons, forgetful of what accompanies it.

Given these circumstances, we are perhaps too quickly inclined, in philosophy, to consider that *vécu* as a not yet explicit knowing or as a still confused representation that reflection will bring to full light. Dark context of the thematized world which reflection, intentional consciousness, will convert into clear and distinct data, like those that represent the perceived world itself.

It is not illegitimate, however, to ask ourselves whether, beneath the gaze of reflective consciousness understood as self-consciousness, the nonintentional, lived contrapuntally to the intentional, retains and renders up its true meaning. The traditional critique of introspection has always suspected that the "spontaneous" consciousness undergoes a modification beneath the scrutinizing, thematizing, objectifying, and indiscreet eye of reflection; a violation and a misreading of some secret. An ever refuted and ever recurrent critique.

What goes on in this nonreflexive consciousness which is taken as merely prereflexive, and which, implicit, accompanies intentional consciousness as the latter intentionally focuses in reflection on its own self, as if the thinking self appeared in the world and belonged there? What goes on in that original dissimulation, in that manner of inexpressibility, in that compounding upon itself of the inexplicit? What can that supposed confusion, that implication, signify positively in some sense? Is there not reason to distinguish between the *envelopment* of the particular in a concept, the *implication* of the presupposed in a notion, the *potentiality* of the possible in a horizon on the one hand, and on the other the *intimacy* of the nonintentional in prereflexive consciousness?

DOES the "knowing" of the prereflexive consciousness of self *know*, properly speaking? A confused consciousness, an implicit consciousness, preceding all intention—or returned from all intention—is not act, but pure passivity. Not only by virtue of its being-without-having-chosen-to-be, or its fall into a jumble of possibles already realized before all assumption, as in the Heideggerian *Geworfenheit*. "Conscience"[5] that, rather than signifying a knowledge of self, is a self-effacement or discretion of presence. Bad conscience: without intentions, without aims, without the protective mask of the character contemplating himself in the mirror of the world, self-assured and affirming himself. Without name, position, or titles. A presence that fears presence, stripped bare of all attributes. A nakedness that is not that of unveiling or the exposure of truth.

In its nonintentionality, on the hither side of all will, before all wrong-doing, in its nonintentional identification, the identity draws back from the eventual insistence that may be involved in identification's return to self. Bad conscience or timidity: accused without culpability and responsible for its very presence. Reserve of the non-invested, the non-justified, the "stranger in the earth," in the words of the Psalmist,[6] the stateless or homeless person, who dares not enter. The interiority of the mental is perhaps originally this. Not in the world, but in question. In reference to which—in memory of which—the self that already puts itself forward and affirms itself, or confirms itself, in the world and in being, remains ambiguous enough—or enigmatic enough—to recognize itself, in Pascal's terms, as being hateful in the very manifestation of its emphatic identity of ipseity—in language, in saying "I." The proud priority of A *is* A, the principle of intelligibility and signifying, that sovereignty, that freedom in the human ego is also, if one may say so, the advent of humility. A questioning of the affirmation and confirmation of being, which is found even in the famous—and easily rhetorical—quest for the "meaning of life," as if the *I* in-the-world which has already assumed meaning on the basis of the vital, psychic, or social purposes were reverting to its bad conscience.

Prereflexive, nonintentional consciousness cannot be described as a realization of this passivity, as if, in it, the reflection of a subject were already distinguished, posited as the "indeclinable nominative," assured of its right to be, and "dominating" the timidity of the nonintentional, as if it were some childhood of the mind to be outgrown, or the momentary weakening of an otherwise impassive psyche. The nonintentional is passivity from the start, and the accusative in a sense its first "case." In fact, this passivity, which is not the correlate of any action does not so much describe the "bad conscience" of the nonintentional as it is described by it. Bad conscience that is not the finitude of existing signified in anxiety. My always premature death thwarts the being that *qua* being perseveres in being, but this scandal does not perturb the good conscience of being, or the morality based on the inalienable right of the *conatus*. In the passivity of the nonintentional—in the very mode of its "spontaneity" and before all formulation of "metaphysical" ideas on this subject—the very justice of position in being which is affirmed in intentional thought, knowledge and control of the now [*main-tenant*][7] is questioned: being as bad conscience; being put in question, but also put to the question, having to answer—the birth of language; having to speak, having to say "I," being in the first person, being precisely myself; but, henceforth, in the assertion of its being as myself, having to answer for its right to be.

Here, the profound meaning of Pascal's line is revealed: The self is hateful.

HAVING to answer for one's right to be, not by appealing to the abstraction of some anonymous law, some juridical entity, but in the fear for the other person. My "being in the world" or my "place in the sun," my home—are they not a usurpation of places that belong to the other man who has already been oppressed or starved by me? Let us quote Pascal again: " 'This is my place in the sun.' Here is the beginning and the prototype of the usurpation of the whole earth."[8] Fear for all the violence and murder my existing, despite its intentional and conscious innocence, can bring about. A fear that goes back behind my "consciousness of self" and despite all returns of pure perseverance in being toward good conscience. A fear that comes to me from the face of the other person. An extreme uprightness of the face of my fellow man, rending the plasticity of the phenomenon. Uprightness of an exposure to death, defenseless; and, before all language, and before all mimicry, a demand made of me from the depths of an absolute solitude; a demand addressed to me or an order issued, a putting in question of my presence and my responsibility.

Fear and responsibility for the death of the other person, even if the ultimate meaning of that responsibility for the death of the other person is responsibility before the inexorable, and at the last moment, the obligation not to leave the other alone in the face of death. Even if, facing death—where the very uprightness of the face that asks for me finally reveals fully both its defenseless exposure and its very facing— even if, at the last moment, the not-leaving-the-other-alone consists, in that confrontation and that powerless facing, only in answering "Here I am"[9] to the request that calls on me. Which is, no doubt, the secret of sociality and, in its extremes of gratuitousness and futility, love of my neighbor, love without concupiscence.

Fear for the other person, fear for the death of my neighbor is my fear, but nowise fear *for* me. It thus contrasts with the admirable phenomenological analysis of affectivity proposed by *Sein und Zeit*: a reflexive structure in which emotion is always an emotion *of* something that moves it, but also emotion *for* oneself, in which emotion consists in being moved[10]—in being afraid, glad, sad, etc.—a double "intentionality" of the *of* and the *for* participating in emotion *par excellence*; anxiety; being-toward-death in which the finite being is moved *by* its finitude *for* that finitude itself. Fear for the other person does not come back to anguish over *my* death. It transcends the ontology of Heidegger's *Dasein*. An ethical disturbance of being, beyond its good conscience of being "with respect to that being itself"[11] whose end and scandal are marked by being-toward-death, in which, however, no scruples are raised.

In the "naturalness" of being-in-respect-to-that-being-itself, in relation to which all things, as *Zuhandenes*— even the other person—seem to take on meaning, the essential being of nature is put in question. A reversal based on the face of the other person, in which, at the very heart of the phenomenon, in its light, a *surplus* of significance signifies what may be termed the glory that challenges and commands me. Does not what we call the word of God come to me in the demand that challenges me and claims me, and before any invitation to dialogue, does it not break through the form of generality under which the individual who resembles me appears to me and only shows himself, and become the face of the other person? Does God not come to the mind[12] in that challenge rather than in some thematization of a thinkable, rather than in I know not what invitation to dialogue? Does not the challenge make me enter into a nonintentional thought of the un-graspable? In relation to all the affectivity of being-in-the-world—the innovation of a non-indifference for me of the absolutely different, other, non-representable, non-graspable; that is, the Infinite, which summons me—rending the representation under which the beings of the human species manifest themselves—in order to designate to me, in the face of the other person, inescapably, as it were, the unique, the chosen. Although it is a call from God, it does not initiate between me and Him who called me a relation; it does not initiate what in any sense could be a conjunction—be it a coexistence, a synchrony, even ideal—between terms. The Infinite cannot signify for a thought that is oriented toward an end point, and the toward-God[13] is not a finality. Perhaps it is this irreducibility of the toward-God, or of the fear of God, to the eschatological—by which, in the human, the consciousness that was oriented toward being in its ontological perseverance or toward death (which it takes to be the ultimate thought) is interrupted—that, beyond being, the word glory signifies. The alternative of being and nothingness is not the ultimate. The toward-God is not a process of being: in the call, I am sent to the other person through whom that appeal signifies, to my fellow man for whom I have to fear.

Behind the affirmation of a being persisting analytically—or animally—in its being, where the ideal vigor of the identity which identifies and affirms and confirms itself in the life of human individuals and in their struggle for existence (vital, conscious, and rational), the wonder of the *I* claimed by God in the face of my neighbor—the marvel of the *I* rid of self and fearing God—is thus tantamount to the suspension of the eternal and irreversible return from the identical to itself and of the inviolability of its logical and ontological privilege. A suspension of its ideal priority, with its negation of all otherness and its exclusion of the third. A suspension of war and politics which pass themselves off as relation of the Same to the Other. In the deposition by the *I* of its sovereignty of self, in its modality as hateful self, ethics, but probably also the very spirituality of the soul, signifies. The human, or human inwardness, is the return to the inwardness of nonintentional consciousness, to bad conscience, to its possibility of fearing injustice more than death, of preferring injustice undergone to injustice committed, and what justifies being to what secures it. To be or not to be is probably not the question par excellence.

From the One to the Other: Transcendence and Time

The One and Intelligibility

Among the four metaphors which, in the Fifth *Ennead*,[1] represent the "movement of the Immobile"— or the emanation of being from the One—by which, according to Plotinus, the various degrees of the multiple produce themselves, the figure of light which is spread by the sun precedes that of heat spread by fire, cold spread by snow, and perfumes spread by the fragrant object. The first multiplicity is the light of the theoretical, of vision, the duality of seeing and seen, of thinking and thought. The first exteriority—the exteriority with regard to the One—is the intelligence of the One, but which, *qua* knowing, is not only multiple because of the distance that separates it from the One; at a distance from the One, its only dealings are with a multiplicity: with the multiplicity of (Platonic) ideas—with the multiplicity that disperses the essence of being—instead of having *in act* to do with the One.

> It does indeed think this principle, but in trying to grasp it in its simplicity, it diverges from it and takes into itself other things, which multiply. . . . It possessed a vague outline of the object of its vision, without which it would not have received it into itself, but that object, from being one, has become many; it is thus that it knows it in order to see it and has become vision in act.[2]

It already lacks or fails to reach the unity of the One in attaining the ideas in act. The unity of the One in fact excludes all multiplicity, even that which is already adumbrated in the distinction between thinker and thought, and even in the identity of the identical conceived in the guise of consciousness of self where, in the history of philosophy, it would one day be sought.

But the intelligence that is the intelligence of multiple ideas, which it reaches in act, is not absolutely separated from the One because of that multiplicity itself: that multiplicity remains a nostalgia for the One, a homesickness. What might be called the movement of knowledge—seeing—or, perhaps, in today's terms, the noetic/noematic intentionality of knowing, filled, but dispersed—is, precisely as dispersion, a state of deprivation compared to the unity of the One; yet, as if the One were anticipated by that deprivation itself; as if knowledge, still an aspiration by the very dispersion of its seeing, went beyond what it sees and thematizes, and thus, were a transcendence because of the very deficiency of its plural rationality; as if its dispersed accession to the multiple essence were a piety—Plotinus speaks of *prayer*[3]—with regard to the inaccessible One. An ambiguity or a risk run at a distance from the One in the knowledge of the intelligence whose multiplicity can keep one far from the "homeland," but thus, as a deprivation, "hollowed out," attached to it. Similarly, in the following degree of hypostasis, the soul, separated from intelligence and dispersing itself among the things of this world, is capable of gathering itself together, and prepares to "hear voices from on high." This "gathering itself together," this "converting into itself," this knowledge in the consciousness of self, is already an aspiring-higher-than-oneself, to intelligence, and thus, to the One.

Hence the necessity of a philosophy to perpetuate nostalgia and "love" of the One, lodged in the "dissatisfaction" of the intelligence, which is its non-indifference toward the One, from which it is separated, toward the One which is still different from it. This is the Classicism of Greek thought, which will be conveyed through Neoplatonism to Western philosophy and seems to have prevented it, even as late as in Hegel, from failing to recognize, in aspiration, its dis-satisfaction. Already an "unhappy" consciousness! All complacent dalliance in dissatisfaction, and even in love, *qua* aspiration, on the pretext that they bring "in hollowed out form" what they are the lack of, all renunciation of wisdom in the simple love of wisdom, or philosophy, will be treated as romanticism, a pejorative label. Philosophy, always dissatisfied with being only philosophy! The return to the One from which it had emanated without diminishing it—the coincidence with the source of "beyond-being"—would be the main thing, in separation, for the philosophy that emerges from it. The aspiration *for the return* is the very breath of the Spirit; but the consummate unity of the One is better than the Spirit and philosophy. The best is that indivisibility of the One, a pure identity in which all multiplicity and all number are abolished at rare "instants" that Plotinus attests to, when the distance, or even the distinction of knowing—even if it is the distinction between knowing and the known in consciousness of self—disappears without a trace. The One to which intelligence piously aspires, beyond the ideas it attains and grasps in their multiplicity (in which, however, it is completed, realized, in act, satis-fied)—the One beyond the noema that is equaled by the noesis of intelligence—would be, according to the neoplatonic schema, better than that aspiration and that approach from which the One is still absent. There is love in the look of *knowing*, but, because of that absence which is again signified by the dispersal of the known, that love is worthwhile only because of the end it seeks and in which the seeking is absorbed, because of the One in which the lover coincides with the loved, because of the goal of ecstasy, in which the movement of ecstasy is abolished and forgotten. The consummate unity of the One, a "satiety of Kronos"[4] is worth more than love, which in Plato's *Symposium*, according to the teaching of Diotimus, remains a demigod.

The Intelligibility of the Return and Time as Privation

Neoplatonism, exalting that consummate unity beyond being and knowing, *better* than being and knowing, offered the monotheism that conquered Europe in the first centuries of our era an itinerary and stations capable of corresponding to mystical tastes and the needs of salvation. Henceforth, piety was understood as modeling itself on the activity of intelligence, on its "vision in act" of a multiplicity of ideas— at once failure and, in failure, a relative culmination; a culmination precisely as *relationship* and, thus, only piety: a religious metaphor of a formal space whose logical genre remained *the relationship*, itself understood in terms of the unity of the One in which it consummates and consumes itself, but the deprivation of which it signifies. One has every right to wonder *whether the devotion that animates this religion, which was originally inseparable from the love of one's fellowman and concern for justice, would not find in this ethics itself the place of its semantic birth and thence the significance of its non-in-difference for the infinite difference of the One, instead of owing it to the non-satisfaction of knowing. A radical distinction which would impose itself between religion and relation!* But, interpreting itself in terms of Neoplatonism, religion understood its piety as nostalgia, as an adventure of return and a coincidence with the origin, whose penultimate stage remained intelligence. Henceforth, it in fact accepted Greek rationalism, and thus found itself forced to respond to the demands of the models of *meaning* in which it exposed itself and which were those of the theoretical, those of knowing, a nostalgia for the unity of the One. Hellenism was thus transmitted to the history of European philosophy, which wound up separating itself from religion to make its way as autonomous thought.

What can this separation—which nevertheless remained loyal to the intelligibility of the *return to the One*—mean, if not, in renouncing the *transcendence* of the One, participation in the model of the unity of the One, and thus, the granting of pride of place to thinking focussed on knowledge about the Intelligence? Has the theoretical event of knowledge in which the act of knowing is obliterated in the discovered truth—in which truth has been *re-discovered* ever since Socrates showed us that learning was only a *return* to a forgotten knowledge—has the theoretical event not remained the analogue or the icon[5]—but why not the unavowed archetype?—of the return to the One, of the culmination of an ecstasy vanishing into attained or rediscovered transcendence? Knowledge as return to presence, that is to say, to being, in the flash of evidence; as return to a multiplicity of ideas, but also always to the assembly of those ideas, to their synthesis, to the unity of their apperception, to their com-prehension; and, in this comprehended presence, return to the very place of meaning, to the significance of the sensed in which temporal dispersion is taken precisely for a deprivation of intelligibility or for its degraded image. Whence the secondary position and pure appearance attributed to time, in conformity with the neo-platonic schema in which time is but a manner of speaking[6] and of exposing the "eternal reality," insofar as that calls for "causality and order." Time as pure deprivation of the eternal; or as its imitation: *"Alles Vergängliche ist nur ein Gleichnis"* [All that passes is but a like-ness]. The fullness of the Greek heritage, transmitted to, and imposing itself on, a philosophy that separates from religion. "But why not the theoretical as unavowed archetype of the One?" we ask timidly and parenthetically, concerning the event of synthesizing and com-prehen-sive knowledge. The very evolution of Western thought, freeing itself from the transcendence of the One and finding itself again absolute in the satis-faction of knowing, perhaps grants some credence to this par-enthetical clause.

In knowledge, there is a relation to presence, that is to say, to being; in ontology, which becomes the original locus or homeland[7] of mean-ing, the very broad and quasi-formal structures of the neoplatonic schema of return and union reappear. Modern philosophy since Descartes[8]—despite all its variations—has preserved that neoplatonic framework, whose contours are still clearly distinguishable at the other end of its history, in the Hegelian and Husserlian thematic in which it culminates so visibly. These structures mark the return of absolute thought to itself, the identity of the identical and the non-identical in consciousness of self recognizing itself as infinite thought, "without other," in Hegel. And in another register, they command Husserl's phe-nomenological reduction, in which the identity of pure consciousness carries within itself, in the guise of the "I think" understood as inten-tionality—*ego cogito cogitatum*—all transcendence, all otherness: "all exteriority" is reduced to or returns to the immanence of a subjectivity which itself, and in itself, exteriorizes itself.[9] The first person present, in the *cogito* which was recognized by Hegel and Husserl as being funda-mental to modern philosophy, vouchsafes knowledge its congenital aggregative urge and its self-sufficiency, prefiguring the systematic unity of consciousness and the integration into the system—into the present, or the synchrony, or the timelessness of the system—of all that is *other*. A philosophical motif in which time is subordinated to eterni-ty, to a present which neither passes nor can be gone beyond, in univer-sal and eidetic laws governing the dispersion of the empirical in the timeless ideality which exists unmoving above the immediate temporality of human patience, in the substitution of dialectic rigor for "incompressible," unavoidable, insurmountable *durée*. Or time is subordinated to eternity by way of another design and project, when the "phenomenological description" ventures forth behind or beneath the abstraction, ideality, or formality of speculative time. Does not the analysis of temporality in Husserl reduce to saying time in terms of presence and simultaneity—of retained or anticipated presents? Various ways of knowing time! As if time exhausted itself in its way of making itself known or of conforming to the demands of its manifestation. That is an analysis in which the meaning of the meaningful is synonymous with its aptitude for the present and for representation, with the simultaneity of a whole entering and spreading itself out in a theme; or, even more radically, with its aptitude for *presence*, that is to say, for being (understood as a verb); as if, in the notion of presence—or in the notion of being expressed by presence—a privileged mode of time were associated with the very birth of knowledge in representation, thematization or intentionality. As if knowledge, concreteness of presence, were the psychic structure of all thought. Manifestation would coincide with the signifying of meaning and would appeal to the understanding. Representation (*Ver-gegenwärtigung*)—reminiscence and imagination—would wrest from the past and the future—simple modes of mis-take, inaccessibility to hand, and thus, incomprehensibility—the already or still ungraspable presence of the bygone or the yet to come. Representation would be the first grasp of it, to which intellect again refers for the com*prehension* it establishes. It would lead these initially ungraspable "presents" of the past and the future back to the simultaneity of the theme. As if, in its diachrony, time returned to a failed eternity, to the "mobile image of immobile eternity" or of the consummate One. Henri Bergson, who, for the first time in the history of ideas, tried to think time outside that failure of eternity, designates the fate of that notion in philosophy as that of a becoming, construed as a privation of eternity.

Thought as Intentionality

The rationality of knowledge, according to this way of thinking, corresponds to the absolute of the One: the knowledge here below—in the immanence of evident manifestation—that attains the known of being, or attains, in reflection, the transcendental concreteness of the self, is full or accomplished: *wird erfüllt*. The equality of the One with itself—a supposedly prototypical equality—in knowing thus becomes adequacy, and hence, satisfaction, and as such, as the significance of the meaningful itself, the secret of a civilization. Knowledge as research is still deprivation, but it is no longer an impotent and pious nostalgia for transcendence of the unattainable or only exceptionally attained One. The presence of being in truth is grasp and appropriation, and knowing a teleological activity.

What remains in thought "*in potentia*" is also a power. A teleology animates consciousness according to Husserl's *Krisis*. Consciousness goes to an end, a term, a given, a world. Knowledge is intentionality: act and will. An *auf-etwas-hinauswollen*, an "I want" and an "I can" which is suggested by the very word intention. An "I want" and an "I present myself" which Husserl at least understands as being part of intentionality. A thought that spends itself [*se dé-pense*] in representing or mastering presence. Being in its presence offers itself to a taking in hand, is a giving. The most abstract lessons of science begin in a world we live in, amidst things that are within reach. These are things given in a given world which Husserl calls a "life-world." The intentionality of consciousness is concrete grasp, perception and concept, an application incarnate in all knowledge, a premature promise of its technical continuations and of consummation. The correlative being of knowledge, already thus signifying in terms of an ontology that might be called idealist, is datum and giving and *to be taken*. The meaning of satis-faction is not simply reduced to the abstract adequacy of something perceived on the scale of perception. The concreteness of satisfaction is enjoyment. The "*vécu*" [lived], which is not simply "content of consciousness," but which is *signifying*: in it the identification of the "I am" takes place, the identification of the *cogito* delighting in itself, and thus, persevering in its being. Identification of the free ipseity of the Western man within the limits of his powers.

A freedom that can be limited only by obstacles: natural and social forces, and death. The obstacles of Nature and Society, which Knowledge can gradually overcome. The obstacle of death: unassumable, in-comprehensible, accrediting the idea of a "finite freedom." But freedom is always measured by powers. The marvel of Western man in his modernity, which is probably essential to him: the ideal of the satisfied man, to whom all that is possible is permissible.

The questions I would ask, given these circumstances, can now be formulated. Does thought think only as an investment of all otherness, effacing itself in the unity of the result or in the identity of the identical and the non-identical, engulfing the attained absolute or extinguishing itself in it, in the ambiguity of philosophical idealism and realism? Does thought thinking the absolute signify only need, lack and nostalgia, or satisfaction, accomplishment and enjoyment? Does the diachrony of time mean nothing but a deficiency of presence and nostalgia? Can thought not approach the absolute otherwise than by knowing it and excel by that approach, *better* than the return to the One and the coincidence with unity? It is the dominant conception of the received philosophy, according to which thought is fundamentally knowing, that is to say, intentionality—will and representation—that I am trying to put in question.[10] My analysis will take as its point of departure a reflection on the intentional act.

Intentionality and Bad Conscience[11]

We will start out from intentionality as it is exposed in Husserlian phenomenology. In it, the equation of thought with knowledge in its relation to being is formulated in the most direct way. While developing the idea of an original, non-theoretical intentionality of the affective and active life of the soul, Husserl maintained representation—the objectifying act—at its base, adopting Brentano's thesis on that point, despite all the precautions he took in his new formulation of this thesis. Now, by itself, knowing is a relationship to an *other* of consciousness and the aim or will of this other which is its object. Investigating the intentionality of consciousness, Husserl wants to know *"worauf sie eigentlich hinauswill"* [what it really wants, what it is getting at]. This will, which is already suggested by the word intention, justifies the term *acts* given to the unities of consciousness. In the intuition of truth, knowing is described as filling, as the satisfaction of an aspiration to the object. An intervention in being, equal to the constitution of that being: Transcendental Reduction, by suspending all independence in *being* other than that of consciousness itself, makes that suspended being be rediscovered as noema, and leads—or should lead—to the full consciousness of self affirming itself as absolute being, confirming itself as a self that identifies itself through all the differences as "master of itself as of the universe" and capable of illuminating all the dark corners in which the *I*'s mastery would be challenged. If the constituting *I* collides with a sphere in which it is carnally implicated in what it is, moreover, supposed to have constituted, it is there in the world as in its skin, according to the intimacy of incarnation, which no longer has the exteriority of the objective world.

But a reduced consciousness—which, in reflection on itself, rediscovers and masters its own acts of perception and knowledge as objects in the world, and thus affirms itself as consciousness of self and absolute being—also remains, supplementarily, as it were, nonintentional consciousness of itself, without any voluntary aim; nonintentional consciousness exercising itself as knowledge, unbeknownst to itself, of the active self that represents world and objects to itself. It accompanies all the intentional processes of the consciousness of the *I* which, in this consciousness, "acts" and "wants" and has intentions. A consciousness of consciousness, "indirect" and implicit, without initiative, proceeding from a nonintending *I*. A passive consciousness, like time, that passes and ages me without me. An immediate consciousness of self, nonintentional, to be distinguished from reflection, from the inner perception to which the nonintentional would certainly be apt to offer itself as an interior object, or which reflection would be tempted to substitute itself for, in order to explain its [nonintentional consciousness's] latent messages.

The intentional consciousness of reflection taking as its object the transcendental self, its mental states and acts, can also thematize and grasp or explain all its modes of nonintentional, so-called implicit, *vécu*. It is invited to do so by philosophy, whose fundamental project consists in illuminating the inevitable transcendental naiveté of a consciousness forgetful of its horizons, of what is implicit in it, and of the very time that it lasts.

Given these circumstances, we are no doubt too quickly inclined, in philosophy, to consider all that immediate consciousness solely as nonexplicit forms of knowledge, or as still confused representation to be led to full light. Dark context of the thematized world which reflection, intentional consciousness, will convert into clear and distinct data like those that present the perceived world itself or absolute reduced consciousness.

It is not illegitimate, however, to ask ourselves whether, beneath the gaze of reflective consciousness understood as self-consciousness, the nonintentional, lived contrapunctually to the intentional, retains and renders up its true meaning. The traditional critique of introspection has always suspected that the "spontaneous" consciousness undergoes a modification beneath the scrutinizing, thematizing, objectifying, and indiscreet eye of reflection; a violation and a misreading of some secret. An ever refuted and ever recurrent critique.

I ask: What goes on in this nonreflexive consciousness which is taken as merely prereflexive, and which, implicit, accompanies intentional consciousness as the latter intentionally focuses in reflection on its own self, as if the thinking self appeared in the world and belonged there? What can that supposed confusion, that implication, signify positively in some sense? It is not enough to refer to the formal notion of potential. Is there not reason to distinguish between the envelopment of the particular in the concept, the implication of the presupposed in a notion, the potentiality of the possible in a horizon on the one hand, and on the other the intimacy of the nonintentional in what is called prereflexive consciousness, and which is duration itself?

Does the "knowing" of the prereflexive consciousness of the self know, properly speaking? A confused consciousness, an implicit consciousness, preceding all intention—or duration returned from all intention—it is not act, but pure passivity. And this, not only by virtue of its *being-without-having-chosen-to-be* or its fall into a jumble of possibles already realized before all assumption, as in the Heideggerian *Geworfenheit*. It is a "consciousness"[12] which, rather than signifying a knowledge of self, is a self-effacement or discretion of presence. It is pure duration of time, which phenomenological analysis describes, it is true, in reflection, as structured intentionally according to a play of retentions and pro-tentions, which, in the duration of time itself, at least remain inexplicit;[13] a duration abstracted from all will of the self, totally outside activity of the self, and which—like aging—is probably the very carrying out of the *passive* synthesis based on the passivity of the *lapse* whose irreversibility no act of memory, reconstituting the past, reverses. The temporality of time escaping *a limine*, through its lapse, all activity of representation.

Does not the implication of the implicit signify here *otherwise* than as knowledge but simply concealed, otherwise than a way of representing to itself the presence or non-presence of the future and the past? Duration as pure duration, as nonintervention, as being-without-insistence, as being-on-tiptoe, as being without daring to be: agency [*instance*] of the instant without the insistence of the *I* and already lapse, which "leaves while entering!" Bad conscience, this implication of the nonintentional: without intentions, without aims, without the protective mask of the character contemplating himself in the mirror of the world, self-assured and affirming himself. Without name, position, or titles. A presence that fears presence, that fears the insistence of the identical me, stripped bare of all attributes.

In its nonintentionality, on the hither side of all will, before all wrong-doing, in its nonintentional identification, identity draws back from its affirmation, worries about the eventual insistence that may be involved in identification's return to self. Bad conscience or timidity; guiltless, but accused; and responsible for its very presence. Reserve of the non-invested, the non-justified, the "stranger in the earth," in the words of the Psalmist,[14] the stateless or "homeless," who dares not enter. The interiority of the mental is perhaps originally this, this lack of boldness to affirm oneself in being and in one's skin. Not being-in-the-world, but being-in-question. In reference to which—in "memory" of which— the self that already puts itself forward and affirms itself, or confirms itself, in being, remains ambiguous enough—or enigmatic enough—to recognize itself, in Pascal's terms, as hateful in the very manifestation of its emphatic identity of ipseity: in language, in the "I-saying" act. The proud priority of A *is* A, the principle of intelligibility and signifying, that sovereignty, that freedom in the human me is also, if I may say so, the advent of humility. A questioning of the affirmation and confirmation of being, which is found in the famous—and easily rhetorical—quest for the "meaning of life," as if the absolute me, which has already assumed meaning from the vital, psychic or social forces, or from its transcendental sovereignty, were reverting to its bad conscience.

Prereflexive, nonintentional consciousness cannot attain a realization of this passivity, as if, in it, the reflection of a subject was already distinguished, posited as the "indeclinable nominative," assured of its right to be, and "dominating" the timidity of the nonintentional, as if it were some childhood of the mind to be outgrown, or the momentary weakening of an otherwise impassive psyche. The nonintentional is passivity from the start, and the accusative is in a sense its "first case." (In fact, this passivity, which is not the correlate of any activity does not so much describe the "bad conscience" of the non-intentional as it can be described by it.) Bad conscience that is not the finitude of existing signified in anxiety. My always premature death may thwart the being which, as being, perseveres in being, but in anguish, this scandal does not perturb the good conscience of being or the morality based on the inalienable right of the *conatus*, which is also the right and the good conscience of freedom. On the other hand, in the passivity of the nonintentional—in the very mode of its "spontaneity" and before all formulation of metaphysical ideas on this subject—the very justice of position in being which is affirmed in intentional thought, knowledge and control of the now [*main-tenant*]¹⁵ is put in question. Here is being as bad conscience, in this questioning; being-put-in-question, but also put to the question, having to answer—the birth of language in responsibility; having to speak, having to say *I*, being in the first person. Being precisely myself; but, henceforth, in the assertion of its being as myself, having to answer for its right to be. We must push our thinking of Pascal's "the self is hateful" to that point.

The Face and the Death of the Other

Having to answer for one's right to be, not by appealing to the abstraction of some anonymous law, some juridical entity, but in the fear for the other. My being-in-the-world or my "place in the sun," my home—have they not been a usurpation of places which belong to the others already oppressed or starved by me, expelled by me into a third world: a repelling, an exclusion, an exile, a spoliation, a killing. "My place in the sun," said Pascal, "the beginning and prototype of usurpation of the whole earth."¹⁶ Fear for all the violence and murder my existing—despite its intentional and conscious innocence—can bring about. Fear from behind my "consciousness of self," and despite the returns of pure perseverance in being toward good conscience. The fear of occupying someone's place in the *Da* of my *Dasein*; an incapacity to have a place, a profound utopia.[17] A fear that comes to me from the face of the other.

In my philosophical essays, I have spoken a great deal about the face of the other man as being the original locus of the meaningful. Will I be permitted to take up yet again rather briefly the description—as I am now attempting to do—of the eruption of the face into the phenomenal order of the appearance?

The proximity of the other is signifying of the face. Signifying from the outset from beyond the plastic forms which do not cease covering it like a mask with their presence in perception. It incessantly penetrates these forms. Before all particular expression (and beneath all particular expression that—already pose and countenance given to self—covers and protects it) a nakedness and stripping away of expression as such; that is, extreme exposure, defenselessness, vulnerability itself. Extreme exposure—before all human intending—as to a shot at "point blank" range. An extradition of the beleaguered and tracked down—the tracked down before all tracking down and before all battue. Face in its straightforwardness of facing things, straightforwardness of exposure to an invisible death and mysterious forsaking. Mortality—beyond the visibility of the unveiled—and before all knowing about death. Expression that tempts and guides the violence of the first crime, whose murderous rectitude is already singularly well adjusted in its aim at the exposure of the expression of the face. The first murderer did not know, perhaps, the result of the blow he was about to strike, but his violent aim made him find the line according to which death affects with undeflectable directness the face of one's fellowman—drawn as if it were the trajectory of the blow that finds its mark and the arrow that kills.

But this facing of the face in its expression—in its mortality—summons me, demands me, claims me: as if the invisible death faced by the face of the other—pure otherness, separated somehow from all unity— were "my business." As if, unknown to the other whom, in the nakedness of his face, it already concerns, it "regarded me" before its confrontation with me, before being the death that looks me square in my own face. The death of the other man puts me in question, as if in that death that is invisible to the other who exposes himself to it, *I*, through my eventual indifference, became the accomplice; and as if, even before being doomed to it myself, *I* had to answer for this death of the other, and not leave the other alone in his death-bound solitude. It is precisely in this call to my responsibility by the face that summons me, that demands me, that claims me—it is in this questioning that the other is my neighbor.

This way of demanding me, of putting me in question and of appealing to me, to my responsibility for the death of the other, is so irreducible a meaning that it is in terms of this that the meaning of death must be understood, beyond the abstract dialectic of being and its negation, to which (once violence is reduced to negation and annihilation) death is reduced. Death signifies in the concreteness of what for me is the impossibility of abandoning the other to his aloneness, in the prohibition addressed to me of that abandonment. Its meaning begins in the inter-human. Death signifies primordially in the very proximity of the other man or in sociality. Just as it is in terms of the face of the other that the commandment through which God who comes to the mind[8] is signified.

Fear for the other, fear for the death of the other man is my fear, but it is in no way a fear for *oneself*. It thus contrasts strongly with the admirable phenomenological analysis of affectivity, of *Befindlichkeit* proposed by *Sein und Zeit*: a reflexive structure expressing itself by a verb in the pronominal form, in which emotion is always an emotion *of* something that is moving, but also an emotion *for* oneself; in which emotion consists in *being* moved[19]—in being afraid *because of* something, glad *because of* something, sorrowful *because of* something, but also *being* glad *for oneself*, *being* sorrowful *for oneself*, etc. I am anxious and care about my death. A double intentionality of the *because of* and the *for* and thus a return to the self, a return to anxiety for the self, to anxiety for its finitude: in the fear of the dog, an anxiety for my death. Fear for the other man does not return to anguish for my death. It overflows the ontology of the Heideggerian *Dasein* and its good conscience of being in view of that being itself. Ethical awakening and vigilance in that affective turbulence. Heidegger's being-toward-death certainly marks, for *beings*, the end of their being-in-view-of-that-being-itself and the shocking nature of that end, but in that end no scruple of being is awakened.

Ethics, or the Meaning of Being

In the naturalness of being-in-respect-to-that-being-itself, in relation to which all things—even the person—seem to take on meaning, the essential nature of being is put in question. A reversal based on the face of the other, in which, at the very heart of the phenomenon, in its light itself, a surplus of significance signifies what may be designated as glory. It demands me, claims me, assigns me. Should we not call that demand or that challenge or that assignment of responsibility the word of God? Does not God come to the mind precisely in this assigning rather than in the thematization of something thinkable, even rather than in any invitation to dialogue? Does not this summons to responsibility break through the forms of generality in which my knowledge, my knowing the other man re-presents him to me as similar to myself, and designate me, in the face of the other, as responsible without any possible escape, and thus as the unique, the chosen one?

The orientation of consciousness by being in its ontological perseverance or in its being-toward-death, in which consciousness is sure that it is going to the ultimate—all that is interrupted in the presence of the face of the other. It is perhaps this beyond being and death which is meant by the word glory, of which I availed myself in speaking of the face.

The human that is behind perseverance in being! Behind the affirmation of a being persisting analytically (or "animally") in its being, and in which the ideal vigor of the identity which identifies and affirms and confirms itself in the life of human individuals and in their struggle for vital, conscious or unconscious, and rational existence—the wonder of the *I* claimed in the face of one's neighbor, or the wonder of the *I* relieved of self and fearing for the other, is also something like the suspension—the *epochē*—of the eternal and irreversible return of the identical to itself, and of the inviolability of its logical and ontological privilege. A suspension of its ideal priority, with its negation of all otherness through murder or through encompassing and totalizing thought. A suspension of war and politics, which pass themselves off as relations of the Same to the Other. In the laying aside by the self of its sovereignty of self, in its modality of detestable self, ethics signifies, but also probably the very spirituality of the soul, and certainly the question of the meaning of being, that is to say, its call to justify itself. It signi-fies—through the ambiguity of the identical which says *I* to itself at the apogee of its unconditional and even logically indiscernible identity, an autonomy above all criterion; but which, precisely, at that apogee of unconditional identity, can also confess itself to be a hateful self.

The self is the very crisis of the being of beings in the human. A cri-sis of being, not because the meaning of this verb would also have to be understood in its secret semantics and would call on ontology, but because I myself already ask myself if my being is justified, if the *Da* of my *Dasein* is not already the usurpation of someone's place.

A bad conscience which comes to me from the face of the other who, in his mortality, uproots me from the solid ground where, as a simple individual, I stand and persevere naively—naturally—in my stance. A bad conscience which puts me in question. With a question that does not await a theoretical answer in the guise of information. A question that calls on responsibility, which is no practical, make-do solution, a conso-lation for the failure of knowledge to equal being. A responsibility that is not the deprivation of comprehension-knowledge and grasping-knowledge, but the excellence of ethical proximity in its sociality, in its love without concupiscence.

The human is the return to the interiority of nonintentional con-sciousness, to bad conscience, to its possibility of fearing injustice more than death, of preferring injustice undergone to injustice committed, and what justifies being to what guarantees it.

Ethics and Time

I have attempted a phenomenology of sociality based on the face of the other, reading in its uprightness, before all mime, a defenseless exposure to the mysterious aloneness of death, and hearing in it, before all verbal expression, from the depths of that weakness, a voice that commands, an order to me signified, not to remain indifferent to that death, not to let the other die alone; that is to say, to be answerable for the life of the other, or else risk becoming the accomplice of that death. The facing of the face of the other, in his honesty, would signify both the defenseless-ness and the opposition of otherness, an authority lacking in the simply logical otherness identifying individuals and concepts and distinguishing them from one another or (mutually) opposing notions by contradiction or contrariness. The otherness of the other is the extreme point of "Thou shalt not commit murder," and, in me, a fear for all the violence and usurpation my existing, despite its intentional innocence, risks committing. From the *Da* of the *Dasein*, a risk of occupying the place of another, and thus, concretely, of exiling him, of consigning him to the miserable condition in some "third" or "fourth" world, of killing him. Thus, in this fear for the other man, an unlimited responsibility would be isolated, that responsibility one is never rid of, which does not cease in the last moment of the neighbor, even if responsibility then amounts only to responding, in the impotent confrontation with the death of the other, "here I am."[20] A responsibility which no doubt preserves the secret of sociality, whose total gratuitousness, even if completely vain, is called love of neighbor, love without concupiscence, but as irrefragable as death.

A sociality not to be confused with some weakness or deprivation in the unity of the One. From the depths of natural perseverance in the being of an entity assured of his right to be, from the heart of the original identity of the *I*[21]—both against that perseverance, and against that identity—awakened opposite the face of the other, rises a responsibility for the other to whom I have therefore been dedicated *before* every vow, before being present to myself or returning to self.

What does this *before* signify? Is it the before of an *a priori*? But would it not henceforth revert initially to an idea which, in a "deep past"[22] of innateness would already have been a correlative presence of the *I think* and which—retained, preserved, or revived in the duration of time, in temporality taken as a flow of instants—would be represented by memory? Thus, the privilege of the present would still be maintained, whose sovereign expression is the Platonic theory of reminiscence, and thus a reference from thought to perception would be guaranteed; and thus, the privilege of eternity, as well as of a present-which-does-not-pass, would again be affirmed in the ideality of the idea; an eternity whose duration or diachrony of time would be only dissimulation or deformation or deprivation in the finite consciousness of man. A privilege also of the *I think*, "stronger" than time, which gathers the dispersal of temporal shades under the unity of transcendental apperception, the firmest and most formal of forms, stronger than all heterogeneity of contents—to identify the diversity of experience by embracing it and grasping it again identified in the knowing of the being into which it enters. Rediscovery of the ancient One. The *I* or the *I think* that identifies would be the reason and the logos of rationality. Ontology should henceforth be interpreted not only as a knowing doubling being, but as the ultimate return of the identity of being to itself, as a return to the One.

It is, on the contrary, a past that cannot be reduced to the present, that seems to signify in the ethical antecedence of responsibility-for-another-person, without reference to my identity guaranteed its right. Here I am, in this rejected responsibility thrown back toward someone who has never been either my fault or my concern, toward someone who has never been in my power, or in my freedom, toward someone who doesn't come into my memory. An ethical significance of a past which concerns me, which "has to do with" me, which is "my business" outside all reminiscence, all retention, all representation, all reference to a recalled present. A significance in ethics of a pure past irreducible to my present, and thus, of an originating past. An originating significance of an immemorial past, in terms of responsibility for the other man. My unintentional participation in the history of humanity, in the past of others which has something to do with me.

The responsibility for the other doesn't return to the thought referring to a formerly given idea of the "I think" and rediscovered by it. The natural *conatus essendi* of a sovereign Self is questioned in the presence of the face of the other, in ethical vigilance in which the sovereignty of the self is recognized as "detestable" and its place in the sun—the "prototype and beginning of the usurpation of the whole earth." The responsibility for the other *signified*—as an order—in the face of my fellowman is not a simple modality of "transcendental apperception" in me.[23]

"In the presence of the face of the other," I said. Properly speaking, can we use the prepositional phrase *in the presence of* here? By speaking this way, haven't we confused the significance of the face with the plastic forms of representation which already mask it, unless in its formal bareness—or bare of forms—the face expresses mortality and signifies a commandment? Haven't we already misunderstood the incessant surplus of meaning which un-does these plastic forms? A surplus that does not represent itself—is not presented—but signifies in the imperative with authority or glory. We must return—if only in a very general and brief way—to the *how* of this glorious significance of the command-ment, to the "imperativeness," if we can call it that, of that original imperative.

The face of the other concerns me, although the responsibility-for-another-person which it orders does not allow me to refer to the the-matic presence of an entity who would be the cause or source of this commandment. In fact, this is not about receiving an order by perceiv-ing it first and obeying it subsequently in a decision, an act of will. In this proximity of the face, the subservience of obedience precedes the hearing of the order. An obedience preceding the hearing of the order—which measures or indicates an extreme urgency of the com-mandment in which the demands of deduction which might be raised by an "I think" taking consciousness of an order is adjourned forever. An urgency by which, "to the exclusion of everything else," the imperative is categorical and subservience irreversible, that is to say, not lending itself to the return from passivity to activity, to the return which char-acterizes intellectual receptivity always inverting itself in spontaneities of reception.

But "subservience of an obedience preceding the hearing of the order"—is this just insanity and an absurd anachronism? Is it not rather the description of the paradoxical modality of inspiration, breaking precisely with the intellectualism of knowing, and in obedience to absolute order, outlining the very diachrony of the future? Is it not the unparalleled way the absolutely irreversible future commands the pre-sent without reducing that way of concerning, that "affection" by com-mandment and that passivity or patience to any "simultaneity" at all, any superposition, even a partial or punctual one, of the "present" and the future, without having the future dominated by the to-come (*à-venir*) or the *grasping* of an anticipation—or of a pro-tention—without obscuring the dia-chrony of time and the audacity and authority of the imperative by the representation of fear or hope? Inspiration breaks precisely with the intellectualism of knowing: as if the order were for-mulated in the voice of the one who obeys it. Beyond all metaphor, such would be the voice of ethical conscience which is not the simple innateness of an instinct or the intentionality in which *I think* would preserve the last word, investing what is imposed on it, impatiently turning its irreversible passivity into initiative, in the "taking of consciousness," being equal to what it receives, destroying all authority. The conversion of the for-self into for-the-other of responsibility could not be played again within an autonomous *for-self*, even in the guise of a simple discovery made by the "I think," inflexible but still reflecting on itself, of a secret, heretofore unsuspected, modality of some "profound nature."

A heteronomy of ethical obedience which, in the guise of inspiration, is not the deployment of a *vis a tergo*; it comes from the *face*: subservience to the order signified in the face of the other man who is not approached as a topic. An obedience to the absolute order—to the perfect authority—an originating obedience to the perfect authority, to the word of God, on condition of naming God only in terms of this obedience. An un-known God who does not assume a body and is exposed to atheism's denials.

But the meaning or the content of that order is inseparable from the obedience to its inspired order: responsibility for the other man is ordered, goodness pulling the self away from its irresistible return to self, pulling the self away from the unconditional perseverance of the entity in its being. It is necessary to underline the unity of the *ethics* of this subservience to a commandment ordering responsibility for the other, and the *diachrony* of the future in this irreversible subservience which cannot be converted into knowledge, and is inspired *beyond* what, in obedience, represents and presents itself. A *beyond* which would signify for obedience by the very "imperativeness" of the commandment and its goodness. A concreteness of the paradox of the idea of the infinite in Descartes's *Third Metaphysical Meditation*.

An ethical and future inspiration—prophecy's significance. I would like to suggest the diachrony of the future as prophetic inspiration, which the impatience of anticipation in the Husserlian idea of goal, intentionality, and pro-tention does not equal. The idea of the Infinite taught by Descartes as paradox, an unparalleled thought, thinking more than it can contain, the concrete wisdom of which I have tried to express as obedience to the commandment that, in the face of the other, devotes me to the other man—there we have "intended future" beyond the to-come (*à-venir*), the true "phenomenology." Thought thinking more than it thinks, or thought that, in thinking, does *better* than thinking since it already finds itself responsible for the other whose mortality—and consequently whose life—concerns me. Thought limited to the categorical imperative, inspired by an unknown God,[24] limited to bearing responsibilities that are inalienable, but thus consecrating my personal uniqueness, my primogeniture and chosenness. Dis-inter-estedness of a responsibility for the other and for his *past*—a past immemorial for me—on the basis of the *future* of prophecy—without which the unknown God would remain inaudible in His glory—breaking His wordless, negative theology—this is the temporality in which the plot of being and ontology are unraveled in ethics.

The Rights of Man and Good Will

entre nous

The discovery of those rights that, under the name rights of man, are associated with the very condition of being a man, independently of qualities by which men differ from one another—such as social rank, physical, intellectual, and moral strength, virtue and talents—and the elevation of these rights to the rank of fundamental legislative principles and social order certainly marks an essential moment in Western consciousness. Even if the biblical imperatives, "Thou shalt not kill" and "Thou shalt love the stranger"[1] had been waiting for thousands of years for rights associated with the humanity of man to enter into the primordial legal discourse of our civilization. Man as man would have the right to an exceptional place in being, and by that very fact, one that was exterior to the determinism of phenomena; the right to independence, or to the freedom of each recognized by all. The right to a position protected from the immediate order of necessities inscribed in the natural laws that command inert objects, living things and thinking beings of a Nature, which, in a sense, however, also concerns and envelops humans. An exceptional place, a right to free will, guaranteed and protected by laws henceforth instituted by man. A right revealing itself in the obligation—incumbent, however, on free men themselves—to spare man the dependence of being but a means to a finality and not its end. An obligation to spare man the constraints and humiliations of poverty, vagrancy, and even the sorrow and torture which are still inherent in the sequence of natural—

physical and psychological—phenomena, and the violence and cruelty of the evil intentions of living beings.

The formal essence of the rights of man seen in terms of the exceptional place of man in the determinism of the real, opening up the right to a free will, thus receives a concrete characteristic and a content. It is not always easy, in defense of the rights of man (and this is an important, but practical, problem) to establish an order of priority for those concrete rights. It may vary as a function of the actual situation in each country.

Whence in any case considerable and already revolutionary work, with its inevitable upheavals, in favor of the rights of man. Work that makes possible the science of modern times, a science of the nature of things, men and collectivities. Work that is encouraged by access to the technical procedures opened up by science. The further refinement of a human order of freedom by the elimination of many material obstacles of the contingent and social structures that encumber and pervert the application and exercise of the rights of man. Rights that may not be capable of eradicating completely the ultimate harshness of the Inhuman in being, which, by the insuperable firmness of the stitching consolidating its cloth—material, physiological, psychological, and social—always thwarts and limits the free will of man.

Man can also stubbornly go on existing while giving up the attempt to acquire and preserve difficult rights. As if the freedom of rights were itself a limit to freedom, as if freedom were itself a necessity of obligation. What is the meaning of the "should be" of this right?

Even if the fact that the possibility of the consolidation and expansion of the rights of man is bound to the scientific progress of modernity seems to me to explain the relatively recent character of its actualization, and the profound origin of the right seems already acquired, as we said, from the earliest time of our Western destiny, the question of the justification of this right, the question of its very "*should be,*" remains open. The answer cannot be reduced to a necessity apprehended inductively on the basis of the extension of the interest raised by the rights of man and the general consent assumed by this extension. Does not the "normative energy" of the rights of man lead us back to the rigor of the reasonable? By virtue of what, and in what way, could the free or autonomous will claimed by the right of man impose itself on another free will without this imposition implying an *effect*, a violence suffered by that will? Or could it be that the decision of a free will conforms to a maxim of action which can be universalized without being contradicted and that, thus revealing the reason that inheres in a free will, this will makes itself *respected* by all other wills, which are free because of their rationality? A will Kant has called practical reason. And could it be that the "intellectual feeling" of *respect* here delineates respect as a *modality* of the true meaning of the situation? An "intellectual feeling" that, precisely as intellectual, would no longer proceed from sensibility, understood as a source of heteronomy by Kant and that attests—rather than to a wound inflicted by one will on the freedom of the other will—to the fullness of peace in reason. The will that obeys the order of a free will would still be a free will, as reason yielding to reason. The categorical imperative would be the ultimate principle of the rights of man.

Is it certain, however, that free will lends itself entirely to Kant's notion of practical reason, that height of universal thought also called good will? Does it allow itself to be contained therein without resistance? Does respect for formal universality appease the irrepressible part of spontaneity, which cannot immediately and conveniently be reduced to the impulses of passion and feeling? An irrepressible spontaneity that still allows us to distinguish between the rigorous rationalism of intelligence and the risks of a reasonable will. But is that irrepressible spontaneity of the will not goodness itself, which, sensibility par excellence, would also be the original and generous project of the infinite universality of reason which is required by the categorical imperative? A generous impulse rather than, in its holy imprudence, the pathological one denounced by Kant, which disqualifies all freedom![2]

Goodness, a childish virtue; but already charity and mercy and responsibility for the other, and already the possibility of sacrifice in which the humanity of man bursts forth, disrupting the general economy of the real and standing in sharp contrast with the perseverance of entities persisting in their being; for a *condition* in which the other comes before oneself. Dis-inter-estedness of goodness: the other in his demand which is an order, the other as face, the other who "regards me" even when he doesn't have anything to do with me, the other as fellow man and always stranger—goodness as transcendence; and I, the one who is held to respond, the irreplaceable, and thus, the chosen and thus truly unique. Goodness for the first one who happens to come along, a right of man. A right of the other man above all. Descartes speaks of generosity. He attaches it both to the "free disposition of [a man's] will" and to the fact that those who are generous "do not hold anything more important than to do good to other men and to disdain their individual interests."[3]

In religion and theology it is said that the right is conferred by God on man, that the right of man corresponds to the will of God. Expressions that in any case indicate the unconditional or extraordinary nature of that right in relation to all legal forms that already rest on human conventions or on the examination of "human nature." Here, without bringing in the famous "proof of the existence of God," are the rights of man constituting a juncture in which God comes to mind,[4] in which the notion of transcendence ceases to remain purely negative and the abusive "beyond" of our conversations is thought positively in terms of the face of the other person. What I have called an interruption or rupture of the perseverance of beings in their being, of the *conatus essendi* in the dis-inter-estedness of goodness does not indicate that the right of man gives up its absolute status to revert to the level of decisions made by I know not what compassionate subjectivities. It indicates the absolute of the social, the *for-the-other* which is probably the very delineation of the human. It indicates that "nothing greater" of which Descartes spoke. No doubt it is important in good philosophy not to think the rights of man in terms of an unknown God; it is permissible to approach the idea of God setting out from the absolute that manifests itself in the relation to the other.

entre nous

The sphere of intelligibility—of the meaningful—in which everyday life as well as the tradition of our philosophic and scientific thought maintains itself, is characterized by vision. The structure of a *seeing* having the *seen* for its object or theme—the so-called intentional structure—is found in all the modes of sensibility having access to things. It is found in the *intellectual* accession to states of affairs or the relationships between things; and also, apparently, in the way human beings interact, between beings who speak to each other, and who are said to see each other. Hence the priory of *knowing*, in which all that we call thought, intelligence, mind, or simply the psyche, is formed.

Knowledge and Presence

Thought, intelligence, mind, and psyche would appear to be *consciousness*, or on the threshold of consciousness. Human consciousness would be their perfected modality: the consciousness of an *I identical* in its *I think*, aiming at and embracing, or perceiving, all alterity under its thematizing gaze. This aiming of thought is called intentionality. This is a remarkable word, which first indicates the thematization of a *seeing* and, after a fashion, the contemplative character of the psyche, its being-at-a-distance from what is contemplated, which one easily takes as a model of dis-interestedness. But intentionality also indicates aspiration, finality, and desire, a moment of egotism or egoism and, at all events, of "egology." It is a moment that surely includes what have been called "drives," however little the latter are differentiated from a purely kinetic phenomenon in the physicist's object. In this sense, consciousness, of which the unconscious is itself a deficient mode, remains truly the dominant characteristic of our interpretation of mind. The *other*, "intentionally" aimed at, and invested and assembled by the apperception of the *I think*, comes— through that which is *thought* qua thought, through the noema—to fulfill, fill, or satisfy the aim, desire, or aspiration of the I *think* or its *noesis*. The other is thus present to the *I*. And this "being-present," or this *presence* of the "I think" to the *I*, is equivalent to *being*.

This presence or being is also a temporal modality. But it thus concretely signifies an ex-position of the other to the *I*, and thus precisely an *offering of itself, a giving of itself, a Gegebenheit*. It is a giving of alterity within presence, not only in the metaphorical sense of the term, but as a giving that signifies within a concrete horizon of a *taking*, already in reference to a "taking in hand." The presence of the present as temporality, an essential "at-handness" [*main-tenance*][1] so to speak, is the promise of something graspable, solid. This is probably the very promotion of the *thing*, the "something," the configuration of a *being* [*étant*] in being [*être*], to presence. And this prototypical trait of the knowledge of things is the necessary forerunner of the abstractions of understanding's idealized knowledge, as we have learned from Husserl's *Krisis*, or already, in theory at least, from his *Logical Investigations*.

Hence the technological potentialities of knowledge and vision contrast less sharply with the alleged theoretical purity and the alleged contemplative serenity of truth and the time of pure presence and pure re-presentation; these potentialities and technological temptations are their horizon. They clash much less with the alleged dis-inter-estedness of theory than is thought by the critics of industrial modernity, denounced as deviation and corruption. Seeing or knowing, and taking in hand, are linked in the structure of intentionality, which remains the intrigue of a kind of thought that recognizes itself in consciousness: the "at-handness" [*main-tenance*] of the present emphasizes its immanence as the characteristic virtue of this sort of thought.

But once that step is taken, intelligibility and intelligence—being situated in thought understood as vision and knowledge, and being interpreted on the basis of intentionality—consist in privileging, in the temporality of thought itself, the present in relation to the past and the future. To comprehend the alteration of presence in the past and future would be a matter of reducing and bringing back the past and future to presence—that is, of re-presenting them. And, similarly, it would be a matter of understanding all alterity, which is brought together, received, and synchronized in presence within the *I think*, and which then is taken up in the identity of the *I*—it is a matter of understanding this alterity that has been taken up by the thought of the identical as *one's own* and, in so doing, of reducing one's *other* to the *same*. The other becomes the *I*'s very own in knowledge, which secures the marvel of immanence. Intentionality, in the aiming at and thematizing of being—that is, in presence—is a return to self as much as an issuing forth from self.

In thought understood as vision, knowledge, and intentionality, intelligibility thus signifies the reduction of the Other to the Same, synchrony as *being* in its egological gathering. The *known* expresses the unity of the transcendental apperception of the *cogito* or of the Kantian *I think*, the egology of presence affirmed from Descartes to Husserl, and even in Heidegger, where, in Section 9 of *Being and Time*, *Dasein*'s "to be" [*à-être*] is the source of *Jemeinigkeit* and thus of the *I*.

Does not the "seeing one another" between humans—that is, obviously, language—in turn revert to a seeing, and thus to this egological significance of intentionality, the egology of synthesis, the gathering of all alterity into presence, and the synchrony of representation? This is the usual way in which language is understood. It is true that, in speaking, knowledge and seeing have recourse to signs and are communicated in verbal signs to other people—which would go beyond the pure egological gathering of the signified into thematized presence. And it is true that the problem remains as to the motive for this communication. Why do we give an account to the other? Because we have something to say. But why is this known or represented something something to say? And, at the same time, the recourse to signs does not necessarily presuppose this communication. It can be justified by the necessity the *I* feels—in its solitary synthesis of apperception—of giving signs to itself, before speaking to anyone else. In its egological work of gathering the diverse into presence or into representation, it can, beyond immediate presence, search for the presence of what is already past or has not yet come about, and then recall them, foresee them, or name them, by signs.

One can, accordingly, even write for oneself. The fact that one cannot have thought without language, without recourse to verbal signs, would not then attest to any definitive rupture in the egological order of presence. It would only indicate the necessity of inner discourse. Finite thought divides in order to question and answer itself, but the thread is retied. Thought reflects on itself in interrupting its continuity of synthetic apperception, but still proceeds from the same "I think" or returns to it. It can even, in this gathering, pass from one term to another term apparently exclusive of the first, but that, owing to its very exclusion, would be announced and already recuperated. The dialectic that tears the *I* apart ends up with a synthesis and system whereby the tear is no longer seen. Dialectic is not a dialogue with the Other, or at least it remains a "dialogue of the soul with itself, proceeding by questions and answers." That is precisely how Plato defined thought. According to the traditional interpretation of discourse that goes back to this definition, the mind in speaking its thought remains no less one and unitary, the same in presence, a synchrony despite its to and fro movement in which the *I* could stand opposed to itself.

This unity and this presence are maintained in the empirical reality of inter-human speaking. For each of the interlocutors, speaking would consist in entering *into* the thought of the other, in fitting into it. This coincidence is Reason and interiority. Here the thinking subjects are multiple dark points, empirically antagonistic, in whom light is produced when they see each other, speak to each other, and coincide. The exchange of ideas will produce presence or representation in the unity of an utterance or an account naming or displaying a field of knowledge. It would fit within a single consciousness, within a *cogito* that remains Reason: universal Reason and egological interiority.

Language can be construed as internal discourse and can always be equated with the gathering of alterity into the unity of presence by the *I* of the intentional *I think*. Even if the other enters into this language—which is indeed possible—linkage to the egological work of representation is not interrupted by this entry. It would not be interrupted even when presence, beyond the re-presentation accomplished in memory and imagination, is confirmed by the work of the historian and the futurologist, or when, in a cultivated humanity, writing gathers the past and future into the presence of a book—a thing between two covers—or that of a library enclosed within a bookcase. This is the gathering of a historical narrative into the presence of a thing, the gathering of the being of beings into a being! It is the key moment of re-presentation and vision as the essence of thought! And this despite all the time that the reading of a book may take, during which this gathering together, or this texture of presence, returns to duration. And especially despite the past that had neither been present nor re-presented by anyone—the immemorial or an-archic past—and despite the inspired future, which no one anticipates. Such a past and future begin to signify time on the basis of the hermeneutic of the biblical "verses" of the text, without prior chronological reference to the metaphor of flux, nor to the still spatial images of the "hither" and "beyond."

Has time *thus* shown its incompressible intrigue? As it has already shown it in certain chiaroscuros of the phenomenology of time whose masterful example Husserl has already given us, in which the intentionality of re-tention and pro-tention would have, on the one hand, reduced the time of consciousness understood as the consciousness of time to the re-presentation of the living present—that is, still as the re-presentation of presence: "the being of beings," which it signifies—but in which, on the other hand, the *retaining* of re-tention differs from the protending of pro-tention only through the comprehension of time already given and pre-supposed in this very constitution—that is, as a time that slips by like a flux. This metaphor of "flux" lives off a temporality borrowed from the *being* [*étant*] that is a liquid whose particles are in movement, a movement already unfolding in time.

It is necessary, then, to ask if even the discourse that is called interior, which thus remains egological and on the scale of representation, despite its scission into questions and answers addressed by the *I* to itself, in which the association of several individuals is possible on condition that "each enter into the thought of the others"—one must ask if this very discourse, despite its allegedly interior scissions, does not already rest on a prior sociality with the other in which the interlocutors are distinct. It is necessary to ask if this effective, forgotten sociality is not nonetheless presupposed by the rupture, however provisional, between self and self, for the interior dialogue still to deserve the name dialogue. This sociality is irreducible to the im-manence of representation, is other than the sociality that would be reduced to the knowledge one can acquire about the other person as a known object, and would already support the immanence of an *I* having an experience of world. Does not the interior dialogue presuppose, beyond the *representation* of the other, a relationship to the other person as other, and not initially a relationship to the *other* already apperceived as the *same* through a reason that is universal from the start?

The moment has come to ask whether this entry of each into the representation of the others, whether this agreement between thoughts in the synchrony of the given, is the unique, original, and ultimate rationality of thought and discourse. One must ask whether this gathering of time into presence by intentionality—and thus whether the reduction of time to the essance[2] of being, its reducibility to presence and representation—is the primordial intrigue of time. And one must ask whether the manifestation of presence, whether appearing, is equivalent to rationality. Is language meaningful only in its *said*, in its propositions in the indicative, everywhere at least latent, in the theoretical content of affirmed or virtual judgments, in pure communication of information—in its *said*, in all that can be written? Is it not meaningful in the sociality of *saying* [*dire*], in responsibility with regard to the other person who commands the questions and answers of the saying, and through the "non-presence" or the "appresentation"[3] of the interlocutor, which thus contrasts strongly with the presence of things according to the underlying simultaneity of the given universe? From me to this interlocutor there is a temporality other than the one that allows itself to be assembled into the presence of the *said* and the *written*, a temporality that is concrete in this "from-me-to-the-other," but that immediately congeals into the abstraction of the synchronous in the synthesis of the "I think" that grasps it thematically.

Must we grant an unconditional priority in the signifying of meaning to this thematizing and theoretical grasp and to the order that is its *noematic* correlation, the order of presence, being as being, and objectivity? Is that where meaning arises? Should not knowledge interrogate itself about itself and its justification? And does not justification—in its semantic context of rightness and justice—thus go back to the responsibility for the other, that is, to the proximity of the neighbor—as to the very domain of intelligibility or original rationality where, on this side of every theoretical explanation, in the human, the being that until then is justified in its natural unfolding as being, and as giving itself out to be the beginning of all rationalization, is brusquely put into question in me and seeks for itself a pre-initial rightness?

I have tried to show elsewhere[4] that the judgments of true knowledge and thematic thought are summoned—or invented—on the basis of or apropos of certain exigencies that depend on the ethical significance of the other, inscribed in his or her face; imperatives in the face of the other who is incomparable to me and is unique; certain exigencies that make justice concrete. The fact that justice is thus found to be the source of the objectivity of logical judgment, and that it has to support the entire level of theoretical thought, amounts to denouncing neither rationality nor the structure of intentional thought, nor the synchronization of the diverse that it implies, nor the thematization of being by synthetic thought, nor the problematic of ontology. But I also think that the latter constitute the rationality of an already derived order, that responsibility for the other signifies an original and concrete temporality, and that the universalization of presence presupposes it. I also think that the sociality in which responsibility is made concrete in justice calls for and founds the objectivity of theoretical language, which "gathers" the diachrony of time into presence and representation through accounts and histories, and—*up to a certain point*—makes reason understandable (in view of justice itself) by *comparing* in knowledge/thought "incomparable and unique" persons; comparing them as *beings* [*étants*]—that is, as individuals of a genus. I also think that institutions, courts, and thus the state, must concretely appear in this derived order of rationality.

But if it is not a matter, setting out from this analysis, of denouncing the intentional structure of thought as alienation, by showing its development from out of the "proximity of the neighbor" and "responsibility for the other," it is nevertheless important to lay stress on this development. The state, institutions, and even the courts that they support, expose themselves essentially to an eventually inhuman but characteristic determinism—politics. Hence it is important to be able to control this determinism in going back to its motivation in justice and a foundational inter-humanity. We have just taken some steps in this direction.

Alterity and Diachrony

Let us begin by inquiring as to whether, for an *I*, the alterity of the other initially signifies a logical alterity; the sort of alterity in which parts of a whole are marked off in opposition to one another, in which, in a purely formal way one, this one, is other to that one, and that one is, by the same token, other to this one. Between the persons included in this reciprocity, language would be but a reciprocal exchange of information or anecdotes, intended and gathered into the statements of each partner. Or whether, as I am inclined to think, the alterity of the other man to the *I* is first—and I dare say, is "positively"—the face of the other obligating the *I*, which, from the first—without deliberation—is responsive to the other. *From the first*: that is, the self answers "gratuitously," without worrying about reciprocity. This is the gratuitousness of the *for-the-other*, the response of responsibility that already lies dormant in a salutation, in the *hello*, in the *goodbye*. Such a language is prior to the statements of propositions communicating information and narrative. The *for-the-other* responsive to the neighbor, in the proximity of the neighbor, is a responsibility that signifies—or commands; precisely the face in its alterity and its ineffaceable and unassumable authority of *confronting* [*faire face*]. (Whom does one confront? Whence the authority? Questions not to be lost sight of!) But the *for-the-other* in the approach to the face—a for-the-other older than *consciousness of*. . .— precedes, in its obedience, all *grasping*, and remains prior to the intentionality of the *I*-subject in its being-in-the-world, which presents itself and gives itself a synthesized and synchronous world. The *for-the-other* arises in the *I* as a commandment understood by the *I* in its very obedience, as if obedience were its very accession to hearing the prescription, as if the *I* obeyed before having heard, as if the intrigue of alterity were woven prior to knowledge.

But now the simplicity of this primary obedience is upset by the third person emerging next to the other; the third person is himself also a neighbor, and also falls within the purview of the *I*'s responsibility. Here, beginning with this third person, is the proximity of a human plurality. Who, in this plurality, comes first? This is the time and place of the birth of the question: of a demand for justice! This is the obligation to compare unique and incomparable others; this is the moment of *knowledge* and, henceforth, of an objectivity beyond or on the hither side of the nakedness of the face; this is the moment of consciousness and intentionality. An objectivity born of justice and founded on justice, and thus required by the *for-the-other*, which, in the alterity of the face, commands the *I*. This is the call to re-presentation that ceaselessly covers over the nakedness of the face, giving it content and composure in a world. The objectivity of justice—whence its rigor—offending the alterity of the face that originally signifies or commands outside the context of the world, and keeps on, in its enigma or ambiguity, tearing itself away from, and being an exception to, the plastic forms of the presence and objectivity that it nonetheless calls forth in demanding justice.

Extra-ordinary exteriority of the face. Extra-ordinary, for order is justice: extra-ordinary or absolute in the etymological sense of that adjective, by virtue of its always being separable from every relation and synthesis, extricating itself from the very justice in which that exteriority is involved. The absolute—an abusive word—could probably take place concretely and have meaning only in the phenomenology, or in the rupture of phenomenology, to which the face of the other gives rise.

Face of the other—*underlying* all the particular forms of expression in which he or she, already right "in character," plays a role—is no less *pure expression*, extradition with neither defense nor cover, precisely the extreme rectitude of a *facing*, which in this nakedness is an exposure unto death: nakedness, destitution, passivity, and pure vulnerability. Face as the very *mortality* of the other human being.

But through this mortality, also, an assigned task and obligation that concern the *I*—that "concern me"—a coming face to face with authority, as if the invisible death to which the face of the other is exposed were, for the *I* that approaches it, his business, implicating him before his guilt or innocence, or at least without his intentional guilt. The *I* as hostage to the other human being is precisely called to answer for this death. Responsibility for the other in the *I*, independent of every engagement ever taken by this *I* and of all that would have ever been accessible to its initiative and its freedom, independent of everything that in the other could have "regarded" this *I*. But here, through the face of the other, through his mortality, everything that in the other does not regard me, "regards me." Responsibility for the other—the face signi-fying to me "thou shalt not kill," and consequently also "you are responsible for the life of this absolutely other other"—is responsibili-ty for the one and only. The "one and only" means the *loved one*, love being the condition of the very possibility of uniqueness.

The condition or (noncondition) of the hostage is accentuated in the *I* approaching the neighbor. But so too is his *election*, the uniqueness of he who does not allow himself to be replaced. Such a one is no longer the "individual within a genus," called *I*, not "a particular case" of the "*I* in general." It is the I who speaks in the first person, like the one Dostoyevsky has say "I am the most guilty of all," in the obligation of each for each, as the most obligated—the one and only. Such is the one whose obligation with regard to the other is also infinite, who, without wondering about reciprocity, without asking questions about the other at the approach of his face, is never done with the neighbor.

The "relationship" from me to the other is thus asymmetrical, with-out noematic correlation of any thematizable presence. An awakening to the other man, which is not knowledge. Precisely the approach to the other man—the first one to come along in his *proximity* as fellowman—irreducible to knowledge, though it may eventually call for knowledge, faced with others in the plural, a knowledge required by justice. Thought that is not an adequation to the other, for whom I can no longer be the measure, and who precisely in his uniqueness is refracto-ry to every measure, but nonetheless a non-in-difference to the other, love breaking the equilibrium of the equanimous soul. A putting into question within me of the natural position of the subject, of the perse-verance of the *I*—of its morally serene perseverance—in its being; a putting into question of its *conatus essendi*, of its existential insistence. Here is indiscreet (or "unjust") presence, which was perhaps already at issue in "The Anaximander Fragment" as Heidegger interprets it in *Holzwege*. A putting into question of that "positivity" of the *esse* in its *presence*, signifying—brusquely—encroachment and usurpation! Did not Heidegger, despite all he wants to teach about the priority of the "thought of being"—here run up against the original significance of ethics? The offense done to others by the "good conscience" of being is already an offense to the stranger, the widow, and the orphan, who, from the faces of others, look at/regard the *I*.[5]

Time and Sociality

I have attempted a "phenomenology" of sociality, taking as my point of departure the face of the other, proximity, by hearing—before all mimicry, in its facial straightforwardness, before all verbal expression, in its mortality, from the depths of that weakness—a voice that commands: an order addressed to me, not to remain indifferent to that death, not to let the other die alone; that is, an order to answer for the life of the other man, at the risk of becoming an accomplice to that death. The look with which the other faces the world, in its rectitude, means both his frailty and an authority not present in a simply logical *alterity*, which, as the counterpart of the identity of facts and concepts, distinguishes one from another, or reciprocally opposes the notions of them, by contradiction or contrariety. The alterity of the other is the extreme point of the "thou shalt not kill" and, in me, the fear of all the violence and usurpation that my existing, despite the innocence of its intentions, risks committing. The risk of occupying—from the moment of the *Da* of my *Dasein*—the place of an other and thus, on the concrete level, of exiling him, of condemning him to a miserable condition in some "third" or "fourth" world, of bringing him death. Thus an unlimited responsibility emerges in this fear for the other, a responsibility with which one is never done, which does not cease with the neighbor's utmost extremity—despite the merciless and realistic expression of the doctor, "condemning" a patient—even if the responsibility comes to nothing more at that time—as we powerlessly face the death of the other—than saying "here I am," or—in the shame of surviving—than pondering the memory of one's wrongdoings. Despite all the modern denunciations of the inefficacy and facileness of a "bad conscience"! It is a responsibility that, without doubt, contains the secret of sociality, whose total gratuitousness—though it be of no avail at the limit—is called "love of one's neighbor"—that is, the very possibility of the uniqueness of the one and only (beyond the particularity of the individual in a genus). It is a love without concupiscence, but as irrefrangible as death.

A sociality not to be confused with some hypothetical lapse or privation supposed to have taken place within the unity of the One, in which "perfection" and the unity of coincidence, having fallen into separation, would aspire to their reunion. From the depths of the natural perseverance in being of a being assured of its *right to be* (to the point of being unaware of the concept and problem)—from the heart of a logically indiscernible identity (because it rests on itself and dispenses with every distinctive sign that would be necessary for identification)—from the depths of the identity of the *I*, precisely, and in opposition to that perseverance of good conscience, and calling into question that restful identity—there arises, awakened by the silent and imperative language spoken by the face of the other (though it does not have the coercive power of the visible), the solicitude of a responsibility I do not have to make up my mind to take on, no more than I have to identify my own identity. A responsibility prior to deliberation and to which I was therefore exposed and dedicated before being dedicated to myself. A vow or a votive offering?[6]

Immemorial Past

A responsibility anterior to all the logical deliberation required by the reasoned decision. Deliberation, i.e., already the reduction of the face of the other to a re-presentation, to the objectivity of the visible, to its coercive power, which is of the world. The anteriority of responsibility is not that of an a priori idea interpreted on the basis of reminiscence—that is, referred to perception and the glimpsed intemporal presence based on the ideality of the idea or the eternity of a presence that does not pass, and whose duration or dia-chrony of time would be only a dissimulation, decline, deformation, or privation, in finite human consciousness.

Here we have, in the ethical anteriority of responsibility (for-the-other, in its priority over deliberation), a past irreducible to a hypothetical present that it once was. A past without reference to an identity naively (or naturally) assured of its right to a presence, in which everything supposedly began. Here I am in this responsibility, thrown back toward something that was never my fault or of my own doing, something that was never within my power or my freedom, something that never was my presence and never came to me through memory. There is an ethical significance in that responsibility—without the remembered present of any past commitment—in that an-archic responsibility. It is the significance of a past that concerns me, that "regards me" and is "my business," beyond all reminiscence, re-tention, re-presenta-tion, reference to a remembered present. The significance, based on responsibility for the other man, of an immemorial past, which has come into the heteronomy of an order. My *nonintentional* participation in the history of humanity, in the past of the others, who "regard/look at me." In the depths of the concreteness of the time that is that of my responsibility for the other, there is the dia-chrony of a past that cannot be gathered into re-presentation.

Responsibility for the other does not amount to a thought going back to an *a priori* idea, previously given to the "I think" and rediscovered by the "I think." The natural *conatus essendi* of a sovereign *I* is put into question by the death or the mortality of the other, in the ethical vigi-lance through which the sovereignty of the *I* can see itself as "hateful," and see its "place in the sun" as the "image and beginning of the usurpa-tion of the whole world."[7] The responsibility for the other, signified as an order in the face of my neighbor is not, in me, a simple modality of "transcendental apperception."[8] The order concerns me without it being possible for me to go back to the thematic presence of a being that would be the cause or the willing of this commandment. As I have said, it is not even a question here of receiving an order by first perceiving it and then subjecting oneself to it in a decision taken after having delib-erated about it. In the proximity of the face, the subjection precedes the reasoned decision to assume the order that it bears. The passivity of this subjection is not like the receptivity of the intellectual operation that turns back into the act of assuming—into the spontaneity of receiving and grasping. Here there is absolute foreignness of an unassumable alterity, refractory to its assimilation into presence, alien to the apper-ception of the "I think" that always assumes what strikes it by re-pre-senting it. Unequaled dia-chrony of the past. Subjection preceding the understanding of the order—which attests to or measures an infinite authority. And without the future's being already given in the "to come" [*à-venir*], in which the grasp of anticipation—or protention—would offend the dia-chrony of time, brought on by the authority of an imperative.

A past that is articulated—or "thought"—without recourse to mem-ory, without a return to "living presents," and that is not made up of re-presentations. A past signifying on the basis of an irrecusable responsibility, which devolves on the *I* and is signified to it as a commandment, without, however, reverting back to an engagement that it would supposedly have made in some forgotten present. Past in the meaning of an inveterate obligation, older than any commitment, taking on its full meaning in the imperative that, in the guise of the face of the other, commands the *I*. A categorical imperative: without regard—so to speak—for any freely taken decision that would "justify" the responsibility; without regard for any *alibi*. An immemorial past, signified without ever having been present, signified on the basis of responsibility "for the other," in which obedience is the mode proper for listening to the commandment. Harkening to a commandment that is therefore not the recall of some prior generous dispositions toward the other man, which, forgotten or secret, belong to the constitution of the *ego*, and are awakened as an *a priori* by the face of the other. This hearing of a commandment as already obedience is not a decision emerging from a deliberation—be it dialectical—disclosing itself in the face of the other, the prescription deriving its necessity from a theoretical conclusion. A commandment whose power no longer signifies a force greater than mine. The commandment here does not proceed from a force. It comes—in the guise of the face of the other—as the renunciation of coercion, as the renunciation of its force and of all omnipotence. Its authority is not submissive to the determinism of formal and ontological structures. Its heteronomy does not inevitably signify enslavement. It is the heteronomy of an irrecusable authority—despite the necessities of being and its imperturbable routine, concerned with its own being. This is precisely the whole novelty of an ethics whose disobedience and transgression do not refute authority and goodness, and which, impotent but sovereign, returns in bad conscience. The latter does not attest to an incomplete thought, manifest in its generous nonviolence, nor to the immaturity of a childish reason. It signifies—beyond the contributions of memory, deliberation, and violent force—an exceptional sonority which, in its irreducibility, suggests the eventuality of a word of God.

Pure Future

The significance of an authority signifying *after and despite my death*, signifying to the finite *I*, to the *I* doomed to death, a meaningful order signifying beyond this death. Not, to be sure, any sort of promise of resurrection, but an obligation that death does not absolve and a future contrasting strongly with the synchronizable time of re-presentation, with a time offered to intentionality, in which the *I think* would keep the last word, investing what is imposed upon its powers of assuming.

Responsibility for the other to the point of dying for the other! This is how the alterity of the other—distant and near—affects, through my responsibility as an *I*, the utmost present, which, for the identity of my *I think*, still gathers itself together, as does all my duration, into presence or representation, but which is also the end of all egological attribution of meaning by intentional thought, an end to which, in my "being-for-death," this attribution of meaning would already be doomed, and which is anticipated in the seamless immanence of its conscious existing. In the paroxysm of the proximity of my neighbor, the face of the other man—which one was therefore right not to interpret as a representation—keeps its own way (imperative) of signifying a meaning to a mortal me, through the eventual exhaustion of its egological *Sinngebung* and the anticipated collapse of all meaning proceeding from this *Sinngebung*. Behold, in the other, a meaning and an obligation that oblige me beyond my death! The futuration of the future does not reach me as a to-come [*à-venir*], as the horizon of my anticipations or pro-tentions. Must one not, in this *imperative* meaning of the future that concerns me as a non-in-difference to the other, as my responsibility for the stranger—must one not, in this rupture of the natural order of being, understand what is improperly called super-natural? Is it not to hear an order that would be the word of God or, still more exactly, the very coming of God to the idea and its insertion into a vocabulary— whence the "recognizing" and naming of God in every possible Revelation? The futuration of the future—not as "proof of God's existence," but as "the fall of God into meaning." This is the singular intrigue of the duration of time, beyond its meaning as presence or its reducibility to presence, as in Saint Augustine himself—time as the to-God [*à-Dieu*] of theology!

Responsibility for the other man, being answerable for the death of the other, devotes itself to an alterity that is no longer within the province of re-presentation. This way of being devoted—or this devotion—is time. It remains a relationship to the other as other, and not a reduction of the other to the same. It is transcendence. In the finitude of time that the "being-toward-death" of *Sein und Zeit* sketches out—despite all the renewals of the received philosophy that this brilliant book brings us—the meaningful remains enclosed within the immanence of the *Jemeinigkeit* of the *Dasein* that *has to be* [*a à être*] and that thus—in spite of the denunciation of being as presence—still belongs to a philosophy of presence. Does not responsibility for the other's death—the fear for the other that no longer enters into the Heideggerian phenomenology of emotion, *Befindlichkeit*—consist in perceiving, in the finite being of the mortal *I* arrived at from the other's face, the meaning of a *future* beyond what happens to me, beyond what, for an *I*, is to come [à-venir]? Thus we have not gone to the end of thought and meaningfulness in dying! The meaningful continues beyond my death. Should we continue designating this non-in-difference of responsibility for the other by the word *relationship* even though the terms of every relationship are already, or still, within the ideality of the system, simultaneous? And does not dia-chrony (more formal than transcendence, but also more significant) prove to be irreducible to any noetic/noematic correlation, by the concreteness of the responsibility of one for the death of the other?

To-God [*A-Dieu*]

Subjection to the order that orders man, the *I*, to answer for the other is, perhaps, the harsh name of love. Love that is no longer what this compromised word of our literature and our hypocrisies expresses, but the very fact of the approach to the unique, and, consequently, to the absolutely *other*, piercing what merely *shows* itself—that is, what remains the "individual of a genus." Love here implies the whole order, or the whole disorder, of the psychic or the subjective, which would no longer be the abyss of the arbitrary in which the meaning of the ontological is lost, but the very place that is indispensable to the promotion of the *logical* category of *unicity*, beyond the hierarchy of genres, species and individuals, or, if you will, beyond the distinction between the universal and the individual.

Subjection to an absolute order, to authority par excellence, or to the authority of excellence or of the Good. Is it not the very occasion, or

the "circumstances," in which, contrasting sharply with the perseverance of a *being* in its being, authority takes on its full sense? It brings
neither promise nor relief, but the absolute of a requirement. It is the
Word of God, perhaps, provided we only name God on the basis of that
authority in which he merely comes to the idea. The "unknown" God
does not take shape in a theme, and is exposed—because of that very
transcendence, that very nonpresence—to atheism's denials. But is it
certain that thematization is appropriate to the Infinite, that vision is the
supreme excellence of the spirit, and that through the egoism and egology of being, the Infinite accedes to that original modality, thought?

The idea of the Infinite, in which thought thinks more than it can
contain and, according to Descartes' Third Meditation, God is thought
in man—is It not like a noesis without a noema? And is the concreteness of responsibility, in its extra-ordinary future of the uncontainable,
not ordered by His Word in the face of the Other?

A subjection that precedes deliberation about the imperativeness of
an order—which gives the measure of, if you will, or attests to, an infinite authority—but also an extreme refusal of coerciveness, a nonviolence turning away from the use of force, turning away with all the
withdrawal of transcendence, with all its Infinity! Retreat of transcendence and indeclinable authority; already the dia-chrony of time? An
infinite and indeclinable authority that does not prevent disobedience,
that leaves time—which is to say, freedom. Such is the ambiguity of
authority and nonviolence. The human, *qua* bad conscience, is the
Gordian knot of this ambiguity of the idea of the Infinite, of the Infinite
as idea. A bad conscience that is not just the sign of an incomplete reason and already the appeasement and the precipitate justification of sin
and already all the good conscience of hypocrisy, but also a chance for
holiness in a society of just men without good conscience, and, in the
inextinguishable concern for justice, consent to the rigor of human justice.

Deformalization of Time

This meaning of a past that has not been my present and does not concern my reminiscence, and of a future that commands me in mortality
or in the face of the other—beyond my powers, my finitude, and my

being-doomed-to-death, no longer articulate the representable time of immanence and its historical present. Its dia-chrony, the "difference" of diachrony, does not signify pure rupture, but also non-in-difference and concordance that are no longer founded on the unity of transcendental apperception, the most formal of forms, which, through reminiscence and hope, joins time up again in re-presenting it, but betrays it. I am not going to speak, however, about these concordances of dia-chrony, about the to-God of time, or about its pro-phecy, whose ultimate concreteness is time itself in its patience. Its "adventure" or "intrigue," which I have especially tried to distinguish from the presence of being, and which I have approached from the angle of the ethical in the human, can neither be constituted nor better said starting from any category or "existential." All the figures and words that try to express it—such as "transcendence" or "beyond"—are already derived from it. The *to-God* is neither the thematization of theologies, nor a finality, which goes toward an end point and not to the Infinite, nor eschatology, preoccupied with ultimate ends or promises rather than obligations toward men. The prepositions themselves, including the *to* and the *pro*, are already only metaphors of time, and cannot serve in its constitution.

It was important to me above all to speak in this study of how, in the human intrigue, past, future, and present are tied together in time, without this being the result of a simple degradation that the unity of the One may somehow (I know not how) have undergone, dispersing itself in *movement*, which since (or according to) Aristotle supposedly lead us to time in its diachrony. On such a view, the unity of time would lose itself in the flow of instants, and find itself again—without truly finding itself—in re-presentation, where the past gathers together instants by way of the memory's images, and the future by way of installments and promises. But I have sought time as the deformalization of the most formal form there is—the unity of the *I think*. Deformalization is that with which Bergson, Rosenzweig, and Heidegger, each in his own way, have opened the problematic of modern thought, by setting out from a concreteness "older" than the pure form of time: the freedom of invention and novelty (despite the persistence of the kinetic image of *running*) in Bergson; the biblical conjunction of "Creation, Revelation, and Redemption" in Rosenzweig; and the "nearness to things," *Geworfenheit*, and *Sein-ʒum-Tode* (despite the still kinetic *ex* of the *ecstases* [*exstases*] in

Heidegger). Is it forbidden to also recall that in *The Two Sources of Morality and Religion*, the "durée" of *Time and Free Will* and *Matter and Memory*, which is conceived of as "élan vital" in *Creative Evolution*, means love of my neighbor and what I have called "to-God"? But does one have the right to avoid this comparison, in spite of all the lessons of the half century that separates us from the publication of *The Two Sources of Morality and Religion*?

What seems in fact to transpire—after the attempts to think time starting from the face of the Other, in which "God comes to our minds,"[9] as an authority that there commands indeclinably, but also refuses to compel and commands while renouncing omnipotence—is the necessity to think time in the devotion of a theology without theodicy. To be sure, this religion is impossible to propose to others, and consequently is impossible to preach. Contrary to a religion that feeds on representations, it does not begin in promise. Should we recognize in it the difficult piety—all the certainties and personal risks—of the twentieth century, after the horrors of its genocides and its Holocaust?

To be sure, one may wonder whether the time of promises ever stands at the beginning elsewhere than in pedagogy, and whether service without promises is not the only one to merit—and even to accomplish—promises. But these two questions seem already suspect of preaching.

fourteen

The Philosophical Determination of
the Idea of Culture

Culture as Immanence

Culture can, first, be interpreted—and this is the
privileged dimension of the Greco-Roman West (and
its possibility of universalization)—as an intention to
remove the *otherness* of Nature, which, alien and previous, surprises and strikes the immediate identity
that is the *Same* of the human self.

Whence the human as the *I* of the "I think" and
culture as *knowledge* extending as far as *consciousness
of self* and identity *in oneself* "of the identical and the
nonidentical." Descartes extends the "I think,"
derived from the "I doubt" (which is a vicissitude of
knowing), to the entire human soul, and Kant will see
in it the unity of transcendental apperception which is
the gathering of the *sensed* into knowledge. The place
of the meaningful and the intelligible will be maintained in knowledge and will be tantamount to the
intrigue of the spiritual in all of Western culture.
Even the relations of man with the other person or
with God will be understood as collective or religious
experiences, that is to say, as contributions to truth. In
knowledge, the radical exteriority of Nature, indifferent or "hostile" to man, is converted into *presence*,
which signifies both the being of the real and its being
placed at the disposal and within reach of the thinking thing in the temporal modality of the present,
which is precisely a breaking free from impenetrable
being and the secrets of the past and the future.
Memory and imagination will be understood as leading the hidden back to the present—as re-presenta-

tion, as regrouping and synchronization of the diachronous in the "eternity" of the ideal present, in the thinkable of law and system and their mathematical expression. Even the absence that makes science incomplete is henceforth present in the opening of the world to research.

Knowledge would thus be the relation of man to exteriority, the relation of the Same to the Other, in which the Other finally finds itself stripped of its alterity, in which it becomes interior to my knowledge, in which transcendence makes itself immanence. Léon Brunschvicg said that mathematics is our inner life! Knowledge is the culture of immanence. It is this adequation of knowledge to being that, from the dawn of Western philosophy, makes us say that one learns only what one already knows and has only forgotten in one's interiority. Nothing transcendent could affect or truly enlarge a mind. A culture of human autonomy, and probably, at the outset, a very profoundly atheistic one. A thought of the equal-to-thought.

Practice as a Moment of Knowledge

But being in the world, in its exposure to knowledge, in the openness and the frankness of presence, is ipso facto a *giving itself* and a *letting-itself-be-taken* to which the com-prehension of truth first responds. But in the fullness of the concrete, the "giving itself" of presence in knowledge is an "offering-itself-to-the-hand-that-takes," and consequently, already in knowing itself, a muscular contraction of the hand that grasps and already has at its disposal the matter it holds, or that the finger of the hand points to. Thus in *perception*, which is still "theoretical," a "goal" is accentuated, a referring to an end, to a thing, to a "something," to a term, to an *entity*. The entity belongs to the concreteness of the comprehension of being. Perception is a holding onto, appropriation, acquisition and a promise of satisfaction made to man; a rising up within the self of an interested and active subject. In a culture of immanence, satisfaction as a hyperbole of that immanence! Metaphors to take seriously: a culture in which nothing can remain other is, from the beginning, turned toward practice. Even before the technology of the industrial age and without the supposed corruption of which that age is accused, the culture of knowledge and immanence is the schematic representation of an embodied practice, of seizure and appropriation, and of satisfaction. The most abstract lessons of future science rest on this manual familiarity with things in which the presence of things is, as it were, "main-tenance."[1] Husserl taught us this in his notion of the "life-world." A "main-tenance" to which the "inner" life of the mathematician, of which Léon Brunschvicg spoke, nevertheless can be traced back—as to a forgotten or obscured foundation.

But a "main-tenance" in which a formation by a hand that shapes or sculpts what it holds—that is, in which a thought expresses itself in the flesh of the hand—is already added to the "taking in hand." A hand that forms, already the act of an artist, or that, in shaping clay or handling a brush, brings forth a form in the material of things, and in which—paradoxically for pure knowledge—thought recognizes its model which has never been seen before! Knowing or non-knowing, an artistic movement, another way than that of knowledge to give *meaning* to *being*, an artistic dimension of culture which we will discuss presently.

But in the culture of knowledge—of the absolute knowledge Hegel glorifies as freedom and a triumph of reason in which, in the *satis* of satisfaction, thought completes itself by equaling and interiorizing the other—culture triumphs over things and men. That is the meaning of being; as in the writings of Husserl, in which, with intentionality, human consciousness gets out of itself, but remains on the scale of the *cogitatum* which it equals and which satisfies it. Culture as a thought of adequation, in which human freedom is guaranteed, its identity is confirmed, in which the subject in his identity persists without the *other* being able to challenge or unsettle him.

The Sensed as Embodied Thought

But does culture as knowledge (in which, between the identity of the Same and the otherness of already constituted being the difference *is reduced*, and in which experience is interpreted as control over the given and as the fact of rediscovering—an ideal of immanence—being in itself as an interior world, as presence and constitution of exterior being in the *noema* of the *noesis*) succeed fully in this envelopment of the *other*? After all, even the perception of things, in their objectivity as thinkable, cannot be accomplished as pure immanence. Perception is not possible without the movements of the eyes, for example, and of the head, without hands and legs moving, without the whole body taking part in the act of "knowledge," in which banal analysis sees nothing but a content of representation. This is not a simple reminder of the physiological conditions of sensibility which psychophysiology has always known. Presence and organic life in its spontaneity of movements adapting to reality must not be invoked as the natural or "naturalist" causes of knowing—they somehow belong to the sensorial "content" itself of what perception brings in the way of objectivity and intelligibility, and which Husserl has already analyzed among the transcendental conditions of perception.

So there is a singular anachronism in the immanent structure of knowledge: the world or a part of the world enveloped by the *I think* or comprehended in experience is in fact already among the enveloping elements, and somehow belongs to the flesh of the *I think*. Which is not a metaphor either, but the very paradox of an embodied *I think* which the notion of a mental synthesis "associating" thought and corporeity does not succeed in justifying. "Transcendental apperception" would not suffice here. Hence the notion of the *body proper* quite *other* than the objectively identifiable body, a part of the world, as it appears to me in the mirror, as a physician sees it while examining me; and, at the same time, the *same* as that body! A relationship between the *Same* of the *I think* and the Other of *Nature*, for which culture as knowing cannot account. Would the hand as the articulation of knowledge, whose "contemplation" becomes hold and grasp—as I said earlier—already be an incarnation of the subject, older than the state of pure interiority of Descartes's *res cogitans*, absolutely distinct from the *res extensa* and which, "without the help of God," can be *known* only through the *cogitatio* of the thinker?

Culture as Expression in Art

Is it a pure failure of universal wisdom understood as a sustained effort for thought to enter into itself and rediscover being there, as *given* in its presence, which may seem to have driven the whole Culture of the West? Or would there be "something new," in the words of Merleau-Ponty in *Signs*, "between transcendent Nature, naturalism's being in itself, and the immanence of mind, its acts, and its noemata"?[2] An immemorial state of living flesh or of embodiment, a concreteness preceding the pure spirituality of the idealist subject and the pure materiality of nature—both constructed abstractions! In the concrete sensibility between the self and the "other" of the self, the initial relationship was not, on this view, opposition or radical distinction, but *expression*, an expression of the one in the other, a cultural event, a source of all the arts. Between the thought of the "I" and the exteriority of matter, the *meaningful* of expression signifies with signifyingness, different from the interiorization of knowledge and from domination of the Other by the Same. Culture in the etymological sense of the term—a dwelling in a world which is not a simple spatial inherence, but a creation of perceptible expressive forms in *being* by a non-thematizing wisdom of the flesh, which is art or poetry.

In the still technical gesture applied to attain a proposed goal, skill and elegance are already delineated; in the voice, already the delineation of a signifying language and the possibilities of song and poem. Legs that can walk will already be able to dance; hands that touch and hold, will be able to feel, paint, sculpt, and play a piano in the surprise of conforming to an ideal never seen previously. A precocious or *original* embodiment of thought, a birth, in all its diversity, of an artistic culture, in which the the meaningful does not refer to the noetic/noematic structure of the transcendental constitution in knowing, nor to any common rule; but in which harmonies and disharmonies in the human occur without recourse or reduction to the universal, and remain in the extreme exoticism of that variety.

There is no arguing about tastes! In the differences between persons and between dispersed collectivities—matter, or nature, or being, reveals or expresses or celebrates, according to Merleau-Ponty, its soul. The human (or man himself) is the very *locus* of that expression and of the whole arrangement indispensable to the manifestation of the Beautiful, to art and poetry, which are the active modes of this celebration or of the original incarnation of the Same in the Other. This is also a manifestation, a manifestation contrasting with the intelligibility of cognitive adequation and which, without leaving the culture of immanence, takes the place of an unknown god and the name of spiritual life in the atheism of our Western culture's knowledge.

But is the alterity of being sufficiently measured and appreciated as the *other* of the human? And is it not itself still too natural? Is the culture of dwelling, in its artistic expression, not threatened with a break in terms of an absolute otherness which cannot be reduced to the Same and which invites to another Culture than that of knowing or of poetry?

The Otherness of the Other Person

In the dimension of culture opened up by knowledge, in which the human assimilates the inhuman and masters it, the *meaningful* is affirmed and confirmed as a return of the Same and the Other to the unity of the One; in an analogous way, the unity of the One is affirmed and confirmed—and is again the meaningful—between the soul and the body in the artistic expression already delineating itself in the ambivalence of the corporeal and the mental and in the communication of taste through the differences themselves. All of that situates Culture, knowing, and art as "devotion" to the Neoplatonic ideal of the One to which the multiplicity of the world piously returns to make itself immanent in the unity of the One, or to imitate it in the autonomy or the freedom of knowledge and technique, and in the superb self-sufficiency of the Beautiful.

The state itself, gathering human multiplicity, is henceforth understood in that culture of knowledge and art as an essential form of this unity, and politics, common participation in this unity, is taken as a principle of interhuman proximity and of the moral law connecting in reciprocity the citizen members of the previous unity of the Whole. One whole side of Western culture consists in conceiving of, and in presenting as deriving from the same history or the same Logos or the same phenomenology, the universal state and the blossoming out of sensation into absolute knowledge.

The Relation to the Otherness of the Other Person: Ethics

One must ask, however, whether intelligibility understood as a solution to the antagonism between the Same and the Other cannot signify otherwise than by the reduction or conversion of the Other to the Same in terms of the Other who lends himself to the Same. One must ask whether in the human multiplicity, the alterity of the other man signifies only the logical otherness of the parts—some vis-à-vis others—in a divided Whole whose strictly mutual relationships are commanded exclusively by the unity of that Whole, that One that has degenerated into its parts; in other words, one must enquire as to whether, in the human multiplicity, the otherness of the other man signifies originally in terms of knowledge (a political knowledge, but essentially knowledge) in which the *I* recognizes itself as being a fraction of a Whole which governs human solidarity, like an organism whose unity guarantees the solidarity of the members. Or—and this would be the second term of an alternative—one must ask: Does the otherness of the other man, the otherness of the other, not have for the *I* from the very first an absolute character in the etymological sense of that term, as if the other were not only other in the logical and formal sense (that is to say, other by virtue of a logically or even transcendentally surmountable authority, lending itself to the synthesis of the unity of the Kantian "I think"), but *other* in an irreducible fashion, with an otherness and a separation that resist all synthesis, prior to all unity, in which the possible relationship between me and the other (the otherness of an undesirable stranger)—in which sociability—is independent of all previous recognition and all formation of totalities? An ethical relationship!

The project of a culture preceding politics, which—in the proximity from me to my fellowman, which that proximity signifies—does not reduce to any deficiency or "deprivation" in relation to the unity of the One. A relationship with the other as such and not a relationship with the other already reduced to the same, to "one of mine." A culture of transcendence, despite the supposedly exclusive excellence of immanence which is considered the supreme grace of the spirit in the West.

The Epiphany of the Face and Culture as Responsibility for the Other

This otherness and this absolute separation manifest themselves in the epiphany of the face, in the face to face. Being a grouping quite different from the synthesis, it initiates a proximity different from the one that presides over the synthesis of data, uniting them into a "world" of parts within a whole. The "thought" awakened in the face or by the face is commanded by an irreducible difference: thought which is not a thought of, but, from the very beginning, a thought for . . . a non-in-difference for the other breaking the equilibrium of the equal and impassive soul of knowledge. Signifyingness of the face: an awakening to the other man in his identity which is indiscernible to knowledge, an approach to the first one to come along in his fellowman proximity, commerce with him irreducible to experience. Before all particular expression of the other, and beneath all expression that, being already a bearing given to oneself, protects, there is a bareness and stripping away of expression as such. Exposure, point blank, extradition of the beleaguered, the tracked down—tracked down before all tracking and all beating for game. Face as the very mortality of the other man.

But in this *facing* of the face, in this mortality—a summons and a demand that concern the *I*, that concern me. As if the invisible death which the face of the other faces were *my* business, as if that death "had to do with me." The death of the other man implicates and challenges me, as if, through its indifference, the *I* became the accomplice to, and had to answer for, this death of the other and not let him die alone. It is precisely in this reminder of the responsibility of the *I* by the face that summons it, that demands it, that claims it, that the other is my fellowman.

Taking as my point of departure this straightforwardness between the other and the *I*, I was once able to write that the face is for an *I*— that the face is for me—at once the temptation to kill and the "Thou shalt not kill" which already accuses it, suspects me and forbids it, but already claims me and demands me. The proximity of my fellowman is the responsibility of the *I* for another. The responsibility for the other man, the impossibility for the other man, the impossibility of leaving him alone with the mystery of death is, concretely, through all the modalities of *giving*, the acceptance of the ultimate gift of dying for the other. Responsibility here is not a cold juridical requirement. It is all the gravity of the love of one's fellowman—of love without concupiscence—on which the congenital meaning of that worn-out word is based, and which is presupposed by all literary culture, all libraries and the entire Bible, in which its sublimation and profanation are told.

Culture as a Breach Made by the Human in the Barbarism of Being

A universally significant culture, like that of knowledge and technique in modernity, and like the one that, emanating from the university, has opened itself to the forms of cultures not belonging to the Greco-Roman heritage. But a culture in which, contrary to that of knowledge, technique and the arts, it is not a matter, for the Same of the human *I*, of confirming itself in its identity by absorbing the other of Nature, or by expressing itself in it, but of challenging that very identity, its unlimited freedom and its power, without making it lose its meaning of *uniqueness*. An ethical culture, in which the face of the other—that of the absolutely other—awakens in the identity of the *I* the inalienable responsibility for the other man and the dignity of the chosen.

A new meaning of *spirit* in this signifyingness of the meaningful. It does not reside in the thought that appropriates the *other* of nature or that, in poetry and art, celebrates, that is to say, manifests dwelling in the world. The barbarism of being threatens in terms of a more radical exteriority, in terms of the transcendence and the foreignness of the other man. A more exterior exteriority than all spatial distance. Culture is neither a going beyond nor a neutralization of transcendence; it is, in ethical responsibility and obligation toward the other, a relation to transcendence *qua* transcendence. It can be called love. It is commanded by the face of the other man, which is not a datum of experience and does not come from the world.

A breach made by humanness in the barbarism of being, even if no philosophy of history guarantees us against the return of barbarism.

The Formal Order

It would seem that the human individual should be thought of first within the formal framework of his belonging to a genus—the human genus. He is part of a whole, divided into species and culminating in an undivided unity, in the logically ultimate identity of the individual, situated among empirical data and recognizable by specific spatial and temporal indices, in which that unity *presents itself* as "a being" in its particularity, and which, according to Aristotle, "alone exists," beyond the ideal or abstract existence of genera.

An individual is other to the other. A formal alterity: one is not the other, whatever its content. Each is other to each. Each excludes all others and exists apart, and exists for its part. A purely logical and reciprocal negativity in the community of the genus.

This positivity of the being that has presented itself and this negativity of exclusion seem to reappear, and at an exalted level—or in a more accentuated manner—in the humanity of the human individual. The positivity of the particular individual is a perseverance in being which is life; the human individual lives in the will to live, that is to say in freedom, in *his* freedom which affirms itself as an egotism of the *I*, whose identity—indistinguishable, on the outside—from the human individual, identifies itself precisely as if from within, in *experiencing itself*. But the human individual is also negativity in his freedom, in excluding the freedom of others which limits his own. An alterity—again, reciprocal—of *I*'s: an eventual war of each against all.

The Autonomy of the Reasonable Individual

But, according to the wisdom of the Western tradition and Western thought, individuals overcome the exclusionary violence of their *conatus essendi* and of their opposition to others in a peace established by *knowledge*, the truth of which is assured by reason. Human individuals, on this view, are human through consciousness. The various *I*'s come to an agreement in the rational truth they obey without constraint, without giving up their freedom. The private will of the individual is raised to the auto-*nomy* of the person in which the *nomos*, the universal law, constrains the conscious and reasonable ego without constraining it. The will is practical reason. Persons, be they strangers to one another or just others, assimilate. The free assembly of particular individuals around ideal truths, especially the Law, is achieved—or at least sought. The individual opens himself up to human peace in terms of the state, institutions, politics. Even the authority of the religious is imposed through theologies, in the truth of Reason, in the freedom of the *I*. Reason, which overcomes the alterity of external nature through science and technology, presides over the equal division of things. Hence consciousness, knowledge, truth, and wisdom, of which consciousness is already the possibility and the love—hence philosophy, in the Greek sense of the word, mother of all science and all politics—would be the very spirituality of the human individual, the humanity of man, the person in the individual, source of the rights of man, and principle of all justification. A spirituality that signifies equality between persons at peace. Peace of the human individual as existence for oneself, as the security of the man satisfied in well-being and freedom. The tranquility of repose in his positivity and his position: a substantiality of substance guaranteed to the *I*. An equality to which the state aspires throughout history, and in which, through reason, human individuals, so differently endowed by nature, are promised the formal equality of individuals within a genus. Human individuals within the human genus offer themselves for judgment and lend themselves to the objectivity necessary for the exercise of justice which eventually re-establishes peace. This is the schema to which, for us Europeans, the human condition and the famous rights of man, the principle and criterion of all justification, originally refer. As a referring of the human right to the state and to the logic of the universal and the particular, man's right is no doubt the ineluctable order in the humanization of the individual, his justice and his peace. Is this, for all that, the original moment of that humanization of the individual? Shouldn't his political fate, affirming itself in, and resting upon, the peace of the private person, recall a different bestowal of right and a more ancient modality of peace? That is my problem.

The European's Bad Conscience

But the European conscience is not at peace, in this time of modernity, which is essential to Europe, and which is also a time of reckoning. A bad conscience after thousands of years of glorious Reason, of the triumphant Reason of knowledge; but also after thousands of years of political—and bloody—fratricidal wars, of imperialism in the guise of universality, of contempt for human beings and exploitation, including, in this century, two world wars, oppression, genocides, the Holocaust, terrorism, unemployment, the never-ending poverty of the Third World, the ruthless doctrines of Fascism and National Socialism, and even the supreme paradox in which the defense of the person is inverted into Stalinism. Has reason always convinced wills? Have wills always been a practical reason remaining unrepentant in a culture in which the sciences' triumphant Reason was the guiding force within history itself, supposedly incapable of any false reasoning? Europe has a bad conscience and is moved even to question its centrality and the excellence of its logic, even to exalt—at the highest levels of its universities—thoughts once considered primitive if not savage.[1] A challenging by Europe itself of its philosophical privilege which was to guarantee its peace! Is Europe not frightened by the social insufficiency of its very truth or by a science that, at its apogee, threatens the human individual in his "being qua being," the problem of which, posed in Greece, illuminated and enlightened its philosophy?

But it is also necessary to ask ourselves whether these elements of bad conscience are not already revealing, and condemnatory of

European humanity, in that they attribute to the human individual a meaning which is not exclusively Hellenic, however necessary (as we shall see) the essential message of the latter may be, at a certain time. A shattering of the universality of theoretical reason, which arose early on, in the "know thyself," and went on to rebuild the entire universe in the mode of self-consciousness. This is testimony to a call coming from a spirit whose love of wisdom does not exhaust all the powers of love, nor even, perhaps, its original powers.

Thou Shalt Not Kill

Indeed, this bad conscience does not reflect a simple disappointment brought about by the contradiction between a certain project of culture, comfortable and calm, and the insufficiency of the "results obtained." Skepticism or a cynical dialectic vainly decry laziness of thinking and fear of death in every crisis of culture; in the malaise of European humanity there is something other than laziness and fear. There is a kind of horror of killing. There is an anxiety about the legitimacy of the suffering inflicted on some by the irrefutable logic of things, even if, in regard to one's own hardships, one imposed a philosopher's consent. There is anxiety about the legitimacy of all that is apparently logical, as to the legitimacy of suffering inflicted in the simple perspective of what Hegel calls "identity of the identical and the non-identical." There is the anxiety of a responsibility which devolves on the individuals who live on after the violent death of the victims. A kind of scruple about surviving dangers which threaten the other. As if everyone, though with clean hands and in presumed or certain innocence, had to answer for the starvation and murders! The fear of each for himself, in his own mortality, does not succeed in absorbing the scandal of indifference toward the suffering of the other.

Could it be that, in our vocation of man in Europe, we did not hear, even louder than the "good news" of real knowledge that purports to dispose of our wills without constraining them and to have oriented them toward peace, the imperative of the Decalogue: "Thou shalt not kill"? Behind the reciprocal and formal alterity of individuals composing a genus, behind their reciprocal negativity (but in which, within the human genus, they are equals among themselves through the community of the genus, and endowed with reason, each one promised by Reason to peace "for his part") a different alterity signifies. It is as if, in the plurality of humans, the other man abruptly and paradoxically— against the logic of the genus—turned out to be the one who concerned *me* par excellence; as if I, one among others, found myself—precisely *I* or *me*—the one who, summoned, heard the imperative as an exclusive recipient, as if that imperative went toward me alone, toward me above all; as if, henceforth chosen and unique, I had to answer for the death and, consequently, the life, of the other. A privilege which the logic of the genus and of individuals seemed to have obliterated. "Thou shalt not kill"—what an extraordinary ambiguity of individuals and genus. An extraordinary ambiguity of the *I*: at once the very point at which being and the effort to be contract and congeal into a *oneself*, into an ipseity twisted back upon itself, primordial and autarchic, and the point at which the strange abolition or suspension of this urgency of existing and an abnegation in the concern for the "affairs" of the other are possible: as if they "regarded" me and were entrusted to me, as if the other person were above all a face. There, the otherness-of-the-individual-in-the-genus has come out of its formality and logical banality in which this relation, a clear and distinct idea, went simultaneously or indifferently from me to the other and from the other to me. As if consciousness here lost its symmetry in relation to the consciousness of the other person!

The Unique Before the Individual

The question must be asked: Is the original semantic situation in which the human individual receives meaning or is invested with rights equivalent to the logical schema genus/individual in which, from one individual to the other, otherness remains reciprocal and in which the notion of the human individual is fixed by the objectification of any human individual of the genus, each being other to the other? Or—a second term of the alternative—is the original access to the individual as a human individual, far from being reducible to a simple objectification of one individual among others—a characteristic access in which the approaching one himself belongs to the concreteness of the meeting without being able to take the distance necessary for the objectifying gaze, without being able to stand apart from the relationship, and in which this not-being-able-to-stand-apart, this non-in-difference with regard to the difference or the otherness of the other—this irreversibility—is not a simple failure of an objectification, but precisely a *doing justice to* the difference of the other person which, in this non-in-difference, is not a formal, reciprocal, and insufficient otherness within the multiplicity of individuals of a genus, but an otherness of the *unique*, exterior to all genus, transcending all genus. A transcendence that is therefore not the simple *failure* of immanence, but the irreducible excellence of the social in its proximity: peace itself. Not the peace of pure security and non-aggression, which guarantees everyone their position in being, but the peace that is already that non-in-difference itself. The peace in which non-in-difference must be understood not as the neutrality of some disaffected curiosity, but the "for-the-other" of responsibility. Response—a first language; primordial goodness which hatred, in its attentions, already presupposes. Love without concupiscence, in which man's right assumes meaning; the right of the beloved, that is, the dignity of the unique.

A proximity of the transcendent in man, which signifies precisely the increase of sociality over all solitude in which the knowledge of individuals disseminated in the genus remains. Increase of sociality in *love*. I do not utter inconsiderately this often misused word. In ethical peace, the relationship goes to the unassimilable, incomparable other, to the irreducible other, the unique other. Only the unique is absolutely other. But the uniqueness of the unique is the uniqueness of the beloved. The uniqueness of the unique *signifies* in love. Not that the uniqueness of otherness is thought of in terms of some subjective illusions of the lover. Quite to the contrary, it is the subjective as such that, in the impassive essence of being, and in the generic miscellany of the objective, is precisely the condition of the possibility of the unique. Through the subjective—which is not only knowledge [*le connaître*] but which makes itself love—there is, through the rigor of logical form, both its genera and its individuals, a penetration that pierces through to the unique. Through the hidden violence of perseverance in being—a beyond. Farther than with the known individual, there is, with the absolutely other, human peace and proximity. A peace different from the simple unity of the diverse, brought together beneath the synthesis that integrates it; peace as a relationship with the other in his absolute otherness, a recognition in the individual of the uniqueness of the person. Love as a logical operation!²

Justice and the Unique

This analysis of the interpersonal relation which tended to show the original signifyingness of the right of the individual in the proximity and uniqueness of the *other* man is in no way a repudiation of politics. A few words in conclusion to indicate how this original right itself leads to the liberal state, to political justice, through the plurality of individuals belonging to the "extension" of the human genus; but also to say how the reference to the face of the other preserves the ethics of that state.

Human multiplicity does not allow the *I*—let us say does not allow *me*—to forget the *third party* who pulls me away from the proximity of the other: away from responsibility prior to all judgment, from the pre-judicial responsibility for my fellowman, in his immediacy of uniqueness and incomparability, away from original sociality. The *third party*, different from my fellowman, is also my fellowman. And he is also the fellowman of the fellowman. What are they doing, these unique ones, what have they already done, to each another? For me, it would be to fail in my first-personal responsibility—in my pre-judicial responsibility with regard to the one and the other—fellowmen—were I to ignore the wrongs of the one toward the other because of this responsibility, prior to all judgment, of proximity. This does not mean the taking account of possible wrongs I may have suffered at the hands of one or the other, and denying my dis-interestedness; it means not ignoring the suffering of the other, who falls to my responsibility.

It is the moment of justice. The love of one's fellowman, and his original right, as unique and incomparable, for which I am answerable, tend of their own accord to make appeal to a Reason capable of comparing incomparables, a wisdom of love. A measure superimposes itself on the "extravagant" generosity of the "for the other," on its infinity. Here, the right of the unique, the original right of man, calls for judgment and, hence, objectivity, objectification, thematization, synthesis. It takes institutions to arbitrate and a political authority to support all this.

Justice requires and establishes the state. There is, to be sure, the indispensable reduction of human uniqueness to the particularity of an individual of the human genus, to the condition of citizen. A derivation. But still its imperative motivation is inscribed in the very right of the other man, unique and incomparable.

But justice itself cannot make us forget the origin of the right or the uniqueness of the other, henceforth covered over by the particularity and generality of the human. It cannot abandon that uniqueness to political history, which is engaged in the determinism of powers, reasons of state, totalitarian temptations and complacencies. It awaits the voices that will recall, to the judgments of the judges and statesmen, the human face dissimulated beneath the identities of citizens. Perhaps these are the "prophetic voices."

An anachronism that may bring a smile to the lips! But prophetic voices probably mean the possibility of unforeseen acts of kindness of which the *I* is still capable in its uniqueness preceding all genus or freed from all genera. They are sometimes heard in the cries that rise up from the interstices of politics and that, independently of official authority, defend the "rights of man"; sometimes in the songs of the poets; sometimes simply in the press or in the public forum of the liberal states, in which freedom of expression is ranked as the first freedom and justice is always a revision of justice and the expectation of a better justice.

entre nou

This book, that wants to be and feels itself to be of phenomenological inspiration, proceeds from a long association with Husserl's texts, and a constant attentiveness to *Sein und Zeit*. Neither Buber nor Gabriel Marcel is ignored in this text, and Franz Rosenzweig is mentioned in the preface. The book also claims, in contemporary thought, a faithfulness to the innovative work of Henri Bergson, who made many of the the essential positions of the masters of phenomenology possible. With his notion of duration, he freed time from its obedience to astronomy, and thought from its attachment to the spatial and the solid, and to its technological ramifications and even its theoretical exclusivism.

Totality and Infinity, an Essay on Exteriority, which appeared in 1961, opens a philosophical discourse which was continued in *Otherwise than Being or Beyond Essence* in 1974, and *De Dieu qui vient à l'idée* [On God Who Comes to the Mind] in 1982. Certain themes of the first work are repeated or renewed, or return in other forms, in the last two; certain intentions are specified in them. For the substance of this discourse, which began twenty-five years ago and which forms a whole, these are non-contingent and no doubt instructive variations, but it is not possible to give an account of them in the brevity of a preface.

Let me note, however, two points to avoid misunderstandings. *Otherwise than Being or Beyond Essence* already avoids the ontological—or more exactly, *eidetic*—language which *Totality and Infinity* incessantly resorts to in order to keep its analyses, which challenge the *conatus essendi* of being, from being considered as dependent upon the empiricism of a psychology. The status of necessity of these analyses certainly remains to be determined, despite its analogy with that of the essential.[1] Moreover, there is no terminological difference in *Totality and Infinity* between mercy or charity, the source of a right of other person coming before mine, in the first case, and justice in the second, where the right of the other person—but obtained only after investigation and judgment—is imposed before that of the third. The general ethical notion of justice is mentioned without discrimination in the two situations.

Here are some remarks on the general spirit that characterizes the discourse begun in *Totality and Infinity*.

This book challenges the synthesis of knowledge, the totality of being that is embraced by the *transcendental ego*, presence grasped in the representation and the concept, and questioning on the semantics of the verbal form of to be—inevitable stations of Reason—as the ultimate authorities in deciding what is *meaningful*. Do they restore or lead to the ability to vouchsafe the harmony of a world and thus to manifest reason to the end? Reason to the end or peace between men. For this peace, it may not be enough to *dis-close* all things and to affirm and confirm them, in their places as *in themselves* and *for themselves* in the true, where they appear in the original, *at home* as guaranteed, and where, in their very exteriority, they already appear as coming to hand and are taken and understood and quarreled about among men, and possessed and exchanged and useful to this one or that one. But how do this one and that one come toward one another? The problem of peace and reason is approached in *Totality and Infinity* in terms of a different and no doubt older conjuncture.

Beyond the *in-itself* and *for-itself* of the disclosed, there is human nakedness, more exterior than the outside of the world—landscapes, things, institutions—the nakedness that cries out its strangeness to the world, its solitude, death concealed in its being. Within the world of appearances, it cries out the shame of its hidden misery, it cries out *with a grieving heart* [*la mort dans l'âme*]; human nakedness calls upon me— it calls upon the *I* that I am—it calls upon me from its weakness, without protection and without defense, from nakedness. But it also calls upon me from a strange authority—imperative, disarmed—the word of

God and the verb in the human face. Face, already language before words, an original language of the human face stripped of the countenance it gives itself—or puts up with—under the proper names, titles, and genera of the world. An original language, already an asking, and precisely as such (from the point of view of the in-itself of being) wretchedness, penury, but also already an imperative making me answerable for the mortal, my fellowman, despite my own death—a message of difficult holiness, of sacrifice; origin of value and good, the idea of the human order within the order given to the human. The language of the inaudible, the language of the unheard of, the language of the non-said. Scripture!

An order that touches the *I* in its individuality *qua a being* still enclosed in the genus to which it belongs according to being; a being still interchangeable in the logical community of the extension of the genus, but already awakened to its uniqueness as irreplaceable, ordered to the logically indiscernible uniqueness of the monad, to the uniqueness of one chosen, in the undeniable responsibility that is love. Love outside all concupiscence, but love that binds to the beloved, i.e., to the "one and only."

From uniqueness to uniqueness—transcendence; outside all mediation, all motivation that can be drawn from a generic community—outside all prior relationship and all *a priori* synthesis—love from stranger to stranger, better than brotherhood in the bosom of brotherhood itself. A gratuity of transcendence-to-the-other interrupting the being that is always preoccupied with that being itself and its perseverance in being. Absolute interruption of ontology, but in the one-for-the-other of holiness, proximity, sociality, peace. A sociality that, although utopian, commands all the humanity in us, and in which the Greeks saw the ethical.

A commandment in the nakedness and poverty of the other, ordering responsibility for the other: beyond ontology. The word of God. A theology which does not proceed from any speculation on the beyond of worlds-behind-the-world, from any knowledge transcending knowledge. A phenomenology of the face: a necessary ascent to God, which will allow for a recognition or a denial of the voice that, in positive religions, speaks to children or to the childhood in each one of us, already readers of the Book and interpreters of Scripture.

The research *Totality and Infinity* takes up certainly does not consist in questioning the phenomenology of the object embraced by that science, of presence lending itself to its grasp, of being reflected in its idea—of that *that which is thought in the thought* [*pensé*] always on the scale of the thought that thinks it [*pensée*]—a correlation and correspondence of the rigorous noetic/noematic parallelism of intentionality that informs transcendent consciousness in Husserl's admirable work. It also informs the theoretical, which, in all forms of this consciousness (thoughts, according to Brentano's philosophical testament), doubtless remains the indispensable base or the privileged mode of all consciousness, whether it is affective, axiological or volitive. But in the discourse of *Totality and Infinity*, we have not forgotten the memorable fact that, in his third *Meditations of First Philosophy*, Descartes encountered a thought, a noesis, which was not on the scale of its noema, its cogitatum. An idea which gave the philosopher *bedazzlement* instead of accommodating itself within the *self-evidence* of intuition. A thought thinking more—or thinking *better*—than it thought according to truth. A thought that also responded *with adoration* to the Infinite of which it was the thought. For the author of *Totality and Infinity*, that was a great source of wonder, after the doctrine of noetic/noematic parallelism in the instruction of his teacher Husserl, who called himself a disciple of Descartes! He then asked himself whether all that was dear to the love of "the love-of-wisdom," or the love that is the philosophy of the Greeks, was the certainty of fields of knowledge directed toward the object, or the even greater certainty of reflection on these fields of knowledge; or whether knowledge beloved of and expected from philosophers was not, beyond the wisdom of such knowledge, the wisdom of love, or wisdom in the guise of love. Philosophy as love of love. A wisdom taught by the face of the other man! Had it not been foreshadowed by the Good beyond essence and above the Ideas of Book VI of Plato's *Republic*? A Good in relation to which being itself appears. A Good, from which being draws the illumination of its manifestation and its ontological force. A Good in view of which "every soul does all that it does." [2]

Paris, January 18, 1987

entre nous

QUESTION: *We know the ethical dimension is at the heart of your thought, a dimension inscribed in the face to face with the other. But can we be content with an abstract discourse on the ethical, when in fact the relation between two people—to which you give the greatest importance, and in which forgiving, forgetting, and unlimited self-giving are possible—is not the real social situation? In brief, don't we risk asking much too much of ethics?*

EMMANUEL LEVINAS: We shouldn't let ourselves be overly impressed by the false maturity of the moderns who do not see a place for ethics—which they denounce as moralism—in reasonable discourse. Perhaps we shouldn't be worried about the importance taken on in my reflection by the "extra-ordinariness" of ethics before realizing the meaning expressed by this departure from the established order of reality. Reality—beings—all that *is*. But the word being has a verbal form which should signify, in principle, a doing or a history. The verbal form of the word being, which, certainly, does not evoke substantive nouns, expresses the advent or the very fact or the event of being; it says that, in being, it is a question of being, of self-preservation, and that in it there is the persistence and the effort of being, as if in the fact of being, a kind of unforgettable seniority of non-being, against which being strives, somehow resonated and threatened. Hence, for being qua life, there is a self-contraction, a for-itself, an "instinct of preservation," already struggling for life, and in the thinking being, a will to be, inter-est, egotism. One might wonder whether the materiality of matter, in its ultimate reaches, underlying the solidity of the atom of which physicists speak, is not the analogue for the interiority of pure being before or without ethics, absorbed in its *conatus essendi* in the guise of thing/self, an analogue for the solidity of the solid, for the hardness of the hard, already a metaphor for the cruelty of the cruel in the struggle for life and the egotism of wars. The permanent temptation of a materialist metaphysics! Ethics, concern for the being of the other-than-one-self, non-indifference toward the death of the other, and hence, the possibility of dying for the other—a chance for holiness—would be the expansion of that ontological contraction that is expressed by the verb to be, dis-inter-estedness breaking the obstinacy of being, opening the order of the human, of grace, and of sacrifice.

This human inversion of the in-itself and the for-itself (of "every man for himself") into an ethical self, into a priority of the for-the-other—this replacement of the for-itself of ontological persistence by an *I* henceforth unique certainly, but unique because of its chosenness for a responsibility for the other man—inescapable and nontransferable, this radical turnabout would take place in what I call an encounter with the face of the other. From behind the bearing he gives himself—or puts up with—in his appearance, he calls to me and orders me from the depths of his defenseless nakedness, his misery, his mortality. It is in the personal relationship, from me to the other, that the ethical "event," charity and mercy, generosity and obedience, lead beyond or rise above being.

But then what about humanity in its multiplicity? What about the one next to the other—the third, and along with him all the others? Can that responsibility toward the other who faces me, that response to the face of my fellow man ignore the third party who is also my other? Does he not also concern me?

In a spirituality which I define by this responsibility for the other—to which the *I* is chosen—or condemned—called to respond for the other (and perhaps that is what mercy and charity are)—I must henceforth compare; I must compare incomparables, uniquenesses. No returning to the "for-oneself of each": it is necessary to judge others. In the meeting with the face, it was not one's place to judge: the other, being unique, does not undergo judgment; he takes precedence over me from the start; I am under allegiance to him. Judgment and justice are required from the moment the third party appears. In the very name of the absolute obligations toward one's fellow man, a certain abandonment of the absolute allegiance he calls forth is necessary.

Here is a problem of a different order, for which institutions and a politics—the entire panoply of a state—are necessary. But a liberal state: always concerned about its delay in meeting the requirement of the face of the other. A liberal state—a constitutive category of the state—and not a contingent, empirical possibility; a state that recognizes, beyond its institutions, the legitimacy—though it be a transpolitical one—of the search for and defense of the rights of man. A state extending beyond the state. Beyond justice, an imperious reminder of all that must be added to its necessary harshness, and that springs from the human uniqueness in each of the citizens gathered in the nation, from resources that cannot be deduced, nor reduced to the generalities of a legislation. Resources of charity that have not disappeared beneath the political structure of institutions: a religious breath or a prophetic spirit in man.

Q: *The* I *as ethical subject is responsible to everyone for everything; his responsibility is infinite. Doesn't that mean that the situation is intolerable for the subject himself, and for the other whom I risk terrorizing by my ethical voluntarism? So isn't there an impotence of ethics in its will to do good?*

E.L.: I don't know if this situation is intolerable. It is not what you would call agreeable, surely; it is not pleasant, but it is the good. What is very important—and I can maintain this without being a saint myself, and I don't present myself as a saint—is to be able to say that the man who is truly a man, in the European sense of the word—descended from the Greeks and the Bible—is the man who understands holiness as the ultimate value, as an unassailable value. Of course it is very difficult to preach this; it is not very popular to preach, and it even makes advanced society laugh.

Q: *In comparison with (and I quote you) "the extravagant generosity of the for-the-other"—aren't politics and, in a more precise sense, law, the only means of instituting society? Moreover, isn't this necessity of the Law, this limitation of an infinite right, one of the political lessons of the Talmud?*

E.L.: I wasn't challenging law or politics—I even tried to deduce the necessity for them—I have also shown their ethical limits. What you say about the Talmud is correct, but the Talmud never limits itself to the concept, which, however, is important to it. When it uses concepts, it never forgets the example from which the concept was drawn. *"Here is the law—it is perfectly good, but what will happen if. . . ."* This *"what will happen if . . ."* is a particular case. The discussion never drops it, and often the concept is reversed and reveals a completely different meaning than the one it "pretended to be" at the beginning.

Q: *After all, whether it is a question of ethics or politics, the first question of the interhuman is certainly a question of justice. You say on this subject, and I quote you again: "The basis of consciousness is justice and not vice-versa." Could you explain?*

E.L.: When we talk about consciousness, we are talking about knowledge: to be conscious of is to know; and in order to be just it is necessary to know: to objectify, compare, judge, form concepts, generalize, etc. Faced with human multiplicity, these operations impose themselves and the responsibility for the other —which is charity and love—can go astray, and therefore seeks truth. I have ventured to write that the very search for objectivity emerges in the ethical conflict, the acuity of which is assuaged by justice, which is based on judgment. What I have tried to bring to your attention today is that consciousness is a spirituality of knowledge, a spirituality of truth; it is not itself a spirituality of love. People say of philosophy that it is love of wisdom; and wisdom is still thought of in terms of knowledge. For the publication of my book *Totality and Infinity* in German, I was asked for a preface.[1] I say there that my teaching ultimately remains very classical; it repeats Plato's doctrine that it is not consciousness that establishes the Good, but the Good which calls forth consciousness. Wisdom is what the Good commands. It is in view of the Good that "every soul does all that it does."[2]

Q: *Is it not true, as Tocqueville feared, that the legal state, the egalitarian society, and individualism constitute, in a sense, the death of ethical concern? Isn't equality the death of the other for the good of the Same, in the sense in which it risks bringing all individuals to one standard?*

E.L.: For Tocqueville, society is certainly a necessary evil, and he has an aristocrat's view of it. No, one cannot wish for the existence of the poor to guarantee a place for charity! Egalitarianism is certainly a conception of justice. Is democracy enough for it? Ricoeur, in *le Monde*, speaking of the recent English elections, expressed his sorrow that, in England, a majority of people, having what they need, vote as landlords, and no one is concerned about the poor. Ricoeur sees that as one of the dangers of democracy: the permanent exclusion of a minority that always exists.

Q: *To what extent can the political preserve "ethical rapture" or, on the contrary, does it destroy "disinterestedness?" Can rights be an achievement of the ethical relationship?*

E.L.: Yes, if it is completely moral. . . . I was talking just now about the liberal state: Isn't it a permanent revisiting of the right itself, a critical reflection on political rights, which are only de facto laws ? The jurists who establish it are certainly highly moral. The man who presided over the Barbie trial is a moral being, but he applies only the established law. But the liberal state is also a state capable of questioning itself. I am not familiar with the technicalities of the life and development of courts of law. My problem consists in inquiring into how to reconcile what I call the infinite ethical requirement of the face that meets me, dissimulated by its appearance, and the appearance of the other as an individual and as an object. How to enter into this comparison of incomparables without alienating the faces? For beings are not compared as faces, but already as citizens, as individuals, as a multiplicity in a genus and not as "uniquenesses."

Q: *In his face, the other is unique, and that is why he is incomparable. . . .*

E.L.: When I speak of uniqueness, I am also expressing the otherness of the other. The unique is the other in an eminent way: he doesn't belong to a genus or doesn't remain within his genus. There is an old talmudic text which has always impressed me. God is absolutely extraordinary. To mint money, states resort to a stamp. With a single stamp, they make many coins that all look alike. God succeeds, imposing His image with a stamp, in creating a multiplicity of dissimilarities: selves, unique in their genus. A Lithuanian rabbi of the eighteenth century, Rabbi Haim of Volozhin, concluded from that that each one of them— a unique person in the world—is responsible for the entire universe![3] Which probably means to suggest also that, above and beyond the right—and once the right is respected in its rigor—infinite, nonde-ducible, unforeseeable resources belong to the mercy of each one: Powers of the unique.

Q: *Professor Y. Leibovitz recently insisted on the error Israel would make in giving a messianic value to the historical realization of the State of the Jewish people. Do you share that judgment?*

E.L.: Professor Leibovitz represents strictly orthodox thought, according to which Judaism consists in the fulfillment of the commandments of the Torah. In Zionism, he opposes the purely political form it has adopted, and from which it expects the fulfillment of the destiny of Israel. According to Leibovitz, there is a fundamental theological error in such a vision. For Leibovitz, the Jewish problem remains a supernatural problem: the promise of the Messiah must be taken literally; eschatology is not a politics. The descendant of David will gather in the Diaspora of Israel, put an end to oppression, and transform the world.

My position is different. Auschwitz was a profound crisis. It concerns the very relationship of man to God; the very problem of the promise is posed. Is one loyal to the Torah because one counts on the promise? Must I not remain faithful to its teachings, even if there is no promise? One must want to be a Jew without the promise made to Israel being the reason for this faithfulness. Judaism is valid not because of the "happy end"[4] of its history, but because of the faithfulness of this history to the teachings of Torah. History that is—as it always was—a Passion in its faithfulness. A history that has remained a Passion since the unforgiven resurrection of the State of Israel. But a history which cannot get through our time, nor testify to its truth without taking on, somewhere, political conditions. This is why the State of Israel is important today to the Torah of Israel and to its meaning for all men.

Ladies and Gentlemen, Director
Thank you for what you have said.[1] My remarks,
extending your speech, will doubtless fall short of
what you, in your generous confidence, appear to
expect of mine. Nevertheless, you will find in them
the echo of a crisis that is more profound, and older,
than what is entailed in the narrative of a conflict
between a youthful admiration, still irresistible today,
inspired by a philosophical intelligence among the
greatest and rarest, and the irreversible abomination
attached to National Socialism, in which that brilliant
man was somehow able—never mind how!—to take
part. A deeper and older crisis. Did this meditation on
Sein—the adventure of being—this questioning of
being and its meaning, this meditation on being in the
guise of the human *being-there*, in the guise of the
Dasein, described so brilliantly, leave us without
ambiguities? Is the adventure of being, as being-
there, as Da-sein, an inalienable belonging to self, a
being *proper*—*Eigentlichkeit*, an authenticity altered
by nothing—neither support nor help nor influence—conquering, but disdaining the exchange in
which a will awaits the consent of the stranger—the
virility of a free ability-to-be, like a will of race and
sword? Or, on the contrary, would not *to be*, that verb,
signify—in *being-there*—non-indifference, obsession
by the *other*, a search and a vow of peace? Of a peace
that would be, not the silence of non-interference in
which the freedom of the artistic act takes pleasure,
and in which the beautiful creates silence, maintains
silence, and protects it, but rather a peace in which the

eyes of the other are sought, in which his look awakens responsibility? A peace that Western man has wished for, and in which he has sought fulfillment just as much as in independence or the artistic act. Does not the memory of ethical values—perhaps grown dim in the "Scriptures," which are proclaimed "obsolete"—solicit humanity even in modern times, in the form of literature, which is inspired by this memory and widely disseminated?

These are questions that remain open. But I cannot forget the year, almost half a century ago, when I was a student in Freiburg and Heidegger's teaching had just succeeded the last semester of Husserl's professorship—at a time when 1933 was not yet conceivable, and I lived under the impression of being present at the Last Judgment of the history of philosophy in the presence of Husserl and Heidegger, my memory still ringing with the perfect harmonies of Bergsonism, which had been taught by my teachers at Strasbourg, intertwined with all that was true for my new teachers, or what could be added to their insights without compromising them. Was not Bergsonism, in its way, a reassignment of the verbal meaning of the word *to be* to the concreteness of duration, in which time is no longer pure form, a heritage of transcendental philosophy, but in which the most profound ultimate meaning of time's diachronic instability consists in being awakened in the representation of all the *beings*, all the solid and extended and stable things that issue from the craftsman's act and that, from the start, come to hand—*ʒuhanden*; a diachrony to be awakened also in those ideas and congealed concepts that are eternal in science; a diachrony that, in the *durée* of *The Two Sources of Morality and Religion* will turn out to be love of one's fellowman?

However that may be, the certainty of the primordial philosophical importance of these prestigious phenomenological discourses and these Bergsonian illuminations have never left me. Despite all the horror that eventually came to be associated with Heidegger's name—and which will never be dissipated—nothing has been able to destroy in my mind the conviction that the *Sein und Zeit* of 1927)[2] cannot be annulled, no more than can the few other eternal books in the history of philosophy—however much they may disagree. Nothing could make us forget that, beneath the paths that had become blurred over the ages by the complex movements, the comings and goings of professors and students, its pages sought the original paths and intentions of philosophy and philosophers: Western thought opened to all men.

You are certainly familiar with the positions taken up in *Sein und Zeit*, and I am not going to sum up their progression today. I will raise only the points relative to the ambiguity or the crisis mentioned at the beginning of my remarks. A work and a discourse of ontology, a project which is not an enterprise of conceptual knowledge produced and manifested on the occasion of some virtuality tempting the famous "curious mind" of man, or an ambition to embrace the universe, the totality of things and living beings, relationships and ideas—all that is; but ontology—primordial reason applied to the understanding of the verbal meaning of the expression *to be*. You know it—the best understood and the least definable of verbs. A verbal meaning of the expression "to be" that indicates being as an event, an adventure, or a *chanson de geste*. Intelligible—snugly at home within the grammatical form of the verb, without signifying, properly speaking, either act or motion or history or event or adventure; yet without being confused with the punctual stability of an eternity, unmoving and already completely different from its "intelligible secret," which it loses beneath the light that illuminates substantives and entities. The understanding of it, according to *Sein und Zeit*, is not reducible to a logical operation. Here, understanding the meaning would already belong to the very event of being, the meaning of which is sought; it would already belong to the adventure—the saga—of being, which is caught up in *existing*, in *being-there* or in *human intrigue*, its essential modality.

In the guise of a *concern for being*, a *being-there*, a *being-in-the-world*, a *being-with-others*, and a *going-to-death*, what is at stake in the "event" of being is that being itself. Without recourse or reduction to an "objectifying subject," to a transcendental subject, being precedes and gathers itself in thought in its own way, in the guise of a concern for being, proper to its "event" of being. Ineluctable nodes of the "event" of being itself, which is already known as thought, already drawn together as a question asked about the meaning of being—without delegating or postponing the question to an act of thought different from or ulterior to being; *being-there*, *being man*, is already that questioning, the persisting-in-being or the concern for being. An understanding of being that would no longer be the objectification of a quiddity or representation of substantives qualified by adjectives and answering the question: "What is it?" Understanding of the "event" of being thinks itself in adverbial modalities, which may be discerned in "existing," "being-there," "being-in-the-world," "being-with-others," "being-for-death"—modalities of being, their "how." Strange adverbs of existence which Heidegger calls "existentials." Existence should not be reduced to some still obscure objectifications of an inner datum. The being-there—the *Da-sein*—of man does not signify a property or a conjunction of properties of a present reality having such and such an aspect, the essence of man glimpsed here is a *mode of being*, an *existence*. The theoretical loses the privilege it holds in the intelligibility of the systematic. Without having had to yield it to an axiology! Objectification itself and science would be possible, and appear in their existential rank, but would no longer be foundational. Ontological intelligibility reveals itself as basic to all rationality.

Man does not, in this scheme of things, play the role of transcendental subjectivity. He is expressed in terms of his *being there* and his *being-in-the-world*, a modality of the *authentic* or the event of being. Philosophy is no longer interested in the man of humanism, or an excellence or a dignity that, as a being, he would derive from some nonphilosophical tradition or doctrine, or from a partiality of man for "everything that is human," or from the privileged nature of evidence derived from reflection on the self in the search for certain truths, and in which man already poses himself as a subject of transcendental idealism. It is as *being-there* in its concern for being that Heideggerian phenomenology brings to the heart of ontology that *essential articulation of the event of being*, which is also understanding of that event, thought in the strong sense of the term, flanked by science, which extends into techniques that absorb it and that would pervert man.

The radical distinction between *beings* and *being* in the verbal sense of the word, which dominates *Sein und Zeit*, Heidegger's bold and powerful speculations seeking the logos of that which, in this verbal sense of the word *being*, had been considered logically empty, the discovery of the "event" signified by that emptiness, and eventually the discovery of temporality and historicity, which, according to the "phenomenological construction" of *Sein und Zeit*, are thought on the basis of that event (a theme I will not go into today), the triumphant virtuosity of Heidegger's existential analysis, the suspension of quiddity in the being of man in order to conceive this *being* as *existence*, as the adverbial modality of the event of being, the new function to which the human finds himself called in the meaningfulness of meaning: all this, which constitutes a new approach to the meaningful, seems to me of primary importance, even if, as I shall show (and that is the major theme of my remarks this evening, titled "Dying For . . . ") the human, as conceived here, makes it possible for a *beyond-being* to take on meaning!

The foregoing should indicate to you with what intellectual humility I reflect on some themes from *Sein und Zeit*, in the form of questions they pose for me: Is *thought*—a modality of the event of being, or an interrogation on the meaning of that event—closed to all primordial axiology which would be first philosophy? Is ontology fundamental even when man is understood as *being-there*—both *being* and *a being*—and when the manner in which his substance takes on the ways of a verb is very different from the materialist confusion of the corporal substance with the physical play of causes and effects? Has not the firmness of this primordial ontology already gone through the axiological alternatives and chosen between values and respected the authentic and disdained the everyday, which, nevertheless, proceeds from it? Even if, to begin with, the fall—the *Verfallen*—was exposed as being existential.

I have already stressed, at the beginning of my remarks—before my attempt to retrace some of the movements characteristic of the phenomenology and ontology of *Sein und Zeit*—the alternative between, on the one hand, the identical in its authenticity, in its *own right* or its unalterable *mine* of the human, in its *Eigentlichkeit*, independence and freedom, and on the other hand being as human devotion to the other, in a responsibility which is also an election, a principle of identification and an appeal to an *I*, the non-interchangeable, the unique. In the interrogation on the meaning of being as analyzed by this work from the beginning paragraphs on, the search sets in for the authenticity in which the *event* of being is situated. *Eigentlichkeit* to which all the meaningful can be traced. Primordial importance is attached to *one's own being*. *Eigentlichkeit* is the *genuineness* of being or of thought as the gathering and articulation of the event of being. An event or adventure or advent of *being that is concerned with being*—or being in which being is at stake. It is a kind of fullness of the mine—a "mineness" or *Jemeinigkeit*, in Heideggerian terms, the original concreteness of which implies an *I* and a *thou*. An authenticity to which all alienation refers, as I have said, that that authenticity undergoes. But where does that alienation come from?

Let us recall the first pages of *Sein und Zeit*, in which the concern for being, interpreted in an *existential* manner, is formulated as *being-in-the-world*, being near things. According to Heidegger, these things, before appearing in the "neutrality" of objects to be known or as things which are only things—as *Vorhandenheit* (things to be perceived, or things of pure essence to be represented) give themselves originally in the mode of appealing to the skill of a hand already grasping one thing as a hammer, another as matter to be worked, or as food to be brought to the mouth. To be ready-to-hand—*Zu-handenheit*—is not a simple property of the real, but its *how*, its way of being. But then other people are already signified in this work implied in things, which are already "equipment," or "our things," and in an already common world. Hence being-in-the-world means being near things having a meaning, and whose coherent significance, in terms of the *concern for being*, precisely constitutes the *world*. And thus, being-in-the-world, in *Sein und Zeit*, is immediately to be *with* others. According to Heidegger, *being-with-others* belongs to the existential *being-there*, *being-in-the-world*.

The phenomenology of Section 26 of *Sein und Zeit* isolates the modalities of that *being-with*. It concerns *others* whose mode of existence—always distinct from that of things, nothing but things, and from that of things ready-to-hand—is the mode of human being-there, sharing the same world, understood precisely in terms of work and around the instrumental order of those things of the world, and thus in which "they are what they do." But the concern-for-being of the human being-there also bears the concern for the other man, the care of one for the other. It is not added onto being-there, but is a constitutive articulation of that *Dasein*. A concern for the other man, a care for his food, drink, clothing, health, and shelter. A care which is not belied by the actual solitude of the solitary or the indifference one may feel for one's fellowman, a solitude and indifference that, being deficient modes of the *for-the-other*, confirm it; just as idleness or unemployment, deficient

modes of existence understood in terms of work, confirm this significance in terms of work.

Thus *being-there*, in which being is always at stake, would appear to
be, in its very authenticity, *being-for-the-other*. The *there* of *being-there* is
world, which is not the point of geometrical space, but the concreteness
of a populated place in which people are *with* one another and *for* one
another. The existential of *Miteinandersein* is a being-together with others in a reciprocity of relationship. Did I go too far, in my opening
remarks, in affirming the peace and love of one's fellowman as an *alternative* to the severity of the authentic?

Yet it is precisely in this relation to others as *Miteinandersein*, signified by *being-in-the-world*, that the human *being-there* in its authenticity
begins to get mixed up with the being of all the others and to understand
itself in terms of the impersonal anonymity of the *"they"* [*On*], to lose
itself in the mediocrity of the everyday or to come under the dictator-
ship of the *"they*," as Heidegger puts it. This *"they*," this "Everyman,"
["Monsieur Tout le Monde"] the impersonal personage, becomes a legislator of morals, fashion and opinion, taste and values. There is a subtle presence of the *"they"* even in its own self-denunciation, suspect in
the unanimity of decisions.

> Thus, the particular Dasein in its everydayness is *disburdened* by
> the "they." Not only that; by thus disburdening it of its Being, the
> "they" accommodates Dasein if Dasein has any tendency to take
> things easily and make them easy. And because "they" constantly
> accommodates the particular Dasein by disburdening it of its
> Being, the "they" retains and enhances its stubborn domination.[3]

Hence the return to the authentic is no longer sought in having
recourse, outside the *"they*," to a substantive and substantial identity of
the *I*, nor through the mediation of some sort of relations that would
reach out toward others through a different path than that of the *with*
and *for*—the *mit*-einander and the *Für*-sorge—which is what is entailed
in *being-in-the-world*. In Heidegger's philosophical project, the relationship to the other is conditioned by *being-in-the-world*, and thus by ontology, by the understanding of "the being of beings" whose *being-in-the-
world* is fundamentally existential. *Eigentlichkeit*—the departure from

the "they"—is recovered through an upheaval, within the everyday existence of the "they" brought about by a resolved and free determination made by *being-there* which is thus *being-for-death*, anticipating death in the courage of anxiety. In the courage of anxiety, not in the fear and evasions of the everyday! Perfect authenticity!

> With death, Dasein stands before itself in its ownmost potentiality-for-being. This is a possibility in which the issue is nothing less than Dasein's Being-in-the world. . . . If Dasein stands before itself as this possibility, it has been *fully* assigned to its ownmost potentiality-for-Being. When it stands before itself in this way, all its relations to any other Dasein have been undone.[4]

An authenticity of the most proper being-able-to-be and a dissolution of all relations with the other! And Heidegger goes on:

> This ownmost non-relational possibility is at the same time the uttermost one.
>   As potentiality-for-being, Dasein cannot outstrip the possibility of death. Death is the possibility of the absolute impossibility of Dasein.[5]

"Ahead-of-itself," "precedence" (*Vorstand*), "unsurpassable precedence" which will be qualified as distinguished (*ausgezeichnete*). An expressive terminology (that would have suited the opening up of "transcendence" through the otherness of a unique without genus, toward the absolute outside—a relation impossible through death), it describes only the structural aspect of concern open to itself "as ahead-of-itself." Concern "has in being-toward-death its most original concreteness." The *Eigentlichkeit* par excellence of *being-there* is not a beyond being.

I have titled my remarks on Heidegger "Dying for . . . ," or "Dying for another," in which certain questions are expressed which seem to me to be posed by his noteworthy work. Here we have ontology through the *being-there* concerned with being, and *being-in-the-world* maintaining a priority and a privilege of *Eigentlichkeit* in relation to care for the other person. A care which is certainly assured, but conditioned by *being-in-the-world*; an approach to the other person certainly, but in terms of occupations and works in the world, without encountering faces, without the death of the other signifying to the *being-there*, the survivor, more than funerary behavior and emotions, and memories. I will not make the naive claim—after having presented a few positions and aspects of *Sein und Zeit*, which are nonetheless remarkable, and after recalling points that have always preoccupied me in these positions—of proposing a "better doctrine." A foolhardy ambition! But perhaps you also know that personal research and, notably, meditation on *Sein und Zeit*, have led me to thoughts which have never lost sight of that primordial book, though I have distanced myself from its thesis on the fundamental priority of ontology. I am not going to substitute these thoughts for the presentation of the Heideggerian ideas that are the main topic of this evening, but I will tell you, as I conclude, what matters to me. Very briefly.

"Dying for," "dying for the other." I also considered calling my remarks "dying together." Despite the separation commonly signified by death and despite the texts of *Sein und Zeit* quoted above in which death, "ownmost potentiality-for-Being," "the most authentic," is also that in which "all relations to any other *Dasein*," to other being-there's, to other men, "have been undone." A biblical verse came to mind—II Samuel 1:23, a verse of the funeral chant of the prophet weeping for the death of King Saul and his son Jonathan in combat: "Saul and Jonathan were lovely and pleasant in their lives, and in their death they were not divided; they were swifter than eagles, they were stronger than lions." As if, contrary to the Heideggerian analysis, in death, all relationship to the other person were not undone. I do not think this verse alludes to "another life" that, after death, can unite those who are no longer there. But neither do I think that these words on "non-separation in death" in the verse amount to nothing more than a metaphorical way of speaking to exalt the love between father and son, which would thus be "stronger than death," and a symbol or sign or image in the impressive simultaneity of their final hours in combat. Or could it be that the terms of this metaphor are more rigorously precise, even telling us the essence of that force of love beyond the quantitative concept of intensity. "Swifter than eagles, stronger than lions"—a surpassing in the human of the animal effort of life, purely life—a surpassing of the *conatus essendi* of life—an opening of the *human* through the living being: of the human, the newness of which would not be reduced to a more intense effort in its "persevering in being"; the human, that, in the *being-there* in which "being was always at stake," would awaken in the guise of responsibility for the other man; the human in which the "for the other" goes beyond the simple *Fürsorge* exercising itself in a world where others, gathered round about things, *are* what they do; the human, in which worry over the death of the other comes before care for self. The humanness of dying for the other would be the very meaning of love in its responsibility for one's fellowman and, perhaps, the primordial inflection of the affective as such. The call to holiness preceding the concern for existing, for being-there and being-in-the-world—utopian, a dis-interestedness more profound than the *with-the-others* or *for-the-others* of the *Fürsorge* involved in the being-in-the world, in which the being of the other equals his occupation and is understood only in terms of "one's things" and vested interest. Care as holiness, which is what Pascal called love without concupiscence. A no-place prior to the *there* of *being-there*, prior to the *Da* of the Dasein, prior to that place in the sun that Pascal feared was "the prototype and beginning of the usurpation of the whole world."[6]

I am not going to overwhelm you with language and special expressions that draw on a whole phenomenology, on a discourse on the face, on the *I*, responsible for the other, whom the face summons forth from the human *being-there* (which it shatters), concerned for its being-in-the-world. Expressions that cannot, after the trials of the twentieth century, be construed as signifying the trite platitudes of a verbose idealism. What they set forth—whatever their speculative audacity—names the seriousness of the human intrigue; the opposite of vanity, the opposite of the vanity of vanities.

"*Sterben für*" is evoked by Heidegger in Section 47 of *Sein und Zeit*.[7] There the philosopher is in search of the existential of *being-for death* and is on his way toward its "*authentic*" meaning in free and courageously anxious anticipation (*Vorweg*), without sharing or association, but "to die for . . . " appears to him only as a "simple sacrifice," and without "death for the other person" being able in truth to release the other person from death, and without challenging the truth of "everyone dies for himself." The ethics of sacrifice does not succeed in shaking the rigor of being and the ontology of the authentic.

Sacrifice cannot find a place for itself in an order divided between the authentic and the unauthentic. Does not the relationship to the other in sacrifice, in which the death of the other preoccupies the human *being-there* before his own death, indicate precisely a beyond ontology—or a before ontology—while at the same time also determining—or revealing—a responsibility for the other, and through that responsibility a human *"I"* that is neither the substantial identity of a subject nor the *Eigentlichkeit* in the "mineness" of being? This would be the *I* of the one who is chosen to answer for his fellowman and is *thus* identical to itself, and *thus* the self. A uniqueness of chosenness! Beyond the humanity that still defines itself as life and *conatus essendi* and concern for being—a dis-interested humanity. The priority of the other over the *I*, by which the human *being-there* is chosen and unique, is precisely the latter's response to the nakedness of the face and its mortality. It is there that the concern for the other's death is realized, and that "dying for him" "dying his death" takes priority over "authentic" death. Not a *post-mortem* life, but the excessiveness of sacrifice, holiness in charity and mercy. This future of death in the present of love is probably one of the original secrets of temporality itself and beyond all metaphor.

entre nous

The idea of the infinite—though it may be named, recognized, and operative, so to speak, only in terms of its mathematical meaning and usage—remains, for reflection, the paradoxical knot that is already tied in religious revelation. The latter, bound from the start in its concreteness to commandments directed toward human beings, is knowledge of a God who, while offering Himself within this openness, also remains absolutely other, or transcendent. Would religion not be the original juncture of circumstances in which the infinite comes to the mind in its ambiguity of truth and mystery? But if that is the case, then can we be sure that the infinite's coming to the mind is a matter of knowledge, a manifestation the essence of which would consist in establishing the order of imma-nence? And above all can we be sure—as a certain consensus and perhaps a venerable tradition tend to say—that immanence is the supreme grace of spiritu-al energy,[1] that the revelation of a God completes itself in the adequacy of truth, in the hold exercised by *thought* [*la pensée*] over *that which is thought in thought* [*le pensée*] and, thus, that meaning or intelligi-bility is an economy in the etymological sense of the word, a house we live in, our home, a certain way of investing, grasping, owning, and enjoying?

The finite thought of man cannot draw from itself the idea of the infinite, according to Descartes, who identifies it with the idea of the perfect and of God. God Himself must have put it into us. But how can this idea be accommodated within finite thought? Regardless of the outcome of the "proof of the existence of God" that Descartes claims to deduce from this putting of the idea of the infinite into us, the coming or the descent or the contraction of the infinite into a *finite* thought names an event that describes the meaning of what is designated by divine existence, rather than the mediate datum of an object adequate or equal to the intention of a knowing, rather than the presence of a being in the world, a being *affirming itself,* that is to say, placing itself firmly on the "unshakable" surface of the earth, beneath the vault of a starry sky. According to a saying of rabbinic wisdom, wherever the exaltation of God is uttered, His humility already proclaims itself.

But the exception of the idea of the infinite implies the awakening of a psyche that cannot be reduced to the pure correlation and the noetic-noematic parallelism which the least prejudiced analysis finds in human thought approached in the context of knowledge. Here is an exception reversing the Aristotelian thesis of a theology reserved for God, Who would be His own and only theologian, the only one capable of thinking Himself, as Pierre Aubenque has emphasized. An exception indicating human thought coalescing precisely as theology! But the *logos* of this theology would differ from theoretical intentionality and the adequacy of thought to that which is thought in thought, which is assured on the basis of the unity of the transcendental apperception of a self sovereign in its exclusive isolation as *cogito,* with its assembling and synthetic reign. An exception to the commonly accepted phenomenology of thought which, in an essential sense, is atheistic precisely as thought equaling the thought that fills and *satis*-fies it, apprehending the datum in the inevitable turning of all passivity of experience into activity of consciousness which agrees to accept what strikes it, which is never violated.

In the idea of the infinite, which as such is the idea of God, the *affection* of the finite by the infinite takes place, beyond the simple negation of the one by the other, beyond the pure contradiction which would oppose and separate them or which would expose the other to the hegemony of the One understood as an "I think." An affection which would have to be described other than as an appearing, other than as a participation in a content, a conception, a comprehension. An irreversible affection of the finite by the infinite. A passivity that is not retrieved in a thematization, but in which—as love and fear of God, or the adoration and bedazzlement Descartes speaks of in the last line of the *Third Meditation*—the idea of God is, from top to bottom, affectivity. This is to be distinguished from the *Befindlichkeit* of *Sein und Zeit*, in which the anxiety of the *Jemeinigkeit* for its finitude of being-toward-death always accompanies the intentionality of the feeling aroused by a being that belongs to the world. The affection of the finite by the infinite is not to be the object of a reduction. It is, with the idea of the infinite, with the theological affection, an emergence from the *Jemeinigkeit* of the *cogito* and its immanence construed as authenticity, toward a thought that thinks more than it thinks, and does better than think. A dis-inter-ested affectivity in which plurality in the guise of *proximity*[2] is in no need of being assembled into the unity of the One—no longer signifies a simple deprivation of coincidence, a pure and simple lack of unity. It is an excellence of love, of sociality and "fear for others" which is not my anxiety for my own death. Transcendence is no longer a failed immanence. It has the sort of excellence proper to Spirit: perfection, or the Good.

The issue of whether this affectivity of adoration and this passivity of bedazzlement can admit of further phenomenological interpretation, or whether they can be attained on the basis of an analysis situated at the level of the interpersonal order and the otherness of the other man, my fellowman, and my responsibility for the other—all this, obviously, is no longer in the province of the Cartesian texts and I will not develop it here.[3] But to do phenomenology is not only to safeguard the signification of language, threatened, in its abstraction or in its isolation, by the subreption, slippage, and substitution of meanings. It is not only to control it by investigating, in reflection, the thoughts it alienates and drives into oblivion. It is especially to research and recall, within the horizons that open up around the first "intentions" of the abstracted datum, the "human" (or interhuman) "plot" that is the concreteness of its unthought, which is the necessary "setting," the abstractions of which have broken off into the said of words and propositions. It is to research the human or interhuman plot as the fabric of ultimate intelligibility. And that, perhaps, is also the path of return of wisdom from heaven to earth.

That the idea of the infinite in its passivity should not be understood as the domain of uncertainty in human finitude, which is preoccupied with itself and incapable of embracing the infinite, and in which the fact of being struck by God would be only a makeshift of finitude—this is probably the misinterpretation of the irreducible originality of otherness and transcendence, and a purely negative interpretation of ethical proximity and love, the stubbornness of saying them in terms of immanence, as if possession and fusion—the ideal of intentional consciousness—exhausted spiritual energy. That the proximity of the infinite and the sociality it initiates and commands may be *better* than coincidence and oneness, that, through its very plurality, sociality has its own irreducible excellence which cannot be said in terms of richness without it reverting to a statement of poverty; that the relationship or the non-indifference to the other does not consist, for the other, in converting to the same, that religion is not a moment in the economy of being, that love is not a demigod—this is certainly also what is meant by the idea of the infinite in us or the humanness of man understood as theology. But perhaps it is already indicated in the very awakening to the insomnia of the psyche before the finitude of being, wounded by the infinite, is moved to withdraw into a hegemonic and atheistic *I*.

twenty

QUESTION: *Your first philosophical works concern phenomenology. Was your reflection formed exclusively through contact with that tradition?*

EMMANUEL LEVINAS: I published one of the first books on phenomenology to appear in France, and a bit later, wrote one of the first articles on Heidegger. This is a purely chronological fact, but one I enjoy recalling. I have related elsewhere[1] my encounter with phenomenology during my training in Strasbourg, at the excellent Institute of Philosophy, a sacred place, with professors bearing the names Pradines, Carteron, Charles Blondel, and Halbwachs—Maurice Halbwachs, a member of the Resistance, who did not come back from deportation. On the other hand, I have hardly emphasized the importance (which was essential for me) of the relationship—always present in the background of the teaching of those masters—to Bergson.

Bergson is hardly quoted now. We have forgotten the major philosophical event he was for the French university and which he remains for world philosophy, and the role he played in the constitution of the problematic of modernity. Isn't the ontological thematization by Heidegger of *being* as distinguished from *beings*, the investigation of being in its verbal sense, already at work in the Bergsonian notion of *durée*, which is not reducible to the substantiality of being or the substantivity of beings? Can we continue to present Bergson according to the alternative suggested by the banal formula in which the philosophy of becoming is opposed to the philosophies of being? Do we not find, moreover, in Bergson's last works, a critique of technical rationalism, which is so important in Heidegger's work? *Creative Evolution* is a plea for a spirituality freeing itself from a mechanistic humanism. And in the *Two Sources of Morality and Religion*, intuition, i.e., *life* itself or the lived of "profound time," consciousness, and knowledge of *durée*, are interpreted as a relationship with the other and with God.

Affection and love are concrete in these relationships! I feel close to certain Bergsonian themes: to *durée*, in which the spiritual is no longer reduced to an event of pure "knowledge," but would be the transcendence of a relationship with someone, with an other: love, friendship, sympathy. A proximity that cannot be reduced to spatial categories or to modes of objectification and thematization. There is, in my view, in the refusal to seek the meaning of reality in the the persistence of solids, and in Bergson's reversion to the *becoming* of things, something like a statement of *verbal being*, of *event-being*. Bergson is the source of an entire complex of interrelated contemporary philosophical ideas; it is to him, no doubt, that I owe my modest speculative initiatives. We owe a great deal to the mark left by Bergsonism in the teachings and readings of the twenties.

Q: *Let's get back to phenomenology. It was also in the course of your training at Strasbourg that you encountered phenomenology. From Mlle. Pfeiffer, who read* Logical Investigations, *which had not yet been translated at that time, you learned who Husserl was; after which you translated* Cartesian Meditations *with her. Your first article in* Revue philosophique *in 1929 dealt with Edmund Husserl's* Ideas *(his 1913 work). And so it came about that in 1928, in Fribourg, you attended Husserl's last semester of teaching and Heidegger's first. How do you now interpret the passage from the founder of the phenomenological movement to his disciple, who is considered to be the more original?*

E.L.: What do you mean by this passage? Is it the fact of *one* or the *other* speaking on phenomenology, or the fact that Husserl's readers were prepared to read Heidegger? There was indeed, for Husserlians reading *Sein und Zeit* in 1927, when it first came out, both an impression of innovation in the enquiry and its horizons, and the certainty that we were approaching that marvel of analyses and projects brilliantly prepared by the phenomenological work of Husserl.

Husserl's own criticisms did not come quickly. From the beginning, the master was dazzled by the wealth of the phenomenological analyses in *Sein und Zeit*, which were still reconcilable with the moves, virtualities and procedures characteristic of the Husserlian method, despite the unexpected perspectives they brilliantly open up, and though some of Heidegger's inspiration may have come from elsewhere. It was only later, on re-reading the book, that Husserl understood or perceived those distances. We apparently have access to marginal annotations which indicate that critical reading. Husserl remained convinced that Heidegger had been his most gifted disciple, but always remained cognizant of the disharmony. Of the one he had deliberately chosen as his successor, he said to Professor Max Müller: "I have always been strongly impressed by Heidegger, but never influenced."

Q: *After Victor Farias's book,[2] a discussion of Heidegger's Nazism took the center of the media stage in France. Whatever one may think of the productivity of that polemic, the question it is tempting to ask you is: Could it have been anticipated since the early discovery of Heidegger's work?*

E.L.: Almost everything Farias said was known. In France, Heidegger's political positions were known even before 1933.[3] Right after the war, there were discussions in Paris that had become overly subtle or languishing, and that Farias rekindled. In 1930, it was hard to foresee the temptations National Socialism could represent for a Heidegger! In my very recent remarks at the colloquium organized by the Collège International de Philosophie—but before Farias's book—I recalled this moral problem, despite my admiration for *Sein und Zeit*.[4] After Farias, a few details were specified, but nothing in it is essentially original.

The essential thing is the work itself or, at least, *Sein und Zeit*, which remains one of the greatest books in the history of philosophy, even for those who reject or dispute it. In its pages there is certainly no formulation specifically traceable to the theses of National Socialism, but the construction includes ambiguous passages in which they might find accommodation. I would mention, for my part, the notion, primordial in this system, of authenticity, of *Eigentlichkeit*—conceived in terms of the "mine," of everything personal, in terms of *Jemeinigkeit*, an original contraction of the me in mineness (*Sein und Zeit*, section 9), in terms of a *belonging to self* and *for self* in their inalienable self-belonging. It is indeed surprising that—in the anthropology of *Sein und Zeit*, in which all articulations characteristic of human concreteness, beyond the traditional attributes of the "reasonable animal," are reduced, as *"existentials,"* to the ontological level—there is no philosophy of commercial exchange, in which the desires and cares of men confront one another, and in which money (which would be a simple *Zuhandenheit*? [readiness-to-hand]) is a means of measurement making equality, peace, and "a fair price" possible in this confrontation, despite and before its *Verfallen* [fall] into an enslaving capitalism and Mammon. Authenticity, based on the notion of "mineness," must remain pure of all influence undergone, without admixture, without owing anything to anyone, outside of everything that would compromise the noninterchangeability, the uniqueness of that *I* of "mineness." An *I* to preserve above all from the vulgar banality of the indefinite pronoun "one" in which the *I* risks degradation, even if the vehement contempt inspired by its mediocre banality may quickly spread its condemnation to the rightful portion of commonality present in the universality of democracy.

I learned quite recently that the philosopher Adorno has already denounced that jargon of authenticity. That jargon, however, expresses a "nobility," that of blood and sword. It therefore presents other dangers in a philosophy without vulgarity. The uniqueness of the human *I*, which nothing should alienate, is here thought in terms of death: that everyone dies for himself. An inalienable identity in dying! To sacrifice oneself for another does not make the other immortal. The *I* exists in the world in relationship with others, but no one can truly die for anyone else. And in this existing-toward-death, in this *being-for-death*, the lucidity of anguish yields to nothingness without vainly escaping it in fear. An originary authenticity, but with nothing more, in which, for Heidegger, all "relations with others" are dissolved or "canceled," and in which the meaningfulness of *being-there* is cut short. Fearsome authenticity! You can see what I would reject.

Would that make me a friend of the inauthentic? But is the authenticity of the *I*, its uniqueness, contingent upon that unadulterated possessive "mineness," of self for itself, that proud virility "more precious than life," more authentic than love or than the concern for another? A uniqueness that is not achieved under the difference manifested by someone or other as distinct from the individuals belonging to the extension of the same logical genus, for, as members of this extension, they are precisely not unique in their genus.

Uniqueness seems to me to assume meaning in terms of the irreplaceability that comes to, or returns to, the *I* in the concreteness of a responsibility for the other: a responsibility that, from the start, devolves upon the *I* in the very perception of the other, but as if in that representation, in that presence, it already preceded that perception, as if it were already there, older than the present, and hence, a responsibility that cannot be refused, of an order alien to knowledge; as if, for all eternity, the *I* were the first one called to this responsibility; nontransferable and thus unique, thus *I*, the chosen hostage, the chosen one. An ethics of the meeting—sociality. For all eternity, one man is answerable for an other. From unique to unique. Whether he looks at me or not, he "regards me"; I must answer for him. I call face that which thus in another concerns the *I*—concerns me—reminding me, from behind the countenance he puts on in his portrait, of his abandonment, his defenselessness and his mortality, and his appeal to my ancient responsibility, as if he were unique in the world—beloved. An appeal of the face of my fellowman, which, in its ethical urgency, postpones or cancels the obligations the "summoned *I*" has toward itself and in which the concern for the death of the other can be more important to the *I* than its concern as an *I* for itself. The authenticity of the *I*, in my view, is this listening by the first one called, this attention to the other without subrogation, and thus already faithfulness to values despite one's own mortality. The possibility of sacrifice as a meaning of the human adventure! Possibility of the meaningful, despite death, though it be without resurrection! The ultimate meaning of love without concupiscence, and of an *I* no longer hateful.

The terminology I use sounds religious: I speak of the uniqueness of the *I* on the basis of a *chosenness* that it would be difficult for it to escape, for it constitutes it; of a debt in the *I*, older than any loan. This way of approaching an idea by asserting the concreteness of a situation in which it originally assumes meaning seems to me essential to phenomenology. It is presupposed in everything I have just said.

In all these reflections, what emerges is the valorization of holiness as the most profound upheaval of being and thought, through the advent of man. As opposed to the interestedness of being, to its primordial essence which is *conatus essendi,* a perseverance in the face of everything and everyone, a persistence in being-there—the human (love of the other, responsibility for one's fellowman, an eventual dying-for-the-other, sacrifice even as far as the mad thought in which dying for the other can concern me well before, and more than, my own death)—the human signifies the beginning of a new rationality beyond being. A rationality of the Good higher than all essence.[5] An intelligibility of kindness. This possibility, through sacrifice, of giving meaning to the other and to the world which, though without me, still counts for me, and for which I am answerable (the great dissolution, in dying, of relationships with everyone else, as stated by Heidegger in Section 50 of *Sein und Zeit,* notwithstanding) is certainly not survival. It is an ecstasis toward a future which *counts* for the *I* and to which it is answerable: but a future *without-me* (both meaningful and future) which is no longer the to-come of a protended present.

These analyses, reduced to their primordial data, do not exhaust the phenomenology of otherness. I can only mention the problematic I glimpsed forty years ago in a little book titled *Time and the Other,*[6] through reflections on eroticism and paternity, and in which meditation on the ambiguity of sexuality and the love without concupiscence of holiness opens up perspectives to be explored.

Q: *This definition of holiness places us in the absolute. Granted, what you have stated here concerns an ethical requirement via your insistence on the notion of gratuitousness, not reward. But in emphasizing that aspect, in yourself singling out the aspect of impossibility, aren't you afraid that your conception will be criticized as utopian, and you yourself, as a philosopher, for neglecting the concomitant political exigencies of this requirement? This is, I take it, where the idea of a "third" intervenes?*

E.L.: The *I* can find the requirement of what I call responsibility for the other, or love without concupiscence, only within itself; it is in its "here I am" of an *I,* in its noninterchangeable uniqueness of one chosen. It is originally without reciprocity, which would risk compromising its gratuitousness or grace or unconditional charity. But the order of justice of individuals responsible for one another does not arise in order to restore that reciprocity between the *I* and its other; it arises from the fact of the third who, next to the one who is an other to me, is "another other" to me.

The *I*, precisely as responsible for the other and the third, cannot remain indifferent to their interactions, and in the charity for the one, cannot withdraw its love from the other. The self, the *I*, cannot limit itself to the incomparable uniqueness of each one, which is expressed in the face of each one. Behind the unique singularities, one must perceive the individuals of a *genus*, one must compare them, judge them, and condemn them. There is a subtle ambiguity of the individual and the unique, the personal and the absolute, the mask and the face. This is the hour of inevitable justice—required, however, by charity itself.

The hour of justice, of the comparison between incomparables who are grouped by human species and genus. And the hour of institutions empowered to judge, of states within which institutions are consolidated, of Universal Law which is always *dura lex*, and of citizens equal before the law.

These chosen ones, above commonality, must, like all things, find a place for themselves in the hierarchy of concepts; there must be a reciprocity of rights and duties. To the Bible—the first to teach the inimitable singularity, the "semelfactive" uniqueness of each soul, there must be added the Greek writings, expert in species and genera. It is the hour of the Western World! The hour of justice—required, however, by charity. To resume what I have said: It is in the name of that responsibility for the other, in the name of that mercy, that kindness to which the face of the other man appeals, that the entire discourse of justice is set in motion, whatever the limitations and rigors of the *dura lex* it may bring to the infinite benevolence toward the other. Unforgettable infinity, rigors always to be mitigated. Justice always to be made more knowing in the name, the memory, of the original kindness of man toward his other, in which, in an ethical dis-inter-estedness—word of God!—the inter-ested effort of brute being persevering in being is suspended. A justice always to be perfected against its own harshness.

That is perhaps the very excellence of democracy, whose fundamental liberalism corresponds to the ceaseless deep remorse of justice: legislation always unfinished, always resumed, a legislation open to the better. It attests to an ethical excellence and its origin in kindness from which, however, it is distanced—always a bit less perhaps—by the necessary calculations imposed by a multiple sociality, calculations constantly starting over again. Thus, in the empirical life of the good under the freedom of revisions, there would be a progress of reason. A bad conscience of justice! It knows it is not as just as the kindness that instigates it is good. But when it forgets that, it risks sinking into a totalitarian and Stalinist regime, and losing, in ideological deductions, the gift of inventing new forms of human coexistence.

Vassily Grossman, in *Life and Fate*[7]—such an impressive book, coming right after the major crises of our century—goes even further. He thinks that the "small goodness" from one person to his fellowman is lost and deformed as soon as it seeks organization and universality and system, as soon as it opts for doctrine, a treatise of politics and theology, a party, a state, and even a church. Yet it remains the sole refuge of the good in being. Unbeaten, it undergoes the violence of evil, which, as small goodness, it can neither vanquish nor drive out. A little kindness going only from man to man, not crossing distances to get to the places where events and forces unfold! A remarkable utopia of the good or the secret of its beyond.

Utopia, transcendence. Inspired by love of one's fellowman, reasonable justice is bound by legal strictures and cannot equal the kindness that solicits and inspires it. But kindness, emerging from the infinite resources of the singular self, responding without reasons or reservations to the call of the face, can divine ways to approach that suffering other—without, however, contradicting the verdict. I have always admired the talmudic apologue that, in the tractate *Rosh Hashanah* 17b, is presented as an attempt to reduce the apparent contradiction between two verses of Scripture: Deuteronomy 10:17 and Numbers 6:25. The first text teaches the rigor and strict impartiality of the justice demanded by God: all *regarding of persons* is excluded in it. Numbers 6:25 speaks otherwise. It foresees the luminous Face of God turned toward the man undergoing judgment, illuminating him with Its light, welcoming him in grace. The contradiction is resolved in the wisdom of Rabbi Akiva. According to this eminent rabbinical scholar, the first text concerns justice as it develops before the verdict, and the second specifies the possibilities of the after-verdict. Justice and charity. This after-verdict, with its possibilities of mercy, still fully belongs—with full legitimacy—to the work of justice. Should we then think that the death penalty doesn't belong by the same token to the categories of justice?

The entire life of a nation—beyond the formal sum of individuals standing *for themselves*, that is to say, living and struggling for their land, their place, their Da-sein—carries within itself (concealed, revealed, or at least occasionally caught sight of) men who, before all loans, have debts, owe their fellowman, are responsible—chosen and unique—and in this responsibility want peace, justice, reason. Utopia! This way of understanding the meaning of the human—the very dis-inter-estedness of their being—does not begin by thinking of the care men take of the places where they want to be-in-order-to-be. I am thinking above all of the *for-the-other* in them, in which, in the adventure of a possible holiness, the human interrupts the pure obstinacy of being and its wars. I cannot forget Pascal's thought: "My place in the sun. There is the beginning and the prototype of the usurpation of the whole world."[8]

Q: *"Ethics would be the reminder of that famous debt I have never contracted." You have developed that idea that my responsibility is recalled to me in the face of the other man. But is every man that "other" man? Is there not sometimes a desertion of meaning, faces of brutes?*

E.L.: Jean-Toussaint Desanti asked a young Japanese who was commenting on my works during a thesis defense if an SS man has what I mean by a face. A very disturbing question which calls, in my opinion, for an affirmative answer. An affirmative answer that is painful each time! During the Barbie trial, I could say: Honor to the West! Even with regard to those whose "cruelty" has never stood trial, justice continues to be exercised. The defendant, deemed innocent, has the right to a defense, to consideration. It is admirable that justice worked that way, despite the apocalyptic atmosphere (*les Dossiers du Globe*, p. 21).

It must also be said that in my way of expressing myself the word *face* must not be understood in a narrow way. This possibility for the human of signifying in its uniqueness, in the humility of its nakedness and mortality, the Lordship of its recall—word of God—of my responsibility for it, and of my chosenness *qua* unique to this responsibility, can come from a bare arm sculpted by Rodin.

In *Life and Fate*, Grossman tells how in Lubyanka, in Moscow, before the infamous gate where one could convey letters or packages to friends and relatives arrested for "political crimes" or get news of them, people formed a line, each reading on the nape of the person in front of him the feelings and hopes of his misery.

Q: *And the nape is a face . . .*

E.L.: Grossman isn't saying that the nape is a face, but that all the weakness, all the mortality, all the naked and disarmed mortality of the other can be read from it. He doesn't say it that way, but the face can assume meaning on what is the "opposite" of the face! The face, then, is not the color of the eyes, the shape of the nose, the ruddiness of the cheeks, etc.

Q: *One last question: what is your major preoccupation today in your work?*

E.L.: The essential theme of my research is the deformalization of the notion of time. Kant says it is the form of all experience. All human experience does in fact take on a temporal form. The transcendental philosophy descended from Kant filled that form with a sensible content coming from experience or, since Hegel, that form has led dialectically toward a content. These philosophers never required, for the constitution of that form of temporality itself, a *condition* in a certain *conjuncture* of "matter" or events, in a meaningful content somehow prior to form. The constitution of time in Husserl is also a constitution of time in terms of an already effective consciousness of presence in its disappearance and in its "retention," its immanence, and its anticipation— disappearance and immanence that already imply what is to be established, without any indication being given about the privileged empirical situation to which those modes of disappearance in the past and imminence in the future would be attached.

Hence, what seems remarkable in Heidegger is precisely the fact of posing the question: What are the situations or circumstances characteristic of the concrete existence to which the passation of the past, the presentification of the present, and the futurition of the future—called *ecstases*—are essentially and originally attached? The fact of being, without having chosen to do so, of dealing with possibles always already begun, without us—an ecstasis of "always already"; the fact of a control over things, near them in representation or knowing—an ecstasis of the present; the fact of existing-toward-death—an ecstasis of the future. This, more or less (for there is a lot more to that philosophy) is the perspective opened up by Heidegger.

Franz Rosenzweig, for his part, and without resorting to the same terminology or referring to the same situations, also sought those "privileged circumstances" of the lived in which temporality is constituted. He thought the past in terms of the idea and religious consciousness of creation; the present in terms of listening to and receiving revelation; and the future in terms of the hope of redemption, thus raising those biblical references of thought to the level of the conditions of temporality itself. The biblical references are claimed as modes of original human consciousness, common to an immense part of humanity. Rosenzweig's philosophical audacity consists precisely of referring the past to the creation and not the creation to the past, the present to revelation and not revelation to the present, the future to redemption and not redemption to the future.

Perhaps what I have told you about the obligation toward the other prior to all contract (a reference to a past that was never present!) and about dying for the other (a reference to a future that will never be my present) will seem to you, after this last evocation of Heidegger and Rosenzweig, like a preface to possible research.

Notes

Author's Preface

"Preface" was published under the title "De l'être à l'autre" in *le Temps de la responsabilité*, conversations on ethics conducted by Frédéric Lenoir, Fayard, 1990.

   1. [*Philosophia* means love of wisdom.—Trans.]

   2. [The French *étant*, Levinas's equivalent of Heideg-ger's *das Seiende*, has been translated as "a being" or "beings" (but never just "being") throughout.—Trans.]

   3. [Here Levinas is arguing from language. The pronoun *se* in French is reflexive; the object of self doubling back upon itself. Reflexives are very frequent in French, comprising many verbs that in English would be intransitive.—Trans.]

   4. [Latin for "the effort to be."—Trans.]

ONE. Is Ontology Fundamental?

"Is Ontology Fundamental?" appeared the in *Revue de métaphysique et de morale*, No. 1, January–March 1951.

   1. [Levinas's term is "embarqué," doubtless an allusion to Pascal's famous injunction to his worldly contemporaries that it is in their interest to "wager" that God exists, since in any case they must bet one way or the other. They are already "launched" into life, so that to refuse to bet is still to bet.—Trans.]

   2. See my remarks on this subject in *Esquisse pour une histoire de "l'existentialisme,"* [1947] Jean Wahl, Éditions de l'Arche, 95–96. [See J. Wahl's *A Short History of Existentialism*, trans. F. Williams and S. Maron (New York: Philosophical Library, 1979), 47–53.—Trans.]

   3. [See Heidegger's *Being and Time*, sections 15–18.—Trans.]

TWO. The *I* and the Totality

"The *I* and the Totality" appeared in *Revue de métaphysique et de morale*, 59 (No. 4, October–December 1954): 353–73.

   1. [The association made by Levinas between the living being and the

"cynic" is an important one. It has nothing to do with the modern, informal use of the term, but refers specifically to the iconoclastic, ruggedly self-reliant, and perhaps even "canine" characteristics (the Greek term is said to be derived from the word for dog) of the lifestyle of the Greek school of philosophy of the Cynics, forerunners of the Stoics.—Trans.]

2. [Condillac hypothesizes a human being in the form of a statue, adding one sense at a time, the first being that of smell. "*It is, in relation to itself, only the odors that it smells.* If we present it with a rose, to us it will be a statue that smells a rose; but to itself, it will be the smell itself of this flower." *Philosophical Writings of Etienne Bonnot, Abbé de Condillac*, trans. F. Philip and H. Lane (Hillsdale, N.J.; London: Lawrence Erlbaum Associates, 1982), p. 175—Trans.]

3. See *Phaedrus* 275bcd.

4. [I have translated *travail* as "labor" and *oeuvre* as "work" throughout. It should be noted that Levinas's use of the term *oeuvre* often denotes (as here) a movement toward the other that does not return to the same. For more specifics, see Levinas's *Humanisme de l'autre homme* (Montpellier: Fata Morgana, 1972), 42–48, where the term is often capitalized.—Trans.]

5. See, however, the remarkable analysis by Paul Claudel in *Le Figaro Littéraire*, March 10, 1951.

THREE. Lévy-Bruhl and Contemporary Philosophy

"Levy-Bruhl and Contemporary Philosophy" appeared in *Revue philosophique de la France et de l'étranger*, 147 (No. 4, October–December 1957): 556–569.

1. "I have been able to account for several facts which up till now have either been unexplained. . . . " *Primitive Mentality*, trans. L. A. Clare (New York: Macmillan, 1923), 13. [This translation will henceforth be referred to as *PM*. I have sometimes modified Clare's translation slightly.—Trans.] *La Mentalité primitive* (Paris: Librairie Félix Alcan, 1922), iii. [This work, the original French version, will henceforth be referred to as *MP*.—Trans.]

2. *The Notebooks on Primitive Mentality*, trans. Peter Riviere (Oxford: Basil Blackwell, 1975); *Les Carnets de Lucien Lévy-Bruhl* (Paris: Presses Universitaires de France, 1949). [The Notebooks will henceforth be abbreviated as *NB*, and *Carnets* as *CN*.—Trans.]

3. *NB*, 125–127 and passim; *CN*, 164–166 and passim.

4. *NB*, 57; *CN*, 72.

5. *How Natives Think*, trans. Lilian A. Clare (Salem, N.H.: Ayer: 1984), 36, 37; *Les Functions mentales dans les Sociétés inférieures* (Paris: Alcan, 1910), 28, 29. [Henceforth the translation, which we have altered slightly, will be referred to as *HN*, and the French as *FM*.—Trans.]

6. *HN*, 36, 37; *FM*, 28, 29.

7. *PM*, 59; *MP*, 47.

8. *NB*, 106; *CN*, 138. [The reference to fingers actually occurs on *CN*

139–140, *NB* 107.—Trans.]

9. *NB*, 192; *CN*, 250–251.

10. *PM*, 37; *MP*, 19.

11. *PM*, 38; *MP*, 21.

12. *NB*, 18; *CN*, 22.

13. *PM*, 91; *MP*, 86.

14. *PM*, 307; *MP*, 350. Moreover, the fact of their being well-made instru ments does not require representation, but simply a manual intuition (*PM*, 44: *MP*, 518) which Lévy-Bruhl allows as being independent of representation.

15. *PM*, 32; *MP*, 14; and passim in the six works devoted to primitive mer tality.

16. *NB*, 51; *CN*, 64.

17. *NB*, 71; *CN*, 92.

18. *NB*, 103; *CN*, 134.

19. *NB*, 193; *CN*, 251.

20. *NB*, 53–54, 59; *CN*, 68, 75.

21. *PM*, 68; *MP*, 52.

22. *NB*, 27; *CN*, 34.

23. *PM*, 60 and passim; *MP*, 48 and passim.

24. *PM*, 136; *MP*, 143.

25. *PM*, 198; *MP*, 219.

26. *PM*, 203; *MP*, 225.

27. *PM*, 197; *MP*, 218.

28. *NB*, 59; *CN*, 75.

29. On this point and on the proximity between the time of primitives and Bergsonian *durée*, as well as on what would be called "lived space" in modern terms, cf. *PM*, 93–96, 208–209ff, and passim; *MP*, 90–93, 231ff, and passim. As in Heidegger, the space of perception and its concrete properties take precedence over Euclidean space and its geometrical properties (*PM*, 208–209; cf. also 445; *MP*, 232; cf. also 520).

30. *PM*, 429; *MP*, 500.

31. *PM*, 429; *MP*, 500.

32. *NB*, 43; *CN*, 55.

33. *PM*, 63; *MP*, 81.

34. *NB*, 83, my emphasis; *CN*, 108.

35. *NB*, 100–101, 126, and 179–180; *CN*, 131, 165, and 234.

36. *NB*, 75 and 81; *CN*, 98 and 106.

37. *NB*, 83; *CN*, 107.

FOUR. A Man-God?

"A Man-God?" This paper was presented during the Week of Catholic Intellectuals held in Paris in April 1968, and published the same year under the title *Qui est Jésus-Christ?* in Editions Desclée de Brouwer, whom we thank.

1. [See 2 Kings 19:12.—Trans.]

2. [French, *"méontologique."* Meontology is the study of nothingness.—Trans.]

FIVE. A New Rationality: On Gabriel Marcel

"A New Rationality: On Gabriel Marcel" is an address delivered by Emmanuel Levinas on January 13, 1975, at the initial meeting of the Gabriel Marcel association.

1. [Bergson maintained that all "disorder" was but an order misunderstood or overlooked. See his *Oeuvres* (Paris: Presses Universitaires de France, 1970), 694, 1338.—Trans.]

2. [An allusion to the difficulties experienced by professors in France in conducting lecture courses in large amphitheaters during and after the student uprisings in May 1968. The riots began at the Université de Nanterre, in the western suburbs of Paris, where Levinas had begun teaching the previous year.—Trans.]

3. [That is, Gabriel Marcel's *Journal Métaphysique* (1914–1923); *Metaphysical Journal*, trans. Bernard Wall (Chicago: Henry Regnery, 1952).—Trans.]

4. [*Metaphysical Journal*, 210–11. Translation slightly altered.—Trans.]

5. [The French text of *Entre nous* has "non-différence" rather than "non-indifférence." This appears to be an error, since (1) the preceding paragraph contains the term "non-indifférence," (2) Levinas refers to a double negation in the term, and (3) Levinas's Foreword to *Noms Propres*, which was published shortly after this address was delivered at the first meeting of the Association Gabriel Marcel and which contains the same passage almost verbatim has "non-in-différence."—Trans.]

SIX. Hermeneutics and the Beyond

"Hermeneutics and the Beyond" was published by the Istituto di Studi Filosofici, Rome, 1977.

1. [Perhaps an echo of Augustine's "interior intimo meo." *Cf. St. Augustine's Confessions*, I, 2 vols. (Cambridge: Harvard Univ. Press, Loeb Edit., 1977), 120.—Trans.]

2. Perhaps it has no meaning in the ontological account one gives of it, since it is a question of a *beyond-being*.

3. We write essance with an *a* to express the act or the event or the process of the *esse*, the act of the verb *to be*.

4. Husserl, *Phänomenologische Psychologie*, in *Gesammelte Werke*, vol. 9 (The Hague: Martinus Nijhoff, Collection *Husserliana*, 1962), 384–85. My emphasis.

5. Husserl, *Cartesian Meditations*, trans. D. Cairns (The Hague: Martinus Nijhoff, 1973), 12; *Méditations Cartesiennes* (Paris: Vrin, 1969), 10. [Levinas quotes Gabreille Peiffer's 1931 translation, in which he himself collaborated. (Levinas translated the fifth and sixth Meditation.) Since Cairns's translation is rather different from Peiffer's, I have chosen to translate her version in the text. Cairn's translation is: "Evidence is . . . an "*experiencing*" of something that is, and is thus."—Trans.]

6. [The French is "maintenance." It is related to both "maintenant" (now) and "maintenir" (maintain; but both pointing back to the Latin "to hold in the hand"). I have tried to suggest this conjunction of meanings in English by the word "manifestation," but it is at best only an approximation.—Trans.]

7. [Levinas's "*âme égale*" is the literal translation of the Latin "aequus animus" or "even mind," the Stoic ideal.—Trans.]

8. ["Originality" in the sense of genuineness or authenticity. As the latter part of the sentence makes clear, Levinas is here thinking in Husserlian terms of what is given "originarily" or "primordially."—Trans.]

9. [This Husserlian term (German "*Appräsentation*") indicates the modality of perception by which we may be said to perceive the hidden side of visible objects and, more pertinently here, other minds through their bodies.—Trans.]

10. I will not reiterate here my analysis of the ethical relationship in which language is born. I have described the *fission* of the *I* before another person to which it responds beyond all involvement, infinitely, as a hostage, bearing witness, through that responsibility, to the Immemorial, on the hither side of time; bearing witness to the Infinite, which, having been witnessed, does not spring forth in the form of objectivity. Witness in terms of the ethical relationship which, unique in its own kind, does not refer to a previous experience, i.e., to intentionality. See my *Autrement qu'être ou au-delà de l'essence*, 179 et seq. [*Otherwise than Being or Beyond Essence*, trans. Alphonso Lingis (The Hague: Martinus Nijhoff, 1981), 140ff—Trans.]; my article "Dieu et la philosophie," *Le Nouveau commerce*, No. 30-31 [in *Collected Philosophical Papers*, trans. A. Lingis (Dortrecht: Martinus Nijhoff, 1987), 153-73—Trans.]; and my lecture at the Castelli Colloquium 1972, titled "Vérité du dévoilement et vérité du témoignage" in *Actes du Colloque sur Le Témoignage* (Paris: Aubier, 1972), 101-10.

SEVEN. Philosophy and Awakening

"Philosophy and Awakening" was presented at the Colloquium of Chantilly in September 1976, and constituted the substance of a presentation to the Centre d'Etudes des Religions of the Faculté des Lettres et de Philosophie of the University of Gand (March 9, 1977) and to the International Center for Advanced Research in Phenomenology in Pérouse, at the Monastery of Monteripido (August 10, 1977). It was published in *Les études philosophiques*, No. 3 (July–September 1977): 307-17.

1. [Deuteronomy 32:15. This apparently passing biblical reference in fact dominates the entire passage that follows, down to and including the word "kicked" (in rebellion), which occurs in the same verse of Deuteronomy.—Trans.]

2. See *Phänomenologishe Psychologie*, in *Gesammelte Werke*, vol. 9 (The Hague: Martinus Nijhoff, Collection *Husserliana*, 1962).

3. Ibid., 209.

4. Descartes' *Meditations*, in *Descartes, Spinoza* (Chicago: Encyclopaedia Britannica, Great Books of the Western World Series, no. 31, 1952), 88–89.

EIGHT. Useless Suffering

"Useless Suffering" was published in the *Giornale di Metatisica* 4 (January–April 1982): 13–26.

1. [The French "mal," having a broad semantic range, has been translated in this article as "woe," or "evil," according to context.—Trans.]

2. See the article by Dr Escoffier-Lambiotte in *Le Monde*, April 4, 1981: "Le premier centre français de traitement de la douleur a été inauguré à l'"hôpital Cochin" ["First French Center for Treatment of Pain Opens at Cochin Hospital"].

3. On this point I refer the reader to Philippe Nemo's fine book, *Job et l'Excès du Mal [Job and the Excess of Evil]* (Paris: Grasset, 1978). Suffering's very resistance to synthesis and order is interpreted as the rupture of pure immanence—in which, essentially, the psychism is enclosed—both as the event of transcendence, and even as an interpellation of God. See also my analysis of this book, "Transcendance et Mal," [Transcendence and Evil] in *Le Nouveau Commerce* 41 (1978): 55–75. [The French text is included in Levinas's *De Dieu qui vient à l'idée* (Paris: J. Vrin, 1989 [1982]), 189–207, and is available in English as "Transcendence and Evil" in *E. Levinas, Collected Philosophical Papers*, trans. A. Lingis (Dordrecht: Martinus Nijhoff, Phaenomenologica 100, 1987), 175–186.

4. There is a talmudic dialogue or apologue (tractate Berakhot of the *Babylonian Talmud*, 5b) which reflects the conception of the radical evil of suffering, its intrinsic and uncompensated despair, its imprisonment within itself, and its turning to the other, to medication *exterior* to the immanent structure of suffering. Rav Hiyya bar Abba falls ill and Rav Yohanan comes to visit him. He asks him: "Are your sufferings fitting to you?" "Neither they nor the compensations they promise." "Give me your hand," the visitor of the ailing man then says. And the visitor lifts the ailing man from his couch. But then Rav Yohanan himself falls ill and is visited by Rav Hanina. Same question: "Are your sufferings fitting to you?" Same response: "Neither they nor compensations they promise." "Give me your hand," says Rav Hanina, and he lifts Rav Yohanan from his couch. Question: Could not Rav Yohanan lift himself by himself?

Answer: The prisoner could not break free from his confinement by himself.

5. This suffering *in me* is so radically mine that it cannot become the subject of any preaching. It is as suffering *in me* and not as suffering in general that *welcome* suffering—attested to in the spiritual tradition of humanity—can signify a true idea: the expiatory suffering of the just who suffers for others, the suffering that illuminates, the suffering that is sought after by Dostoyevsky's characters. I think also of the Jewish religious tradition that is familiar to me, of the "I am love-sick" of the *Song of Songs*, of the suffering about which certain talmudic texts speak and which they name "yissurim shel ahavah," suffering through love, to which is joined the theme of expiation for others. This suffering is often described at the limit of "its usefulness." See note 4, above, in which, in the test of the just, suffering is also what "does not fit me." "Neither it, nor the 'recompense' attached to it."

6. [Levinas appears to be availing himself of an etymological connotation of this Latin-based verb: *exasperare* from *ex* (entirely) and *asperare* (to make rough).—Trans.]

7. Maurice Blanchot, who is known for his lucid and critical attention to literature and events, notes somewhere: "How can one philosophize, how write in the memory of Auschwitz, of those who have said to us sometimes in notes buried near the crematoria: 'Know what has happened,' 'Do not forget,' and, at the same time, 'You will never know'?" I think that all the dead of the Gulag and all the other places of torture in our political century are present when one speaks of Auschwitz. [These words of Blanchot appear in his article "Our Clandestine Companion," trans. D. Allison, in *Face to Face with Levinas*, ed. R. A. Cohen (Albany: State University of New York Press, 1986), 50.—Trans.]

8. [Emil Fackenheim, *God's Presence in History: Jewish Affirmations and Philosophical Reflections after Asuchwitz* (New York: New York University Press, 1970), 69–70. This work was translated into French by M. Delmotte and B. Dupuy (Lagrasse: Verdier, 1980.)—Trans.]

9. I said above that theodicy in the broad sense of the term is justified by a certain reading of the Bible. It is evident that another reading of it is possible, and that in a certain sense nothing of the spiritual experience of human history is foreign to the Scriptures. I have in mind here in particular the book of Job, which attests at once to Job's faithfulness to God (2:10) and to ethics (27:5,6), despite his sufferings for no reason, and his opposition to the theodicy of his friends. He refuses theodicy right to the end and, in the last chapters of the text (42:7), is preferred to those who, hurrying to the safety of Heaven, would make God innocent before the suffering of the just. It is a little like Kant's reading of this book in his quite extraordinary short treatise of 1791, *Über das Mißlingen aller philosophischen Versuche in der Theodicee* ["On the Failure of All the Philosophical Attempts at a Theodicy"], in which he demonstrates the theoretical weakness of the arguments in favor of theodicy. Here is the conclusion of his way of interpreting what "this ancient book expresses allegorically." In this state of mind Job has proven that he did not found his morality on faith, but his

faith on morality; in which case faith, however weak it may be, is nonetheless one of a pure and authentic kind, a kind that does not found a religion of solicited favors, but of a well-conducted life (*"welche eine Religion nicht der Gunstbewerbung, sondern des guten Lebenswandels grundet"*).

NINE. Philosophy, Justice, and Love

"Philosophy, Justice and Love." Remarks recorded by R. Fornetand A. Gómez on October 3 and 8, 1982.

1. ["Let him give his cheek to him that smiteth him . . ." Lamentations 3:30.—Trans.]

2. [This expression, which forms the title of Levinas's book *De Dieu qui vient à l'idée* (Paris: Vrin, 1986), has presented a challenge to translators because it draws at both on a colloquial French expression meaning "to come to mind," or "to occur to," and on the more literal "God who comes to the idea." We have taken a middle path, in hopes that "God who comes to the mind" will evoke both God's personal, psychological mode and the conceptual guise in which God appears in philosophy.—Trans.]

3. [The reference seems to have been corrupted. Two possible references in Genesis that would make Levinas's point are Genesis 11:7 and Genesis 18:21.—Trans.]

4. [See Merleau-Ponty's *Phenomenology of Perception*, trans. C. Smith (London: Routledge & Kegan Paul, 1962), 93, and *The Visible and the Invisible*, trans. A. Lingis (Evanston: Northwestern University Press, 1968), 141, 147–148.—Trans.]

5. [*Humanisme de l'autre homme* (Montpellier: Fata Morgana, 1972). Although this work has not been translated as a separate volume, the three essays that it contains are available in English in *Collected Philosophical Papers*, trans. A. Lingis (Dordrecht: Martinus Nijhoff, Phaenomenologica Series No. 100, 1987), 75–107, 127–139, 141–151.—Trans.]

6. [*Le temps et l'autre* (Montpellier: Fata Morgana, 1979) is the publication of four lectures given by Levinas at Jean Wahl's Collège Philosophique in Paris. It has been translated as *Time and the Other* by Richard A. Cohen (Pittsburgh: Duquesne University Press, 1987).—Trans.]

7. [*Totalité et infini: Essai sur l'extériorité*, by Emmanuel Levinas, Phaenomenologica 8 (The Hague-Boston: Nijhoff, 1961); translated as *Totality and Infinity* by Alphonso Lingis (Pittsburgh: Duquesne University Press, n.d. [1969]).—Trans.]

8. [The *Geviert* is the fourfold, a late Heideggerian concept of a oneness that would include the four entities: man, earth, sky, divinities. See Heidegger's *Poetry, Language, Thought*, trans. A. Hofstadter (New York: Harper & Row, 1971), 150–151.—Trans.]

9. [See "Heidegger, Gagarin, and Us," in Levinas's *Difficult Freedom,*

Essays on Judaism, trans. S. Hand (Baltimore: Johns Hopkins University Press, 1991), 231–234.—Trans.]

10. [Stéphane Mosès, *Système et Révélation* (Paris: Editions du Seuil, 1982). Preface by Emmanuel Levinas, pp. 7–16.—Trans.]

11. [The article in question is doubtless "Apropos of Buber: Some Notes," originally published in the collection *Qu'est-ce que l'homme? Philosophie/ Psychanalyse. Hommage à Alphonse de Waelhens (1911–1981)* (Brussels: Facultés Universitaires Saint Louis, 1982). Included in Levinas's *Outside the Subject*, trans. M. B. Smith (Stanford: Stanford University Press, 1994), 40–48. See esp. 41–42.—Trans.]

12. [See Jean-Luc Marion, *God Without Being: Hors Texte*, trans. T. A. Carlson, trans. (Chicago: University of Chicago Press, 1991).—Trans.]

TEN. Nonintentional Consciousness

"Nonintentional Consciousness" appeared in *Philosophe critiques d'eux-mêmes*, published under the auspices of the Féderation internationale des Sociétés de Philosophie, vol. 10, Berne, 1983. It incorporates material from the study by E. Levinas on *Dialogue*, which appeared in *Christlicher Glaube in der modernen Gesellschaft*, published by the Herder company in Freiburg-am-Breisgau, and a paper published by the journal *Exercice de la patience*, No. 2 (Winter 1981): 109–113 in the issue devoted to Blanchot.

1. ["Le présent se fait maintenant." Literally, "The present makes itself now." "Maintenant," the normal French word for "now," is composed of "main" (hand) and "tenant" (holding).—Trans.]

2. Friedrich Hegel, *Science of Logic*, trans. W. H. Johnston, L. G. Struthers, vol. 2 (London: George Allen and Unwin, 1929), 218.

3. [A formulation that echoes Heidegger's characterization of Dasein as "[d]as Sein, *darum* es diesem Seienden in seinem Sein geht" ([t]hat Being which is an *issue* for this entity in its very Being . . . " See *Sein und Zeit* (Tübingen: Niemeyer, 1986), 42; *Being and Time* (New York: Harper and Row, 1962), 67.—Trans.]

4. [Literally, "lived." We have retained the French term because of the awkwardness of "the lived" in English, and because "lived experience" adds a concept that would imply a possible accumulation of knowledge and eventual conscious mastery that is precisely what Levinas wishes to exclude from "nonintentional" consciousness.—Trans.]

5. [The French word "la conscience" is used for both consciousness and conscience. Given Levinas's characterization of it as the indirect or implicit "consciousness," it seems to shade off into "conscience," as its traits become more ethical in nature, and it is eventually qualified as "bad." This is at any rate the assumption we have made in translating latter part of this essay.—Trans.]

6. [Psalm 119:19.—Trans.]

7. [See n. 1, above.—Trans.]

8. [Pascal's *Pensées*, in *Pascal* (Chicago: Encyclopaedia Britannica, Inc., Great Books of the Western World Series, no. 33, 1952), 226.—Trans.]

9. [A recurrent phrase in Levinas's work, of biblical origin. See Isaiah 6.8.—Trans.]

10. [More literally, in "moving oneself." This verb ("s'émouvoir") and the ones that follow are reflexive verbs in French, as are the ones Heidegger uses in the passage to which Levinas refers.—Trans.]

11. [See above, n. 3.—Trans.]

12. [See above, ch. 9, n. 2.—Trans.]

13. [The "à-Dieu," to or toward God, appears to be a contrastive parallel to Heidegger's *Sein zum Tode* (Being-toward-death) or *Sein zum Ende* (Being-toward-the-end).—Trans.]

ELEVEN. From the One to the Other: Transcendence and Time

"From the One to the Other. Transcendence and Time" was first published in *Archivo di filosofia* 51 (Nos. 1–3, 1983): 21–38; reprinted and modified in *Encyclopédie philosophique universelle*, Presses Universitaires de France, 1989.

1. Plotinus's *Enneades*, Treatise V, ch. 1, para. 6.

2. *Enneades*, Tractate 5, ch. 3, para. 11. [In order to remain as close as possible to Levinas's interpretation, we translate his French version of the text, but append, for purposes of comparison, the translation of S. MacKenna and B. S. Page, published in the Great Books of the Western World Series, No. 17: *Plotinus: The Six Enneads* (Chicago: Encyclopaedia Britannica, 1952), 222.—Trans.]

It knows the Transcendent in very essence but, with all its effort to grasp that prior as a pure unity, it goes forth amassing successive impressions, so that, to it, the object becomes multiple. . . . If it had not possessed a previous impression of the Transcendent, it could never have grasped it, but this impression, originally of unity, has become an impression of multiplicity; and the Intellect-Principle, in taking cognisance of that multiplicity, knows the Transcendent and so is realized as an eye possessed of its vision.

3. *Enneades*, Tractate 5, ch. 1, para. 6.

4. *Enneades*, Tractate 5, ch. 1., para. 4.

5. *Enneades*, Tractate 5, ch. 1., para. 7.

6. *Enneades*, Tractate 5, ch. 1., para. 6.

7. [Here we have followed the version of this text published in *L'Herne: Emmanuel Levinas*, ed. Chalier and Abensour (Paris: Editions de l'Herne, 1991), 85, which has "patrie" rather than "partie."—Trans.]

8. Descartes's *cogito*, initially a theoretical "event" of doubt, covers all the modalities of thought. Let us recall the text expanding on the *cogito* in the Second *Méditation Métaphysique:* "A thing that thinks. What is that? A thing

that doubts, understands, affirms, denies, is willing, is unwilling, that also imagines and feels. " We can presume that *to feel* here means both *sensation* and *sentiment*. According to our present ways of speaking, significance [signifiance] coincides with knowing [savoir]. All the human *vécu* is called experience, that is to say, instruction or a received lesson. The relation to the other would be social experience. Theologians who no longer trust syllogistic deduction and do not dare quote Scripture validate the hypothesis of *God* in religious *experience*.

9. See particularly Husserl, *Krisis der europäischen Wissenschaften* . . . (The Hague: Martinus Nijhoff, 1962), 116: "*Innenbetrachtung der sich selbst im Außen äusserenden Subjektivität*" [Introspection of the subjectivity that expresses itself in the outer world]. For a slightlly different translation, see Husserl's *The Crisis of European Sciences* . . ., trans. D. Carr (Evanston: Northwestern University Press, 1970), 113.

10. That the questioning of knowledge is raised in a philosophical mode of thought which is still knowledge is not a refutation of this questioning. The questioning of knowledge as a part of meaning is not the absurd attempt which would consist in wanting to show the falsity of it or even in failing to appreciate its role in thought. Knowledge reveals meaning and allows expression. But, for all that, it is not the site of the ultimate articulation of the meaningful. It does not leave traces in the meaning it reveals. The forms necessary for revelation do not transform the revealed.

11. I repeat here more broadly the ideas on bad conscience developed in the context of the preceding essay.

12. [See above, ch. 10, n. 5.—Trans.]

13. [Here I follow the version of the text published in *L'Herne: Emmanuel Levinas* (Paris: Editions de l'Herne, 1991), p. 89, which has "inexplicites," which is clearly required by the sense, rather than "explicites."—Trans.]

14. [Psalm 119:19.—Trans.]

15. [See above, ch. 10, n. 1.—Trans.]

16. [See above, ch. 10, note 8.—Trans.]

17. [This should probably be interpreted as a utopia in the literal sense of "no-place."—Trans.]

18. [See above, ch. 9, n. 2.—Trans.]

19. [See above, ch. 10 n. 10.—Trans.]

20. Vigil of charity, which is probably also the latent birth of medicine, awakened, on the hither side of all knowledge, by the face or mortality of the other man.

21. Original identity, since identifying oneself without recourse to any distinctive particular sign. The latter, in fact, would not resolve the problem of identification for it, too, would demand to be retained as identical. The self recognizes itself as the same without recourse to any signs. It is a logically indiscernible identity.

22. [The expression, frequent in Levinas's work, is from Paul Valéry. See

the latter's *Oeuvres*, vol. 1 (Paris: 1957), 118—Trans.]

23. The identity of the ego justifying the pronoun "*me*" in such an expression as "*me voici rejeté vers un passé immemorial*," [literally: see me here thrown back toward an immemorial past] signifies, in its "accusative" of "*me*," an identity that is already indebted to the historical fraternity introduced by responsibility for the other. ["Here I am thrown back toward an immemorial past." Levinas's philosophical point is based on, or at least illustrated by, the linguistic circumstance that the French for "Here I am" uses "*me*" in the accusative case rather than the nominative, as in English.—Trans.] The idea of humanity and of its unity is not purely generic, as is the case with *animality*. It already presupposes the history that emerges from responsibility for the other, responding from an immemorial past. A responsibility in which "the spirit of a people" takes shape, and from there, humanity. Does not history, then, an unremembered past, signify the originary concreteness of the past?

24. An un-known God, abstracted from thematization and pure directness of addressability as Thou, as if He had disengaged Himself from that, or transcended Himself in the third person, as He.

TWELVE. The Rights of Man and Good Will

"The Rights of Man and Good Will" was published in the anthology *Indivisibilité des droits de l'homme* (Friburg, Switzerland: Editions Universitaires, 1985), 35–45.

1. [Deuteronomy. 5:17 and 10:19, resp.—Trans.]

2. [See Kant's *Critique of Practical Reason*, in the *Great Books of the Western World Series*, no. 42 (Chicago: *Encyclopaedia Britannica*, 1952), 327; *Kritik der praktischen Vernunft*, in *Kants Gesammelte Schriften*, vol. 5, ed. Paul Natorp (Berlin: Königliche Preußischen Akademie, 1908), 151–154.—Trans.]

3. "The Passions of the Soul," art. 153, 156, resp. [We use the translation in *The Philosophical Works of Descartes*, trans. Hildane and Ross, vol 1 (London and New York: Cambridge at the University Press, 1968), 401, 403. In French, cf. *Descartes, Oeuvres et lettres* (Paris: Editions Gallimard, 1953), 769, 770.—Trans.]

4. [See above, ch. 9, n. 2.—Trans.]

THIRTEEN. Diachrony and Representation

"Diachrony and Representation." Text of a lecture delivered in honor of Paul Ricoeur, in Canada, published in the *Revue de l'Université d'Ottawa* 55 (no. 4, October–December 1985): 85–98.

1. [The French word for "now" is "maintenant." Levinas draws attention to the etymology of the term, which is derived from the word "main," or "hand,"

by hyphenating it and making it into a noun. See above, ch. 6, n. 6.—Trans.]

2. [In an introductory note on page xli to his *Otherwise than Being or Beyond Essence* (The Hague: Nijhoff, 1981; published in French in 1978), Levinas explains this spelling in the following terms. "[T]he term *essence* here expresses *being* different from *beings*, the German *Sein* distinguished from *Seiendes*, the Latin *esse* distinguished from the Scholastic *ens*. We have not ventured to write *essance* as would be required by the history of the language, where the suffix *-ance*, deriving from *-antia* or *-entia*, gave birth to abstract nouns of action." See above, ch. 6, n. 3.—Trans.]

3. ["Apprésentation" the French version of Husserl's "Appräsentation," is "the indirect perceptual presentation of an object mediated through the direct presentation of another, e.g., of the rear through the frontal aspect, or of other minds through their bodies." (H. Spiegelberg, *The Phenomenological Movement* [The Hague: Nijhoff, 2d ed., 1971], vol. 2, p. 712).—Trans.]

4. See my *Otherwise than Being or Beyond Essence*, 161ff.

5. But what an encumbrance of language or what an ambiguity in the *I*! Here we speak of the *I* as a concept even though in each *I* the "first person" is uniqueness and not the individuation of a genus. The *I* is "I," if one may say so, not when spoken about, but when it speaks in the first person: the self escaping from the concept despite the power that the concept regains over it the moment we speak of this escape, this uniqueness, or this election.

6. ["Un voeu ou une dévotion?" The French "voeu" is still quite close to "vouloir," to want or to will. It seems relatively clear from the context that Levinas's implied answer to the question is "une dévotion," i.e., not a free will, but a having been consecrated (to responsibility in the sociality described in this section), in the manner of a votive offering.—Trans.]

7. [Pascal, *Pensées*. See ch. 10, n. 8.—Trans.]

8. [See Kant's *Critique of Pure Reason*, A 107–108.—Trans.]

9. [See ch. 9, n. 2.—Trans.]

FOURTEEN.   The Philosophical Determination of the Idea of Culture

"The Philosophical Determination of the Idea of Culture" is an exerpt from the procedings of the Seventeenth World Conference of Philosophy, held in Montreal in 1983; published in *Editions du Beffroi/Editions de Montmorency*, 1986.

1. [The French "main-tenance," is here broken down into its component parts, "main," meaning hand, and "tenance" the action of holding. See ch. 10, n. 1.—Trans.]

2. Maurice Merleau-Ponty, *Signs*, trans. Richard C. McCleary (Chicago: Northwestern University Press, 1964), 166.

FIFTEEN. Uniqueness

"Uniqueness" was published in *Archivio di Filosofia*, Nos. 1-3, 1986.

1. [A not-so-veiled allusion to Claude Lévi-Strauss's *The Savage Mind* (1962).—Trans.]

2. A subjectivity that, in this *for-the-other* of love, is no longer—or not yet—either the self of the Fichtean *I think* or the transcendental. But it is possible that these latter owe their ex-ception to ontology—the uniqueness that corresponds to their mode of "non-interchangeability" or of their having been "chosen" for this mode—to nontransferable and unimpeachable responsibility. Ethics, as if it were the "individuation" of the *I*, a consecration of its strangeness to all being, is "anterior" to the thematization of the *knowing* resulting from this status.

SIXTEEN. *Totality and Infinity:* Preface to German Edition

Totality and Infinity. Preface to the German Edition. *Totalität und Unendlichkeit* (Freiburg im Breisgau: Verlag Karl Alber; 1987), January 18, 1987.

1. [I take it that this statement, critical of the "ontological" language still used in *Totality and Infinity*, is meant to indicate that after that work Levinas will consider the connection between "essential" and "necessary" a mere analogy. "Essential" will be used, if at all to mean having to do with being, and the latter will no longer be equated with a *summum bonum* or any sort of absolute truth or necessity. As Levinas states in a prefatory note to *Otherwise than Being or Beyond Essence*, he will "carefully avoid using the term essence or its derivatives in their traditional usage. For essence, essential, essentially, we will say eidos, eidetic, eidetically, or nature, quiddity, fundamental, etc." (*Otherwise than Being*, p. xli).—Trans.]

2. *Republic*, 505e.

SEVENTEEN. Dialogue on Thinking-of-the-Other

Remarks recorded by Jöel Doutreleau and Pierre Zalio, 1987. "Dialogue on Thinking of the Other." Quoted from *Cité: Revue de la Nouvelle Citoyenneté* (17 rue des Petits Champs), December 1987, No. 17. Originally titled *Entretien avec Emmanuel Lévinas*.

1. [See ch. 16 of this volume.—Trans.]

2. *Republic*, 505e.

3. [Cf. Rabbi Hayyim de Volozhyn's *L'Ame de la vie*, with Introduction by Emmanuel Lévinas (Lagrasse: Editions Verdier, 1986), 10ff.—Trans.]

4. [The expression "happy end" is in English in the original.—Trans.]

EIGHTEEN. "Dying for. . ."

"Dying For . . ." is the text of a lecture delivered in March 1987 at the Collège International de Philosophie in Paris. The then director of the Collège, Professor Miguel Abensour, chaired the colloquium and introduced the lecturer by recalling the dramatic horizons opened up by reflections on Heidegger. First published in *Heidegger. Questions ouvertes*, ed. E. Escoubas (Paris: Editions Osiris, 1988), 255–264.

1. Professor Miguel Abensour, then director of the Collège International de Philosophie in Paris, who hosted the colloquium "Heidegger" on March 12, 13, and 14, 1987, has just introduced Levinas.

2. [Martin Heidegger, *Being and Time*, trans. John Macquarrie and Edward Robinson (New York: Harper and Row, 1962); *Sein und Zeit*, 16th ed. (Tübingen: Max Niemeyer Verlag, 1986) —Trans.]

3. I quote from the Martineau translation, p. 108. For *Dasein*, I will sometimes use his translation, "*être-là*" [being-there]. [*Being and Time*, 165; *Sein und Zeit*, 127–128.—Trans.]

4. *Being and Time*, 294; *Sein und Zeit*, 250; Martineau's French translation, 185, 186.

5. Ibid.

6. [Pascal, *Pensées*, see ch. 10, n. 8.—Trans.]

7. *Sein und Zeit*, 240; page 178 of the Martineau translation. [*Being and Nothingness*, 284.—Trans.]

NINETEEN. The Idea of the Infinite in Us

"The Idea of the Infinite in Us." Text published in *La Passion et la Raison*, Presses Universitaires de France, 1988.

1. This investigation is not intended to dismiss the valuable analyses of Michel Henry in his admirable—and indispensable— *Essence de la Manifestation*. [Michel Henri, *The Essence of Manifestation*, trans. Girard Etzkorn (The Hague: Martinus Nijhoff, 1973).—Trans.]

2. See the elaboration of this concept in J. Libertson, *Proximity* (The Hague: Martinus Nijhoff, 1982).

3. See my book *De Dieu qui vient à l'idée* (Paris: Vrin, 1982), particularly the essay "Dieu et la philosophie." [This essay is available in English in *E. Levinas: Collected Philosophical Papers*, trans. A. Lingis (Dordrecht: Martinus Nijhoff, Phaenomenologica Series, No. 100, 1987), 153–173.—Trans.]

TWENTY. The Other, Utopia, and Justice

Remarks recorded by J.M. and J.R. "The Other, Utopia, and Justice." A conversation with the journal *Autrement*, No. 102, November 1988.

1. [See Levinas's 1981 interview with Philippe Nemo, *Ethics and Infinity*, trans. Richard A Cohen (Pittsburgh: Duquesne University Press, 1985), 25ff, and his 1986 interview with François Poirié, *Emmanuel Lévinas, Qui êtes-vous?* (Lyon: La Manufacture, 1987), 70ff. See also, for the Strasbourg period, Marie-Anne Lescourret's biography, *Emmanuel Levinas* (Paris: Flammarion, 1994), 51–72.—Trans.]

2. [Victor Farias, *Heidegger et le nazisme* (Lagrasse: Verdier, 1987); in English, *Heidegger and Nazism*, ed. J. Margolis and T. Rockmore, trans. P. Burrell and G. R. Ricci (Philadelphia: Temple University Press, 1989)—Trans.]

3. [Two relevant texts by Levinas with respect to Heidegger's affiliation with the Nazis are: "Reflections on the Philosophy of Hitlerism," trans. Seán Hand, originally published in *Esprit* in 1934 (*Critical Inquiry* 17, Autumn 1990, 63–71) and "As if consenting to Horror," trans. Paula Wissing, originally published in *Le Nouvel Observateur* in 1988 (*Critical Inquiry* 15, Winter 1989, 485–88).—Trans.]

4. [Levinas is alluding to the lecture on Heidegger ("Dying for . . . ") he gave the previous year; see above, ch. 18.—Trans.]

5. [I follow Levinas's usage here, in which "essence" carries the verbal sense of being. See ch. 16, n. 1.—Trans.]

6. [See *Emmanuel Levinas: Time and the Other, and Additional Essays*, trans. R. A. Cohen (Pittsburgh: Duquesne University Press, 1987), 29–94; *Le temps et l'autre* (Paris: Presses Universitaires de France, 2d ed., 1985); originally published as "Le temps et l'autre," in J. Wahl, *Le Choix, Le Monde, L'Existence* (Grenoble-Paris: Arthaud, 1947).—Trans.]

7. [*Life and Fate*, trans. from Russian by R. Chandler (New York: Harper and Row, 1987), esp. 405ff.—Trans.]

8. [Pascal's *Pensées*. See ch. 10, n. 8.—Trans.]

Index